OMEGA

ăn: to eat

ăn: to eat

RECIPES AND STORIES FROM A VIETNAMESE FAMILY KITCHEN

By **HELENE AN,** Executive Chef of Crustacean Beverly Hills
and **JACQUELINE AN**

Food Photography by
EVAN SUNG

RUNNING PRESS
PHILADELPHIA · LONDON

Photo credits for pages 16-17: Simon Dannhauer / Thinkstock.com; page 117: Maciej Bledowski / Thinkstock.com; page 191: Photo by Emma McGowan
The following pages contain images from the An family archives: front endpaper, 2, 9, 13, 14, 15, 20, 22, 43, 48-49, 55, 72, 73, 74, 78, 80, 89, 97, 106, 109, 112, 115, 116, 118, 151, 157, 158, 159, 161, 162, 175, 194, 196, 199, 200, 202, 203, 229, 231, 235, 245, 264, 284, 285, 292, 295, 296

Published by Running Press,
A Member of the Perseus Books Group

Books published by Running Press are available at special discounts for bulk purchases in the United States by corporations, institutions, and other organizations. For more information, please contact the Special Markets Department at the Perseus Books Group, 2300 Chestnut Street, Suite 200, Philadelphia, PA 19103, or call (800) 810-4145, ext. 5000, or e-mail special.markets@perseusbooks.com.

ISBN 978-0-7624-5835-6
Library of Congress Control Number: 2015958289

E-book ISBN 978-0-7624-5836-3

9 8 7 6 5 4 3 2 1
Digit on the right indicates the number of this printing

Design by Susan Van Horn
Edited by Jennifer Kasius
Photography, unless otherwise noted, by Evan Sung
Prop styling by Nidia Cueva
Food styling by Helene An and Tony Nguyen
Typography: Merlo and Archer

Running Press Book Publishers
2300 Chestnut Street
Philadelphia, PA 19103-4371

Visit us on the web!
www.offthemenublog.com

contents

introduction

my mother's food
by JACQUELINE AN

I grew up listening to the stories of my mother's childhood in Vietnam: the adventures, the dangers, and the elegance of a lost world. Her early years were a time of plenty and a time of peril. She told me about her aristocratic family's plantation estate in the unspoiled countryside, four smaller houses surrounding one big one where my great-grandfather addressed everyone from a balcony on high. She recounted the night her own father was pulled from his bed by Communist invaders and tied to a tree, his life spared only when the local villagers pleaded for it. She remembered the delicious grasshoppers she enjoyed as a small girl at harvest festivals, and the time she fell off a basket boat and almost drowned when her family was making yet another unplanned escape.

Helene and baby Jacqueline, 1979.

Most of her stories were told as she was making food, which, since our family is in the restaurant business, was almost always. Forced to flee Vietnam after the fall of Saigon with little more than the clothes on her back, my mother started her new life in America as a cook in a small, converted Italian deli purchased years before on a whim by her mother-in-law. Life in the restaurant business is not easy, and my parents and grandparents worked around the clock to support my sisters and me. Our own early years were not filled with material things. There was not a lot of money, but there was always food.

As she made a dish, my mother would tell the story behind it, bringing to life once again the people and ingredients back home that inspired her.

Food was such a part of our lives that when I was younger, I thought it was such a funny coincidence that ăn, so like our own last name, meant "to eat" since we owned eating establishments, and my parents and grandparents likened almost everything to eating. (As it turns out, our last name An without the breve over the a means "security," but really, in our lives, eating and security were one and the same.)

My parents never thought they would be in the restaurant industry—my father was a colonel in the Vietnamese Air Force and my mother dreamed of being a politician—but they were raised with a deep appreciation of food. My father's motto is: "If you're going to eat, you might as well eat well." My mother likes to remind us that my father's quest for the perfect ingredient goes back decades. When he flew his plane to Hong Kong, he made sure to bring back the famous roast duck; from the Philippines he brought cases of rich butter; from Singapore, the freshest melons and exotic fruits. Even now when he no longer has a plane at his disposal, he still adheres to the same philosophy, driving an hour away to Orange County to get a certain special ingredient for my mother to cook. My mother jokes that before they've finished today's breakfast, my father has already started thinking about tomorrow's meals.

For my family, food is life and life is food. The only day my mother (known as "Mama" to everyone she meets) didn't cook a full meal for us was on Monday, the one day that our restaurant was closed. My father designated it as her day off, and he would take all of us out for a family dinner. Even now she wakes up early every morning to make breakfast for whomever is staying with her before she heads out to our restaurants, and on the weekends when she's not working she'll make everyone lunch. There is always food at Mama's house, and it is the hub that keeps us together.

Although my mother worked sixteen hours a day when we were growing up, we always felt her presence and her love. We felt it through her cooking, through the mouthwatering meals she made for us daily.

As she made a dish, my mother would tell the story behind it, bringing to life once again the people and ingredients back home that inspired her. It was a peek into a time and a culture that we will never get back. Ultimately, that's what cooking and eating together is all about. It's not just a way to pass down recipes and techniques that would otherwise be lost; it's an opportunity for family history to be shared among generations. Coming together to make and break bread (or rice, in our case) helps us keep the memories and legacy of our loved ones alive.

Traditionally in Vietnam, recipes aren't written down. Instead, they are passed along orally. You learn from your mother and your aunt and your sister who learned from theirs. I wanted to break from this tradition, though, in order to save it. I wanted to preserve my mother's recipes and story for my children the same way she had preserved the culture and traditions of her home country for my sisters and me. Writing this book was a way to permanently chronicle her life and recipes as well as the lifestyle of a forgotten time.

I want the people who love my mother's food and those just learning about it to know what inspired her and learn how to bring some of the same magic into their own kitchens. I want to share what her food meant to us children growing up, how it taught us about love and commitment and dedication. And most of all, I want to record her culinary creations, because they are so unlike anything ever imagined before—with clean flavors, simple techniques, and unique twists that could only have come from her personal story. My mother saw the loss of not one but two family fortunes. She was born as bombs were falling, and she gave birth years later the same way. Yet she never gave up.

This book is a record of our family's journey, told for the first time since my mother began her culinary odyssey in America forty years ago. It chronicles her transformation from aristocrat to refugee to restaurateur. While she now oversees our family's five restaurants and catering business, hers was not an overnight success. It came from hard work, sheer determination, and the willingness of our entire family to come together to build a new life. It's my hope that we will inspire you to preserve your own family traditions and create new ones, to come together and tell your story through food.

Above all, this is an invitation to our family's table. We'll share some of our most beloved dishes, from traditional Vietnamese recipes with classic French underpinnings to modern takes on American food with an Asian twist. We'll spill kitchen secrets, pass along restaurant insider tips, and teach you how to make simple, healthy cuisine that will transport you across continents and cultures.

It is our honor to have you as our guest.
Welcome!

the journey
by HELENE AN

FOOD SHOULD TAKE YOU ON A JOURNEY.

O*urs begins in Indochina in the early twentieth century, in the northern province of Kiến An, home to privileged Vietnamese and Europeans. It was a world known for its exotic beauty, envied for its imported French glamour, and legendary for its hospitality. It was a time when dinners were conducted with a sense of ritual and an aura of elegance.*

OPPOSITE, TOP LEFT: Grandmother Diana's parents, posed with their children, servants, and soldiers (Baby Diana is in the arms of a servant.) **TOP RIGHT**—Helene and Danny in Nha Trang on their honeymoon, 1963. **BOTTOM RIGHT**—The An Family, 2015. Clockwise from left: Monique, Hannah, Danny, Helene, Jacqueline, Catherine, Grandma Diana, and Elizabeth. **BOTTOM LEFT:** San Francisco's Chinatown, 1976. From left: Family friend, Danny, Diana, Hannah, Helene, Monique, Elizabeth and Grandpa John.

My father, as his father and his father before him, was a provincial ruler and member of an aristocratic family that for centuries had served as high-level Mandarins, advisors of the royal court. As the youngest of his seventeen children, I lived the life of a princess.

When I was a child, I would spend hours in the kitchen mesmerized as the chefs prepared opulent meals for the many dignitaries and businessmen that visited our home. There were three chefs to represent the cultural influences of the time: one Chinese, one French, and one Vietnamese.

I was fascinated by their art, and peppered them with questions. I'll admit, I've always been a fussy eater, and I wanted to try something new every day. When I asked my mother, I was told, "If you want something more exciting, change the menu." And so I did. At a very early age, I learned how to create menus, manage a kitchen, and entertain in a style spectacular in its simplicity and elegance.

When I was a child, I would spend hours in the kitchen mesmerized as the chefs prepared opulent meals for the many dignitaries and businessmen that visited our home.

From the Chinese chef, I learned that eating is more than a necessity; it's a way to enjoy life. From the French chef, I learned that cooking is an art. From the Vietnamese chef, I learned how to use my country's native herbs, spices, and roots. They taught me that herbs must be used in every dish; some to take the oil out of fish during cooking to make it healthier, others to eliminate the gaminess from fowl.

For the first eleven years of my life, I was privileged and pampered. Then North Vietnam fell under Communist rule, and my family lost everything. In 1955, we fled south to Saigon and began to rebuild our lives.

Ten years later, I married Danny An, a colonel in the Vietnamese Air Force. His father was a wealthy industrialist who loved to be surrounded by people and frequently threw lavish banquets. I was back to planning exquisite menus for visiting dignitaries and guests. My mother-in-

law Diana mentored me in the kitchen and schooled me in the fine art of entertaining.

With me to help manage the household, Diana began to explore her independence. In 1968, she took a trip around the world, stopping in San Francisco near the end of her travels to visit her cousin. One day, they got lunch from an Italian deli at 46th and Judah, and on a whim Diana decided to buy the place. It made no sense at the time, as our family had no designs on the restaurant business, let alone a tiny Italian deli on the other side of the ocean. The Ans were part of the elite class, and the service industry was not becoming of their station, especially for a woman. But Diana had a vision, and she wanted it. Picturing my tiny mother-in-law bargaining with the Italian owner for the best price still tickles me.

A few years later, my husband was away on active duty when I answered a knock at the door of our home. I was told I had one hour to gather my things and evacuate. Saigon was falling. I was so terrified that the only things I grabbed were my children: I had three daughters at the time. We left with only the clothes on our backs.

Our family's transition was swift and brutal. We were squeezed into a refugee camp in the Philippines. My daughters had never been outside the house without attendants, and now they had to fend for themselves. Instead of coddling them, I taught them to be strong, sending them out to fetch their own food, and sending them back again when they were unsuccessful. With hundreds of people waiting in food lines an hour long, they had to quickly learn to fight for what they wanted.

My husband met up with us in the Philippines, and we were reunited with his parents who had left for San Francisco before the evacuation. All we had left in the world was the strange, small Italian deli. None of us had ever cooked professionally before, but that didn't matter. We went right to work.

For two years, my family of five and our in-laws all shared a one-bedroom apartment near the restaurant. I taught French in the morning, worked as an accountant in the afternoon, and cooked in the restaurant all evening. We worked sixteen-hour days, seven days a week.

At first, we kept the menu the same, but slowly, I started to supplement it. I noticed that the most popular dishes were pastas laden with cream and butter, and I wanted to do better. I chose a lighter noodle and flavored it with herbs and garlic instead of a heavy sauce. I knew that garlic, being fat- and cholesterol-

free, would make a more waistline-friendly dish, but that it also wards off colds, improves circulation, and lowers triglycerides. Customers gobbled up my new creation, and our famous garlic noodles were born.

Being a good hostess is important to me; it's part of my life's blood. Whether I'm managing the kitchen or making the dumplings myself, I care about my customers and their well-being. So I began devising healthier twists on American favorites using my knowledge of herbs and the lessons I had learned as a child. This slow fusion of ingredients helped introduce a new generation to Asian flavors elevated by French cooking techniques—a tradition that I was afraid would die out in my homeland.

We changed the name of our restaurant to reflect its new direction, and chose *Thang Long* which means "ascending dragon." We were devastated when the first batch of menus returned from the printer with the name incorrectly spelled *Thanh Long*, until my mother-in-law determined the new translation (green dragon) was an auspicious omen since green is symbolic of happiness and prosperity. It has lived up to its name, as we just celebrated the restaurant's forty-second anniversary.

In 1991, twenty years after my mother-in-law first purchased Thanh Long, we opened our second restaurant in San Francisco, Crustacean. Six years later we celebrated the opening of our first Southern California restaurant, Crustacean Beverly Hills. In 2009 we ventured a little farther south and opened AnQi in Costa Mesa, a gourmet bistro and noodle bar that combines cuisine and couture. And in 2010 we

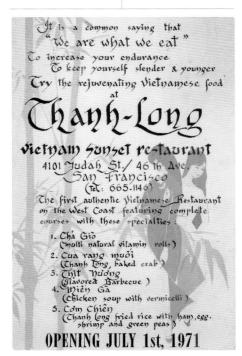

It is a common saying that
"We are what we eat"
To increase your endurance
To keep yourself slender & younger
Try the rejuvenating Vietnamese food
at

Thanh-Long

Vietnam Sunset restaurant

4101 Judah St. / 46th Ave.
San Francisco
(Tel. 665-1146)

The first authentic Vietnamese Restaurant on the West Coast featuring complete courses with these specialties:

1. Chả Giò
   (multi natural vitamin rolls)
2. Cua rang muối
   (Thanh Long baked crab)
3. Thit nướng
   (flavored Barbecue)
4. Miến Gà
   (chicken soup with vermicelli)
5. Cơm Chiên
   (Thanh Long fried rice with ham, egg, shrimp and green peas)

OPENING JULY 1st, 1971

OPPOSITE: In front of Helene's father's estate in Kiến An, 1930s. Helene's father Trần Lưu Mậu is in car, with servants at front of gate.
ABOVE: An early ad for Thanh-Long.

opened Tiato, a market garden café, allowing me to fulfill my dream of growing my favorite herbs in an open-air garden right in the restaurant.

As my daughters—I now have five!—have grown up and gone to college, I encouraged them to try their hand at other jobs and endeavors, but they all somehow ended up back in the family business. They are now managing partners with me in the House of An, each dedicated to their own specialties. Working with the people I love most in the world and serving delicious food to our wonderful customers is my dream come true.

For me, the journey with food never ends. Every day is a chance to try something new: to add a new ingredient to a beloved dish, to learn a new technique for an old way of doing something. The slightest tweaks can make all the difference and lead to a delicious discovery. I have spent years happily honing my own recipes and tinkering with our traditional family dishes. My favorite recipes are combinations of the old and the new: crab marinated in a broth of three wines with cracked pepper and scallions; Maine lobster flambéed in a brandy and shallot–basil sauce served over our garlic noodles; shrimp, garlic, and fennel ravioli served inside rice crepes with a soy and sesame white wine emulsion; tamarind crab in a sweet-and-sour sauce of tomatoes, fresh dill, chile, and herbs.

I believe that food must not only taste good, but also be good for you. I call this balance the Yin and Yang of cooking. I use a ginger sauce on my coconut prawns not just because the zip of the ginger balances the sweetness of the coconut, but also because of ginger's anti-inflammatory properties. Ginger is a natural antihistamine and can help reduce a possible allergic reaction in someone who doesn't know they are sensitive to shellfish.

How food feels on the palate is also very important to me. Food shouldn't be heavy, sticky, overpowering, fatty, or oily. Complex flavors and textures must always be balanced with freshness and lightness.

My culinary philosophy is easy to follow. Aim for simple, refined, and light flavors and textures. Use local ingredients whenever you can, but only when they are in season and at their freshest. And infuse respect, harmony, purity, and tranquility into every dish. Don't be afraid to experiment, and above all, trust yourself. With a good recipe, everyone can be a chef!

My hope is that this cookbook will inspire you on your own culinary journey. After all, today's discoveries are tomorrow's traditions.

vietnam: a brief history

Much has been written about French cooking and cuisine, and Chinese food (albeit what we get in America is not quite traditional) is also fairly well known. However, the tastes of Vietnam are much less recognized, most likely because the late twentieth-century war eclipsed all other news. Allow us to introduce you to a different side of the country, the one covered in lush, green vegetable fields and tropical fruit groves where almost everyone has a kitchen garden, where miles of coastline yield delicious, sustainable seafood, and the use of fresh ingredients contributes to one of the healthiest native diets in the world.

The tradition of simple, fresh flavors and the fragrance of Vietnamese food comes from the country's unique location, climate, and history. It is perhaps no coincidence that the country that strives for balance in all things—life, food, health—itself is shaped like a bamboo pole with baskets at both ends. The skinny middle is only twenty-five miles wide, flanked by the Red (Hong) River Delta in the north and the Mekong Delta in the south.

Situated on the eastern section of Southeast Asia's Indochina Peninsula, Vietnam is bordered by China to the north, the South China Sea to the east, and Laos and Cambodia to the west. It is nearly the same size as Italy, with more than 2,000 miles of coastline. Sixty percent of the population is engaged in agriculture, forestry, and fishing. The lush, fertile, tropical land made it a sought-after prize for civilizations for thousands of years, but its unique geography—the country is bound by mountains, jungles, and the sea—protected it from foreign conquest.

While it only came to the attention of the West in the last century, Vietnam is actually one of the oldest inhabited places on Earth, and believed to be one of the first agricultural societies. In 12,000 B.C., prehistoric nomads gave up their wandering to settle along the Hong River valley. By 3,000 B.C., the first Vietnamese states were created as tribes converged to establish trade, ward off invaders, and manage the persistent flooding of the river. The Bronze Age ushered in a new era of civilization, including the Đông Sơn culture, which was known for its advanced artistic skills especially in regard to elaborate metal drums. The largest drum recovered from Cổ Loa, standing almost two feet tall and weighing 150 pounds, would have required the smelting of several tons of copper.

In the second century B.C., the Chinese conquered the Red River delta and ruled the area for 1,000 years until the collapse of the Tang Dynasty in the early tenth century. The native people then rose up and ruled themselves for the next 200 years.

For the next several hundred years, Vietnamese independence was solidified under the enlightened emperors of the Lý Dynasty. The centralized monarchy introduced the first written laws, including the outlawing of slavery and the protection of animals; opened the country's first university; and expanded public architectural and hydraulic projects.

WARRIOR SISTERS

One of my favorite stories from ancient Vietnam is that of the Trưng sisters, Trưng Trắc and Trưng Nhị. In the early first century A.D., Vietnam was ruled by the Chinese Han Dynasty. Although women in Vietnam were able to own property and had many personal and civil rights that they inherited through their mothers' line, Chinese teachings at the time reflected the opposite. As the Chinese oppression increased, Trưng Trắc's husband took a stand against the invaders and was promptly executed. His wife and her sister took up his cause and encouraged people to stand up for their country for the first time in 250 years. They organized a rebellion of 80,000 led by thirty-six women generals, including their own mother. (I think I love this tale so much because I can definitely see Mama riding an elephant and taking on anyone!)

The Trưng sisters' army was successful in reclaiming their lands, which they ruled as co-queens for five years. In 42 A.D., the Chinese returned with a vengeance. The Trưngs put up a terrific fight, but they were ultimately unsuccessful. One of their close friends, a woman named Phung Thị Chính, led the resistance army while pregnant. Legend has it that she gave birth on the battlefield, scooped her baby up onto her back, and continued fighting.

The Trưng sisters are celebrated in a national holiday every year in February.

The Ly rulers recognized the importance and sacredness of agriculture. At the beginning of each planting season, with great ceremony, the king would till a field himself. In 1038, when King Lý Thái Tôn was advised that the custom was demeaning to his station, he answered, "If I myself do not do some plowing as an offering to the god, how can I set an example for the entire people?" This national sense of service by all classes is still a hallmark of the country.

The Chinese returned and retook control in the early fifteenth century, imposing heavy taxes and reinstating slave labor, but only for twenty years. After watching Ming soldiers destroy a local village, a local nobleman's son, Lê Lợi, rallied the people to revolt against their foreign rulers. Victorious, Lê Lợi became the emperor, thus starting the longest-ruling dynasty in Vietnam, the Lê Dynasty. It lasted, with only minor interruption from the Mạc Dynasty, until 1788.

The sixteenth and seventeenth centuries were marked by periods of civil war between the Trịnh lords in the north and the Nguyễn lords in the south, the beginning of trade with European countries, and the arrival of French Jesuit missionaries. In 1777, Nguyễn Ánh, the 15-year-old nephew of a Nguyễn lord, went into hiding when his family was killed by supporters of the northern Trịnhs. He befriended a French Catholic priest who petitioned the French government to help him reclaim his lands. With French aid, Nguyễn Ánh not only succeeded, but also marched north and took control of the entire country. In 1802, he became Emperor Gia Long, the head of the last dynasty of Vietnam, and united the country.

However, once invited in, the French were reluctant to leave. Starting with military conquests in 1859, the French slowly took over the country, formally annexing it into the French empire in 1887. France ruled the newly christened French Indochina until World War II, when Japan invaded. In 1941, the Việt Minh, a communist nationalist independence coalition was led by Hồ Chí Minh to fight French and Japanese occupation. Although the Japanese surrendered in 1945, one year later the French and

FAMOUS BOSTON BAKER

Before leading the Viet Minh, Hồ Chí Minh traveled the world, stopping for extended periods in France, the United Kingdom, the Soviet Union, and China. In 1911 he took a job as a cook's helper on a ship and came to America. For two years he lived in Boston, where he was a baker at the Parker House Hotel. His brief apprenticeship is marked by a historical plaque in the hotel lobby.

Việt Minh were engaged in a full-scale war, The First Indochina War, which lasted for eight years.

In 1954, the Geneva Accords split the country in two: North Vietnam ruled by Hồ Chí Minh for the Việt Minh, and South Vietnam led by Ngô Đình Diệm. The plan called for reunification of the country two years later, but fighting between the two territories escalated into the Second Indochina War, commonly known as the Vietnam War in America.

The Soviet Union aided the North to propagate Communism, while the United States aided the South to stop it. Following the Paris Peace Accords in 1973, the United States withdrew all combat forces. Northern forces continued to invade the south, culminating in the fall of Saigon in 1975. In July of 1976, the country was once again united as the Socialist Republic of Vietnam. Vietnam has since enjoyed almost forty years of peace. Diplomatic relations with all countries were restored, and Vietnam is now part of the World Trade Organization.

Today, 30 percent of Vietnam's exports are agricultural. Currently the world's second largest rice exporter, Vietnam also produces sugarcane, sweet potatoes, nuts, pepper, and soybeans. Banana, coconut, and citrus tree plantations flourish in the Mekong delta, while coffee and tea are grown in the highlands.

WOMEN ON THE FRONT LINE

In a country that battled oppression and invasion for 1,000 years, Vietnamese women did not have the luxury nor desire to be passive observers of history. When they weren't actually fighting alongside the men, they were holding down the home and business fronts both during and after war.

The majority of able-bodied men were away for decades at a time, and if they ever returned they would most likely come back broken in body or spirit. It was up to the women to keep everything running—farms and fields, children and households, finances and industries. As a result, Vietnamese society empowered women in many ways far earlier than Western cultures did. Women could legally own property in Vietnam 500 years before American women were granted that right. Today, female entrepreneurs own 25 percent of all private companies in Vietnam.

This deeply embedded matriarchal confidence and resourcefulness is a legacy proudly carried forward by subsequent generations. In the early 1970s, when the Culinary Institute of America was just starting to admit women for the first time, my mother and grandmother had no reservations about opening and running their own restaurant. Forty years later, my mother is still a pioneer in the culinary world, one of just a handful of women running a female-owned culinary empire in the United States.

Giặc đến nhà đàn bà phải đánh.
"When the enemy is at the gate, the woman goes out fighting."
- TRADITIONAL VIETNAMESE SAYING

vietnamese culinary traditions

As in most countries, there are regional differences in the food of Vietnam. Crab is king in the North, while the dishes in the central mountains are known for their spiciness. Garlic and shallots are used more in the South, where food tends to be sweeter thanks to coconut milk and sometimes sugar. Yet there is homogeny in the way people prepare their food: with care to balance taste, texture, presentation, and health benefit. Fundamentally, Vietnamese food is a harmony that blends the sweet and the salty, the hot and the cold, the fresh and the fermented.

The country's tropical climate, rich soil, and coastal treasures all contribute to Vietnam's delectable and unique national cuisine. This is the home of tender, savory, caramelized fish braised in a clay pot (*cá kho tộ*). Of crispy crêpes bursting with sweet shrimp, pork, scallions, and herbs (*bánh xèo*). Of succulent water spinach stir-fried with slivers of garlic (*rau muống*).

Noodle soups and broths are a serious business. Mothers have been known to size up the cooking competency of potential daughters-in-law based on their ability to conjure up a perfect pot. An expert can judge just by sniffing.

Sticky rice (*xôi*) made with coconut milk, topped with shallots, mixed with almost anything is generally served as a side or a starter but can easily be a full meal. A simple sandwich served on a French baguette in Vietnam is transformed into the benevolent bánh mì, stuffed with grilled meat, pickled carrots, cilantro, garlic aioli, and fresh vegetable slaw. No place has better fresh seafood rolls wrapped in rice paper (*gỏi cuốn*), banana blossom salads (*nôm hoa chuối*), or honey marinated chicken fired over an open grill (*gà nướng*).

And we cannot forget the condiment for everything: Vietnam's ubiquitous, umami-fired fish sauce (*nước mắm*). As patriotic to Vietnamese cooks as olive oil is to Italians, fish sauce is likewise regulated and labeled for quality; the best comes from the first, virgin extraction of liquid from the salt-brined, fermented fish. The island of Phú Quốc bottles some of the best in the world, harvested from anchovies fat from the local plankton-covered seaweed. The aromatic ingredient is used as almost an elixir to elevate any dish to a gorgeous gourmet status.

In the past, cooks outside of Southeast Asia had to venture into their city's Little Saigon or Chinatown to find specialty ingredients, but thankfully, staples such as fish sauce, rice flour, and bean paste are now easily found in local gourmet markets, the international aisle of many grocery stores, and online. While Vietnamese recipes typically call for more ingredients than other cultures' dishes, each element required is inexpensive, used in small quantities, and contributes mightily to the delicious, mouth-magic blend that is Indochine cuisine.

THE SECRET OF FRESH

It makes me so happy that the national obsession with processed fast food is giving way to a desire to eat local, organic food, as it was always that way in my family. Growing up, we had kitchen gardens and also chicken and fish farms, ponds for raising shrimp, and a family fishing boat. Using our natural resources was not only about self-reliance and sustainability, but it was also the healthiest way to cook and eat. There is nothing like fresh produce or fresh protein in a dish. French cooking is very beautiful, but heavy sauces can overpower food's natural flavor. Starting with the freshest, locally grown or produced ingredients you can find can elevate even the simplest dish into a masterpiece. —HELENE AN

our recipes

Throughout the years as we have moved and married, mastered new techniques, and mingled with other cultures, our family's culinary style has evolved. It is no longer strictly "traditional Vietnamese"—although with our unusual background and fondness for reformulating things, was it ever?

Vietnam is a part of our cultural heritage and a cornerstone for the way we cook, but it is only a part of our make-up. We, like most modern citizens, identify equally with our American home as with our homeland. We are happily influenced by flavors from around the world, excited by fusion in all its forms. Above all, we are devoted to good food.

We seek to preserve ancient traditions and explore new culinary possibilities. The recipes in this cookbook reflect that dual ideal. Some are traditional Vietnamese, some have French colonial influences, and some are modern day creations inspired by our life experiences. While we are restaurateurs, we are also home cooks, and have taken great care to ensure that these meals can be made in any kitchen. Most of the recipes are straightforward and simple. You do not have to be a master chef, just a cook with passion and patience.

We've included recipes for all occasions, from elegant entertaining to just hanging out at home. And like all things, they take you on a journey—from our kitchen, through the unique story of each of our restaurants, to your own table. This is the food that inspires us. We hope it will do the same for you.

1
simple divinity

the original farm-to-table diet

The same way American chefs shudder at the thought of fast food representing their national palate abroad, anyone with exposure to true Vietnamese cooking is dismayed by the lumping of our cuisine with what passes for Asian in this country. The steamy buffet lines in mall food courts and ubiquitous take-out places in strip malls have created a false impression of Asian food: that it is all either greasy or salty (sometimes both); that the only color in the limp and unrecognizable ingredients comes from a thick, unnaturally neon sauce; and that it requires a fussy, deep-fried preparation that is bad for the heart and makes one feel uncomfortably, yet temporarily, full. While this might be a fair and even deserved description of most mass-produced, fast-food type "Asian" entrées, it bears no resemblance to the style, substance, or flavor profiles of Vietnamese cooking.

Vietnamese cooking is the opposite of "Asian" fast food in almost every way. To start, it is one of the healthiest diets on the planet. True Vietnamese food is based on simply mixing good meat, especially lean seafood, with lots of fresh vegetables. Typically, food is cooked in water or broth instead of oil. Flavor comes from aromatic herbs rather than heavy sauces. Vietnamese cooking is organic, paleo, and naturally gluten-free—the original farm-to-table cuisine.

Vietnamese cooking is also unscientific and decidedly forgiving, a blessing to both the inexperienced and the perpetually busy cook. Unlike in baking, the measurements don't have to be precise. Everyday meal preparation is about throwing together whatever you have on hand in the kitchen, mixing and matching flavor profiles to make almost anything work. The heart of Vietnamese cooking isn't all rolling and steaming, it's a light stir fry in a good, homemade stock that pairs different proteins with fresh vegetables in whatever ratio you prefer.

While traditional Chinese cooking can be oily and heavy, and Thai can be either very sweet or very spicy, Vietnamese cuisine is all about balance. It is not too salty, too sweet, too spicy, too oily, or too filling. It is not "too" anything. It is balanced for flavor with a subtle blend of sweet, salty, and umami, the fifth, secret savory taste. It is balanced for the seasons, highlighting what's fresh and locally available alongside preserved foods from previous harvests. And it is balanced for the body, employing ingredients that work together for optimum digestion and wellness.

All of that said, Vietnamese cooking is still a mystery to most home cooks. While the patrons of our restaurants—some of the first Vietnamese establishments in America—have enjoyed our food for more than forty years, most of them confess that it is intimidating to try making these kinds of dishes on their own. Since the process itself is not hard—both American and Italian cooking are more complicated!—the reason can only be because it is unfamiliar. Most Americans don't grow up knowing how to stir-fry in stock or caramelize in a clay pot, just as most Asians don't grow up grilling hot dogs and hamburgers. World traveler Anthony Bourdain, who lists "life-changing" Vietnam as his favorite food destination, confirms that the country was "all so new and different to my life before and the world I grew up in … It just seemed like another planet; a delicious one that sort of sucked me in and never let go." The unknown is only intimidating, however, while it remains unknown. Our hope is that this book will help unmask the secrets of our special way of cooking in a language that everyone can relate to. And just like learning a new language, once you master the foundations and get comfortable with the basic techniques, you'll find that Vietnamese cooking will become fast, easy, and a new, very delicious addition to your life.

kitchen tools

You can generally tell how complicated a cooking style will be based on the list of tools required. When gram-specific kitchen scales, pressure cookers, and sous vide machines are mentioned, you know the process will be meticulous and labor intensive. The difficulty level of Vietnamese cooking is similarly revealed by what is needed to create it: mainly the pots, pans, and knives you already have on hand. This makes sense considering that most Vietnamese refugees left with little more than the shirts on their backs and were able to still conjure up the incredible tastes and flavors with what they found in their new homes. Everything in this book can be made without purchasing a single new item or gadget. Stir-frying can be done in a sauté pan; rice can be cooked in a regular pot. However, if you wish to streamline the process even further, we recommend having just two essential items: a wok and an electric rice cooker.

Selecting Your Wok

While a sauté pan or cast iron skillet can be used to successfully stir-fry, using a wok is preferable for many reasons. Although Vietnamese recipes use little oil, using a wok will require less of it than a regular pan. The high, sloped sides of a wok allow for faster, more even cooking. And only the wok will produce what Chinese cooks call *wok hei*, or "the breath of the wok," the special taste that comes from food seared perfectly in the perfect pan.

The magic of the wok comes from its shape: the slope provides extra cooking surface area while allowing heat to flare up around the pan. Ideal wok cooking requires extremely high heat. There are many choices to consider when selecting a wok for home use in a Western kitchen. Here are our recommendations:

MATERIAL: CARBON STEEL

Carbon steel will heat up and cool down quickly, and it is durable and inexpensive. Cast iron tends to be too heavy to lift and flip food; stainless steel is not recommended as it takes too long to heat up and cool down, and it is difficult to clean.

NONSTICK SURFACE: NO

There are two problems with nonstick woks. The first is that they're unnecessary: properly seasoned woks are by nature nonstick. Secondly, wok cooking requires high heat that artificially applied nonstick coatings can't safely handle.

BOTTOM: FLAT

While a rounded bottom will allow for a smoother internal surface that can assist in cooking, it's not helpful if the wok won't balance on your stove. In Vietnam, kitchens are equipped with special wok burners or wok rings that can be added to accommodate these special pans. In Western kitchens, however, especially when cooking with induction, glass top, or electric burners, flat-bottom woks are a better choice.

HANDLES: ONE LONG HANDLE, PREFERABLY WOODEN

Woks come with two styles of handle: two small loops on either side (called Cantonese-style) or one longer handle paired with one short loop. We recommend the ones with longer handles, since they are much easier to lift and allow you to flip foods for even cooking. The longer handle can be made of either wood or metal, but remember that metal handles get hot. Never grab one without a potholder! If you think you might forget this in the passion of cooking, go for wooden.

SIZE: 14 INCHES

Woks come in many different sizes. The standard workhorse and a good starter wok is one with a 14-inch diameter.

LID: YES

Having a lid that fits your wok will help you get more use out of it when simmering, braising, or steaming.

USEFUL ACCESSORY: STEAMER TRAY

While you can steam food any number of ways, doing so in your wok is especially convenient and fast. You can set bamboo steamers right inside a wok, but we prefer an aluminum steamer rack.

ELECTRIC WOKS: NO

To avoid the hassle of fitting a wok on a Western stove, you might think about turning to a freestanding electric wok. Don't, since most have non-stick coatings and are hard to clean.

HOW TO SEASON A WOK

Much like a beloved cast-iron skillet which was passed down from a grandmother and works better than anything you could ever buy new, woks that have been used frequently become prized possessions. While new woks will start out light gray in color, over time they will develop a lovely, deep black patina that will make them even more non-stick and will enhance the flavors of whatever you cook in them. Like cast-iron skillets, before they can be used, new woks must be seasoned. Here's how:

WHAT YOU'LL NEED

Steel wool scrubber

Heat-resistant BBQ brush

¼ cup vegetable oil

4 inch piece fresh unpeeled ginger, sliced in ½-inch pieces (½ cup)

½ bunch garlic chives or scallions, cut into 2-inch pieces and patted dry with paper towels (¼ cup)

1] New woks come with a protective coating to prevent rusting during shipping and storing that must be thoroughly removed before use. To do this, scrub both the inside and outside of your new wok with hot water, dish soap, and a steel wool scrubber. *This is the only time you will ever use a soap or a scrubber on your wok.* Rinse well but do not towel dry. Instead, set the wok on a burner over low heat until all of the water evaporates and the wok is completely dry.

   Note: The next step requires heating oil and aromatics in the wok at high temperatures. This can cause excessive amounts of smoke and possibly a chemical smell from the leftover sealant. Make sure all windows are open and exhaust fans turned on. If you are worried about the smoke and/or smell, you can season your wok outdoors over an open flame on a grill or camp stove.

2] Place the dry wok on a burner turned up to high heat. Let the empty wok heat up for a few minutes. You'll know it's hot enough when a drop of water in the pan evaporates in seconds.

3] Remove the wok from the heat. Brush oil over the inside of the wok to form thin coating, all the way up the sides, being careful not to spill any. Return the wok to high heat and cook for 3 minutes. Remove the wok from the heat; allow it to cool slightly. Carefully wipe the oil from the wok with a paper towel. Repeat this step one more time.

4] Brush the inside of the pan with another coating of oil. Turn the heat down to medium and return the wok to the stove. Add the ginger and chives or scallions and stir-fry for 15 minutes, making sure to rub the herbs onto every part of the interior; this will help remove any metallic taste from the wok. The pan should be changing colors from gray to brown to black; it might even look splotchy or "ruined," but don't worry, this is what you want!

5] Remove the wok from the heat; allow it to cool to room temperature. Discard the ginger and scallions. Once the wok is cool, wash it with a soft sponge and hot water, then return it to low heat to dry for 1 to 2 minutes. Remove the wok from the heat and allow it to cool again. Using a paper towel, spread a very thin layer of oil around the inside surface of the wok before storing. Your wok is now ready to use.

CARING FOR YOUR WOK

Woks should only be washed in water with soft sponges; no soap whatsoever. You can soak the wok in water to help soften and remove stubborn food, but over time this shouldn't be necessary, as your wok develops its own nonstick surface. Always dry the wok on the stove over low heat, otherwise it will rust. And rub a very thin layer of cooking oil over the surface before storing it to help protect the finish. To remove stuck-on food or rust spots—which are perfectly natural in a newer wok but will decrease with time—sprinkle kosher salt over the offending spot and scrub with a paper towel.

Electric Rice Cooker

The second kitchen item we recommend for Asian cooking is an electric rice cooker.

Using one will free up a spot on your stove, allow you to cook large quantities of rice, and perhaps best of all, eliminate the need to monitor the process. It's a welcome relief to be able to just pour in dry rice and water and walk away knowing that you will get a perfect batch every time.

Small rice cookers with basic functionality can be purchased for around $30, but if you plan on cooking rice frequently, it might be worth investing in a higher-end model. The best ones offer a host of fabulous features including digital controls, delay timers, keep warm functions, and quick cook and simmer capabilities, and some can even cook oatmeal, one pot meals, and dessert, too.

Additional Tools

There are two other relatively inexpensive items that can be useful for frequent Asian cooking: a **mortal and pestle** and a **steamer pot**.

While a food processor can be used to grind herbs, there's something so inherently satisfying about crushing them with an ancient bowl and stick. A mortar and pestle set can be purchased almost anywhere for just a few dollars. Look for one made of stone, especially the pestle, that is neither too smooth nor too grainy.

While we generally use a steamer tray set inside our wok, you can also use a separate, stainless steel steamer pot, which is essentially just a large stockpot and lid with a steamer "basket" that fits inside. To get the most use out of it, choose a three-tier or double stacked one, also called a Chinese steamer; this will allow you to steam two

CLAY POT COOKING

For centuries in early Asian and Mediterranean civilizations, clay pots were the only available vessels for cooking, and today many dishes still rely on this ancient cooking method for one simple reason: clay pots do a wonderful job! Clay is porous so it soaks up steam and keeps food tender and moist. clay pots can be used either in ovens or on stovetops and require very little, if any, oil. The traditional clay pot—which can be purchased at most kitchen stores or online—helps in the caramelization process for many dishes, but it isn't essential. A Dutch oven, covered casserole, terra cotta pan, or Korean stone pot will work just as well.

different groups of food at the same time. You can also use traditional bamboo steamers, but they are a little trickier to work with: They require liners, are a bit more difficult to clean, and won't last as long. The bamboo will soak up some of the moisture during the steaming process, and while some believe this adds to the crispness of the food, others argue that it takes away some of the flavor. It is purely a matter of preference, but no matter how you like to steam your food, a dedicated system can save time.

Helpful Utensils

While your kitchen probably has enough ladles and spoons and spatulas to make any of the recipes in this book, if you want to purchase additional, traditional utensils to assist with Asian cooking, here are a few of our favorites:

A **wok brush**, also called a bamboo brush or cleaning whisk, is a short, stubby brush that looks like a tiny broom made of bamboo. Available for just a couple of dollars, it is the perfect tool for cleaning your wok with hot water and saving your sponges from shredding. A shorter rather than a longer one will be easier to use. Simply swirl it in circles over your dirty wok under hot water. To clean, swirl the bristles in a pot of hot water and hang the brush to dry.

A **wok turner** or **stir-fry spatula** is exactly what it sounds like: a spatula specially designed for the shape of a wok to help quickly turn food while stir-frying. Make sure the end is adequately curved to reach food in any part of the wok (a too-straight edge won't do), and pick a product that will not conduct the high heat up to your hand. Get one big enough for your wok—at least as long as the diameter of your pan. We prefer a natural material such as bamboo over silicone because it is harder and therefore easier to move food with, and won't ever melt.

A **spider strainer**, also called a steamer strainer or skimmer, is a basket on a handle meant to retrieve dumplings, wontons, or other food from hot liquid.

A CUT ABOVE

There are dozens of specialty knives out there styled to cut things from sashimi to watermelon—nice to have, but certainly not necessary. And while you can make do with what you already have in your kitchen, Vietnamese cooking is made easier with these four knives:

Santoku or Chef's knife: An all-purpose knife, great for cutting everything from steak to vegetables. Though these come in many different sizes, an 8- to 10-inch blade is best. This is the only knife worth spending a considerable amount of money on.

Paring knife: A 3- to 4-inch knife used for fruits, garnishes, and small, soft vegetables. Great for mushrooms, scallions, and strawberries; not so much for carrots.

Boning knife: A flexible knife for de-boning fish, meat, or poultry; meant to cut around bones, not through them.

Meat Cleaver: A knife meant to hack through bones and cartilage, especially useful when making homemade stock. Heavy is more important than sharp in this case; a good cleaver can be purchased for under $30. Beware of "Chinese cleavers," as these are actually chef's knives and not sharp enough for butchering.

basic techniques

Cutting

Vietnamese food is easy to cook and to prepare, but it does require more ingredients and prep work than you might be used to. In particular, a lot of things must be cut up before cooking can begin. The secret to a smooth and quick preparation is three-fold: Use the right knife, cut on the right surface, and chop your ingredients into uniform pieces.

Make sure you are using the right knife for the right job. A boning knife is meant to cut around bone, not through it. A paring knife is meant for small, soft foods. If you have to use pressure to cut something with a paring knife, you're using the wrong knife; choose something bigger.

It doesn't matter how fancy your knives are, or whether they are full or partial tang, as long as you are comfortable using them and they are sharp. Sharp knives make for fast, clean, and safe cooking. Use a home sharpener or take your knives to have them professionally sharpened every three to four months.

Nothing will dull a blade faster than cutting down onto a too-hard surface. For this reason, avoid glass or stone cutting boards. Plastic cutting boards are cheap and convenient, but they can harbor bacteria in the surface cuts, even after dishwashing. The best choice is a solid wood cutting board, preferably maple. Some people prefer eco-friendly bamboo, but those boards do split and can retain odors. You should ideally have two cutting boards, one for foods that can be eaten raw like fruits and vegetables, and another for meats and fish to avoid cross-contamination. And always hand wash wood cutting boards (along with any other wooden utensils) rather than putting them in the dishwasher, as they can absorb chemicals from the detergent.

Finally, uniform cutting is important in Vietnamese cuisine, not because it has to look like it came out of a restaurant kitchen (although it will), but because food of the same size will have the same cooking time and consistency. Of course, perfect cuts will leave some extras, but there's no need to waste them: save the scraps for salads or stock. Good knife skills take practice; the more you cut, the better you'll become.

Stir-Frying

Stir-frying is essentially just searing food quickly on all sides at a very high temperature. Doing so locks in flavor, color, and moisture, requiring little, if any, oil to be added to the dish. For this reason, stir-frying is extremely healthy and delicious. Rather than being transformed into something else or buried in sauce, stir-fried foods retain their original fresh flavor.

Cooks new to stir-frying can get nervous because of the high temperatures and quickness of the cooking process, but like everything, it will get easier with time and practice. After just a few recipes, this technique will seem like second nature to you. As you are learning though, be careful around the high heat. If you ever feel that your pan is getting out of control, remove the pan to a cold burner and turn the heat down. While stir-frying uses high heat, that doesn't mean leaving a pan on the highest setting indefinitely. Every stove and every pan will handle heat differently. You want your food to sear but not burn. When it is necessary, lower the heat or remove the pan for a few seconds.

Here are some more tips for stir-frying success:

Prep First

Since food will cook so quickly in a stir-fry, all ingredients must be pre-chopped, pre-measured, pre-marinated, and right on hand for adding to the wok or pan. You will not be

able to walk away from your stir-fry once it's started, so read through each recipe thoroughly and have required items ready and set up in the order that you will use them.

Preheat the Pan

The delicious sizzle you hear when adding food to a pan for stir-frying comes from the fact that the pan is already nice and hot. To achieve this, you must preheat the pan first, and preheat it empty. If you add oil too early, it can reach its smoking point too soon, and if you add food too soon, it can cook too slowly and break down before it ever has a chance to sear. You will know the pan is hot enough when a drop of water evaporates almost immediately.

Adding Liquid

When adding broth, oil, or any other liquid to a hot pan, if you are a new cook, it is advisable to first lift the pan off the burner to avoid excessive smoking or the possibility of spilling onto the heating unit. Add the liquid and swirl it around the pan, and then return to the burner for a few seconds to let the liquid heat up.

Adding Aromatics

As in Italian cooking, where the garlic and onions are added first to help flavor the broth, in stir-frying we do the same, adding shallots, garlic, onion, and ginger first. Make sure to keep stirring and flipping them, though, to keep them from burning. Aromatics are ready when they start to get tender and you can smell them—after about 1 to 2 minutes of cooking.

Adding Protein

The next step is to sear the protein. Add any meat, fish, or poultry to the pan in a single layer and let it sit for 1 minute to form a "crust." Then flip it to sear the other side, tossing it frequently with the aromatics. Once the protein is almost but not quite cooked, remove it from the pan and set it aside on a separate plate.

To sear quickly and correctly, food needs enough room. Don't overcrowd the pan, as that can lead to food steaming instead of searing. Generally, you should only sear 1 pound of protein at a time. Work in batches if you need to make more, but know that the process will go very quickly.

Adding Vegetables

Return the pan to the heat, adding more liquid if the recipe requires it, and toss in the vegetables. Vegetables do not need to be spread out in a single layer, but they do need to be kept in constant motion. That is the true secret of stir-fry: to keep the food tumbling around, so all sides of it hit the hot pan ever so briefly. You can achieve this motion with a spatula, by lifting and shaking the pan, or with a combination of both.

Vegetables must be completely dry before they are added to a hot stir-fry, as any moisture will make them soggy. During prep, use a salad spinner if you need to remove excess water.

Adding Protein Back to the Pan

Once the vegetables are almost but not quite done, add the protein back to the pan to finish cooking the ingredients all together. If extra liquid needs to be added, pour it down the side of the pan rather than in the middle of the stir-fry to keep from lowering the heat of the entire pan. You should hear a constant sizzle throughout your stir-fry, a sign that the pan is hot enough.

Serve Immediately

Stir-fried food is best when it's served and eaten immediately, while it's still steaming hot. Time your meal so that all sides and accompaniments are ready to go when the stir-fry is done.

Steaming

Steaming is another cooking technique often used in Vietnamese cooking because it preserves the vitamins and minerals of food while allowing it to also maintain its flavor, shape, and color.

The secret to steaming food to a wonderful crisp-tender state is to cut the ingredients into uniform pieces so they cook at the same rate, and to avoid over-steaming. The denser the food, the more slowly it will cook, so broccoli will be done before carrots. To compensate, either add the denser food to the steamer a few minutes before the rest, or cut the denser food into smaller pieces.

Add an inch or two of water to the bottom of the pot and place the steamer basket on top, well above the water's surface. Bring the water to a boil and then add the items you wish to steam. Vegetables will continue to cook after you remove them from the pot, so take them out when they still have a little crunch left in the center. Over-steaming will cause sogginess.

Boiling, Simmering & Poaching

Boiling, simmering, and poaching are also frequently used cooking techniques in Vietnamese cuisine. All entail cooking in a liquid using moist heat; the difference lies only in the temperature of the water. Poaching uses the lowest temperature water of these cooking techniques—between 160°F and 180°F—and is used for more delicate foods like eggs and broths. A poach is a really light simmer with barely any bubbles. A simmer is a gentle boil used for tougher food items that need a longer cooking time; this is achieved between 185°F and 200°F and is indicated by small, slow bubbles. Boiling happens at 212°F, when liquid can't get any hotter before it turns to steam. Boiling liquid is full of large, busy bubbles. The only secrets to successful boiling, simmering, and poaching are to cook at the right temperature and to leave enough room in your pot for the liquid molecules to expand as they heat up.

Stewing & Braising

In these two moist-heat techniques, food is cooked submerged in a liquid at a medium to low temperature for a long time to build flavor and tenderness. The only difference lies in how much liquid is used: food that is cooked completely covered in liquid is stewed, and food that is cooked partially covered in liquid is braised. Both stewing and braising are done in heavy pots with lids.

our favorite ingredients

Herbs, Spices, Nuts & Seeds

We have always grown our own herbs and vegetables—from our family's large plantations in Vietnam to kitchen gardens at our restaurants—and thanks to the globalization of cuisine, whatever items we cannot grow ourselves are now readily available at Asian, whole food, and specialty markets and even in the international sections of national chain grocery stores. Plus, almost any Eastern ingredient can also be found online, shipped fresh from Asia, directly to your door. To save money, reduce waste, and ensure that you always have the right ingredients on hand, you can always freeze unused portions. For instance, fresh kaffir lime leaves can be tossed in a plastic bag and stored in the freezer; when removed, they thaw at room temperature in a matter of minutes.

Food is carefully selected in Vietnam. Hot items are balanced with cold, yin with yang, and items known to be hard on digestion are paired with those that aid it. A dish is only as good as its ingredients, so take care to choose the freshest and best items; don't be afraid to cut and discard less-than-perfect pieces. A browned or curled leaf is just a leaf; throw it in your compost bin rather than in your stomach.

Here are some of the herbs, spices, nuts, and seeds we use regularly and why:

Banana Leaves

It's not just the fruit of the banana plant that is healthy—the flowers, stems, and leaves are good for you as well. In Vietnamese cooking we use large, flat, green banana leaves much the same way Westerners use aluminum foil: to wrap food as it cooks. This process is not only more environmentally friendly, but it's also prettier, as the leaves can stay on when food is served. While we don't eat the banana leaves, they do release antioxidants with anti-inflammatory and anti-cancer properties that may even help you live longer.

Banana leaves can be found fresh or frozen. Wash them in hot water (which will bring out the bright green color) and pat them dry before using. Use sharp scissors to cut them into the shape you need. They can be kept in the freezer and thawed in just 30 minutes.

Banana leaves can be used in place of aluminum foil to wrap food when baking or steaming. Just remember that because their porous juices can leak out, be sure to

place the wrapped packets on a pan or dish with sides. They can also be used as decoration, in place of plates for a fun twist, and even on the grill as a mat for delicate items like fish. Use toothpicks to secure them while baking. You can also fold the leaf in half lengthwise and staple the ends closed to turn it into a small canoe shape for serving food in a "banana boat." After using, banana leaves make great compost.

Bean Sprouts

Bean sprouts can come from a variety of beans, but the most common sprouts used in cooking are mung and soybean sprouts. The small, crunchy stems have a huge nutritional benefit, as they contain good amounts of fiber, folate, protein, and vitamins B and C.

They can be eaten raw on salads and sandwiches, and they are tough enough to withstand stir-frying.

Cardamom

Unique, smoky, and aromatic, cardamom seeds are used in both savory and sweet dishes around the world. In many cultures, cardamom is used to treat digestive issues and is even thought to help combat the common cold. It's best to buy cardamom still in pods (which you discard) because the pods keep the seeds fresher and better tasting.

[VIETNAMESE CORIANDER]

[DILL]

[WATER SPINACH]

[KAFFIR LIME LEAVES]

Culantro (ngò gai)

Also called "saw-leaf herb" because of its serrated-edged leaves and "long coriander" or "spiny coriander" because of its taste, *ngò gai* is a common herb used in Asia, the West Indies, and Latin America. The dark green, glossy leaves look thorny, but that's just a protective measure for the plant. *Ngò gai* contains healthy servings of iron, calcium, riboflavin, and carotene.

Dill

This aromatic herb is a member of the parsley family. The feathery green leaves have a sweet taste, while the seeds are tangy. Dill has an antibacterial quality similar to garlic and is more commonly used in northern Vietnam.

Fennel

Fennel has wispy green stalks that look similar to those of the dill plant, but the big difference is in the subterranean white bulb that has a bright, anise-like taste. All parts of the fennel plant are used in Vietnamese cooking: the bulb, the fronds, the leaves, and the seeds. Fennel has antioxidant, anti-inflammatory, and anti-cancer properties. The fennel bulb is also a great source of vitamin C and fiber.

When shopping for fennel, choose ones with unmarred white or pale green bulbs and bright green stems and leaves without flowers (flowering buds are a sign that the fennel is past its prime). Fennel should be stored in the crisper drawer of the refrigerator. Unlike other herbs, it does not retain its flavor very well when frozen, so it's best used fresh or in dried form.

Galangal

Galangal (pronounced guh-LANG-guh) is an aromatic root similar to ginger but larger, lighter in color, harder, and with a more pungent or peppery taste and hints of citrus. Like ginger, galangal must be peeled before it's used in cooking; a potato peeler or a knife will do the trick. Also like ginger, galangal helps temper the pungency of seafood.

[THAI BASIL]

[VIETNAMESE PARILLA]

[RICE PADDY HERB]

[VIETNAMESE BALM]

[GALANGAL]

[GINGER]

[TURMERIC]

[LEMONGRASS]

{GARLIC}

{TARO STEMS}

{OKRA}

{TAMARIND}

{FRIED
SHALLOTS}

{TURMERIC
POWDER}

{CARDAMOM}

{CINNAMON}

{STAR ANISE}

Galangal has antioxidant properties known to settle stomach upset and ease nausea, and anti-inflammatory properties that help alleviate arthritis. While it's not used frequently in Europe today, in the Middle Ages, galangal was employed as an aphrodisiac and believed to repel evil spirits.

Galangal should be stored in the refrigerator in a plastic bag. It also freezes well; simply place peeled chunks in a plastic bag.

Ginger

Ginger is a wonder, not just because of its unique sweet and savory taste but also because it has a myriad of health benefits. The root is loaded with powerful anti-inflammatory and antioxidant agents that strengthen immunity, combat gastrointestinal distress and chronic indigestion, and help fight infection. Around the world, ginger is used to treat headaches and toothaches, upset stomach, flatulence, halitosis, colds, flus, morning sickness, motion sickness, and menstrual pain. All that and it tastes amazing, too!

Ginger is a wonderful addition to many dishes, from fish and stews to desserts and cocktails. It should be peeled before using, although since its skin is soft, the best method is to use a teaspoon to scrape the outside, leaving as much pulp behind as possible (remove the nubs with a small knife first). Ginger is used in recipes cut into pieces or sticks, sliced, shredded, or in powder form. Store fresh ginger in a plastic bag in the refrigerator; cut pieces will also keep well in the freezer.

Kaffir Lime Leaves

Kaffir lime leaves, dark green "doubled" leaves that look like two leaves in one, come from the kaffir lime tree, which produces fruit similar to a Western lime but with a textured, bumpy rind. The rind is used for oil; the juice is too acidic and the fruit is too bitter for most recipes. The leaves, however, are indispensable to Vietnamese cooking, much like bay leaves are in Mediterranean cooking. They impart a fresh, citrus zeal to recipes that cannot be replicated by Western lemons or limes.

You can buy kaffir lime leaves fresh, frozen, or dried. Always get them fresh or frozen if you can, since the dried leaves aren't as flavorful, but if dried is your only option, make sure you crush them before using. Fresh leaves freeze well; just toss them in a plastic bag in your freezer. Kaffir lime leaves can be thrown into recipes whole or cut into thin, 1-inch strips with the center vein removed and unlike bay leaves may be eaten.

Kaffir lime leaves are believed to act as a digestive aid, cleanse the blood, and help maintain healthy teeth and gums.

Lemongrass

This stalky green plant has a zesty lemony flavor and aroma as well as antiseptic, antimicrobial, antifungal, and healing properties. Full of vitamins A, B, and C, lemongrass is used to treat the flu, colds, and digestive issues, relieve pain, calm the nerves, treat insomnia, and even help battle depression.

When shopping for lemongrass, look for firm, not soft or rubbery, stalks. The bottom should be pale yellow or white, the top green; avoid any with brown leaves. When cooking with lemongrass, first cut off the root and remove the tough outer stalks. The remaining stems must be "bruised" to release flavor, either by bending them a few times or pressing them under the flat side of a large knife. Lemongrass should be stored in the refrigerator and will freeze well in a plastic bag.

Rice Paddy Herb (ngò ôm)

A tropical flowering plant native to Southeast Asia, *ngò ôm* thrives in hot, wet environments and is often seen sprouting in flooded rice paddies, hence its name. The fuzzy green stems and leaves have an intense flavor perhaps best described as a cross between citrus and cumin.

Sweet and savory, *ngò ôm* pairs perfectly with fresh water fish and is frequently used in Vietnamese fish soups.

Tamarind

Another legume frequently used in Asian cooking is tamarind, delicious sweet-and-sour seeds encased in brown pods. Tamarind is usually used in paste form, much like peanut butter, and can be purchased that way year round in specialty stores or online.

Tamarind is a good source of iron and magnesium, and is believed to help strengthen the immune system.

Turmeric

Turmeric root looks like a skinny cousin of ginger on the outside, but inside it is bright orange. It has a powerful flavor and is a natural food dye, so it is mainly used in its powdered form as a spice. If you purchase it whole, you must peel the outer skin away, and be careful: the bright orange interior will stain everything from your fingertips to your dishtowels.

Turmeric has a peppery, warm flavor and is one of the main ingredients in curry powder. It's also a powerful anti-inflammatory and antioxidant. Fresh turmeric should be stored in the refrigerator.

Vietnamese Balm [kinh giới]

Also called *kinh giới* or Vietnamese lemon mint, Vietnamese balm has delicate, light-green serrated leaves and both a lemony flavor and scent. Although its aroma and flavor are similar to the lemon balm of Europe and Africa, the plants are not related. Fresh leaves will keep for three to four days in a plastic bag in the refrigerator crisper drawer. Vietnamese balm is frequently eaten raw and added to hot tea and is known for its anti-aging and antioxidant properties. If you can't find Vietnamese balm in your local ethnic market, lemon balm can be substituted in most recipes.

Vietnamese Coriander [rau răm]

Also known as Vietnamese mint and Vietnamese hot mint, although it doesn't look like a coriander plant or come from the mint family, *rau răm* is an herb whose leaves resemble thinner, pointed mint leaves—dark green with brown or burgundy markings. *Rau răm* has a slightly spicy and lemony flavor. It is ideally eaten fresh and frequently used in salads and summer rolls as well as in soups and stews. Fresh leaves will freeze well in a plastic bag.

Rau răm has antibacterial and anti-inflammatory properties and is frequently used to treat digestion issues and skin conditions.

Vietnamese Parilla [tía tô]

One of our family's favorite herbs and the namesake of our restaurant in Santa Monica, *tía tô* is a member of the mint family but is unique in that its beautiful leaves are green on top and purple on the bottom. The savory leaves are rich in vitamins and minerals as well as omega-3 fatty acids. *Tía tô* is believed to keep the yin and the yang of the body in balance and has anti-inflammatory and anti-cancer properties as well.

Tía tô should be used fresh, and will keep well in the freezer. Look for brightly colored leaves on both sides. *Tía tô* is extremely easy to grow in the ground or in containers and makes a lovely edible addition to any garden.

Fruits

Many tropical fruits used in Vietnamese cooking, like coconut, are well-known outside of Asia and easy to find in many forms, such as fresh, shredded, and dried. Here are some of the more exotic fruits we use, though, which are typically found in gourmet, specialty, or Asian markets if you can't find them in your local supermarket. They are also available online.

Diana with chayote in her garden.

Chayote

Part of the melon and cucumber family, chayote has a mild taste and a crispy crunch which makes it a perfect vehicle for many dishes. It can be added to salads or pickled for an accompaniment to almost anything. The pale green, pear-shaped fruit has a wrinkly skin covered with tiny prickles that must be peeled off (wearing gloves for this task is advised). An excellent source of folate, chayote is believed to be good for the heart and brain.

Ginkgo Nuts

Female ginkgo bilboa trees have round, plum-sized fruits that honestly smell quite awful. However, inside is the delicious ginkgo nut that is believed to help ward of dementia and lower cholesterol levels. Ginkgo nuts should be cooked before eating; they can be toasted, roasted, or boiled.

Goji Berries

Considered a "superfruit" because of their high nutrient and antioxidant content, the bright orange-red berries, also called wolfberries, have long been used in both Eastern medicine and cuisine. They have a slightly tart taste, like a cross between a cherry and a cranberry, and are usually sold in dried form.

NOTE: *Goji berries can interact with certain medications for blood thinning, blood pressure, and diabetes, so check with your doctor if you are on any of these medications.*

Lychee

Lychee fruit are something of a treasure in packaging, taste, and nutritional benefits. The oval or round fruit is covered with a leathery pink skin that is easily peeled off to reveal juicy, white flesh, much like a peeled grape. Inside that is a dark brown seed that should not be eaten.

Lychees are sweet, juicy, and have a cooling effect on the body. They have many nutrients, vitamins, and antioxidants, and they are thought to even have anti-influenza virus properties.

Star fruit

Star fruit hold true to their name in appearance: they are fruit shaped like stars. Inside, they have soft, juicy flesh like a kiwi but with seeds that must be removed, similar to those found in an apple. Many feel that the flavor of star fruit reminds them of apples, too. Like an apple, the peel can be eaten or removed. Star fruit are filled with antioxidants and rich in copper.

NOTE: *Star fruit contain oxalic acid, which should be avoided by people with kidney disease, and like grapefruit, they can interact with certain prescription medications.*

Vegetables

Allow us to introduce you to a few of our favorite vegetables, packed with both taste and nutrition. If you've never had these, they are well worth incorporating into your diet.

Bok Choy

Bok choy, also known as Chinese cabbage, is a green, leafy vegetable with leaves that grow in a cluster like celery. Look for firm, unspotted stalks and dark green leaves. To prepare, simply cut off the bottom inch of the stalk—the rest is edible. Store bok choy in the refrigerator crisper drawer.

Bok choy is crispy and refreshing, like a cross between lettuce and cabbage. It can have a slightly bitter taste when eaten raw, although baby bok choy is sweeter. It outmatches almost every other cruciferous vegetable in nutritional value, boasting more than twenty-one different nutrients and seventy different antioxidants. In fact, the US Centers for Disease Control and Prevention ranked it second among all nutrient dense "powerhouse" fruits and vegetables, just behind watercress.

Chinese Long Beans

Also called asparagus beans, garter beans, snake beans, and yard long beans, these long, curling beans resemble Western green beans but are slightly thinner and much, much longer—from 12 to 20 inches. They have a mild taste slightly reminiscent of asparagus, and they are prepared similarly to green beans but require less prep time. Long beans are frequently used in stir-fries because they hold up very well to the heat.

Daikon

Daikon is a root vegetable that looks like a very large white carrot and is prepped in much the same way as carrots—cut into sticks or slices, diced, or shredded—although it tastes quite different. Daikon has a delicious, slightly spicy bite. It can be eaten raw or cooked and is wonderful roasted. Daikon is used in salads, slaws, sandwiches, noodle dishes, soups, sushi, and spring rolls. Daikon can be stored in the refrigerator, but it does tend to emit a stink, so be sure to wrap it well in plastic.

Lotus Root

Beneath the beautiful freshwater lotus flower lies a root that resembles an elongated potato. However, unlike a potato, lotus root has cylindrical tubes running through it that form a pretty flower design when cut into slices (children in Asia make wonderful prints using cut lotus root dipped in paint).

Full of fiber and potassium, lotus root is widely used in the East to treat insomnia, irritability, and fatigue and is especially favored by new mothers.

Okra

Although it's technically a fruit, we eat it like a vegetable, much like we eat green beans. Okra has a mild flavor similar to eggplant and is great in stir-fries. High in antioxidants, okra is also a good source of fiber, vitamin C, and calcium.

Taro Stems (dọc mùng)

Also called Indian taro and giant elephant ear, taro stems are tuberous, sort of like celery, but much larger and spongier. Typically sold already cut and wrapped in plastic to keep in the moisture, taro stems can be as thick as your wrist or forearm, but they weigh next to nothing. They don't really have a taste—it's the nice, crunchy texture Vietnamese cooks love—and the way the built-in straws soak up soups and broths. Unlike celery, however, taro stems cannot be eaten raw. They contain a natural toxin that can severely irritate the throat unless it is neutralized during cooking.

Water Spinach

Water spinach, also called river spinach, Chinese spinach, and kang kong, looks nothing like Western spinach, although it does share a similar taste. Water spinach has thin, pointed, arrow-shaped leaves on top of very long, hollow stems. Both the leaves and tender shoots are used in stir-fries, and eaten as a common side dish in Vietnam. Water spinach should always be cooked, as bacteria can hide in the hollow shoots and isn't easily washed away.

Water spinach is an excellent source of vitamins, folate, iron, copper, and manganese.

Wood Ear Mushrooms

Unlike shiitake or portobello mushrooms, wood ear mushrooms don't have a rounded cap, gills, or much of a stem. Instead, they look like wavy, dark brown ears. They have a subtle woody flavor and aroma, but they are most used in cooking for their color and crisp, squeaky texture.

To keep their firmness, wood ear mushrooms shouldn't be cooked for very long; always add them to dishes toward the end of cooking. Dried wood ear mushrooms will last for years if kept out of the sunlight in a sealed container. Once constituted, however, they should be used right away.

Wood ear mushrooms are rich in dietary fiber and protein, high in iron, and contain the powerful antioxidant riboflavin.

Meats

In Vietnam, we do not waste any part of the animal. Almost everything is edible, from the tip to the tail. Most of us are so far removed from having to butcher our own animals, however, that we have become uncomfortable with less frequently used or unknown parts. There is no reason to be! If you like any part of a particular animal protein, chances are you will like it all. Do not shy away from any cut because of its name, since the nomenclature of butchery is arbitrary and changes frequently. There are currently more than fifty cuts of beef commonly sold in the United States and many of them have multiple names. Top sirloin cap steak used to be called "coulotte steak"; what used to be known as merlot steak is now labeled "bottom round heel side." In Asian cooking we tend to use cuts that are named for where they originate on the animal. Remember, a name is just a name and all cuts are just inches away from others. If brisket were called pectoral steak or if skirt steak were called front belly cut, that wouldn't make them any less delicious.

Duck

Duck is a staple protein around the world, from France to Vietnam. The exception seems to be in America where duck is viewed as an extravagant extra. Perhaps this is due to the large beef and chicken industry in the United States or misconceptions about the nutritional content of duck. Darker and with a bolder taste than chicken, duck is also juicier because of a higher concentration of oil in the skin. Some people mistakenly believe that this means

FINDING "EXOTIC" MEATS

Less common proteins can often be found fresh or frozen at many different locations around the country, including:

○ *Specialty stores like Whole Foods Market and Trader Joe's*

○ *Local butcher shops*

○ *Ethnic groceries: Asian, Italian, or Mexican*

○ *Local farms*

○ *Farmers' markets, especially large downtown ones*

○ *Online meat purveyors like D'Artagnan Gourmet Food*

duck is fattier than chicken. However, skinless duck breast has less fat and significantly fewer calories than chicken has. One hundred grams of skinless duck breast contains 123 calories and 4 grams of fat, compared to 100 grams of skinless chicken breast, which contains 195 calories and 7.7 grams of fat. Duck is not only delicious, it's also a superb source of protein, iron, and vitamin B3.

Jidori Chicken

Jidori, often referred to as the Kobe beef of poultry, is a new breed of free-range, fruit-and-vegetable-fed chicken that originated in Japan. These all-natural chickens are never frozen and are delivered to customers the day after they are slaughtered, which gives them a wonderful taste and also a better texture than chickens frozen during transport. Jidori chickens taste like really, really good chicken. You can get a similar quality from your local, organic farm.

Pork Belly

Pork belly is simply bacon before it's been dried, salted, and cured. The same cut of meat fresh, unsalted, and uncured is the filet mignon cut of the pig: tender and delicious. Like bacon, however, pork belly does have a lot of flavor and a lot of fat. But a little goes a long way. Rather than cutting into a slab of pork belly like a steak, it is best to use it as a flavor enhancer or addition to an otherwise healthy dish. Pork belly is often sold in large chunks, and it freezes beautifully; just thaw it overnight in your refrigerator.

Pork Cheek

This small cut of meat is very lean but also quite tough—until it is cooked, that is. Once braised or slow cooked, it becomes so tender it will practically melt in your mouth. Pork cheek's moist texture has long been appreciated by both chefs and nose-to-tail connoisseurs, but because it is a smaller, less popular cut, you may need to order it ahead of time from your butcher. The good news, though, is that it's one of the cheapest cuts of meat you can buy.

Quail

A smaller bird than a chicken or duck, quail stands right in between the two in terms of taste: it has a stronger flavor than chicken, but isn't quite as strong as duck. It is, however, extremely succulent and more tender than both chicken and duck. Since whole quails are small, care must be taken not to let them dry out when cooking. The secret is to cook them quickly to keep the juices sealed inside. The result: fall-off-the-bone tenderness.

Sauces

Instead of soaking food in sauce or oil while it is cooking, Vietnamese cooks tend to focus on heating the food first—by stir-frying, poaching, steaming, or baking—and then complementing the main ingredients' natural flavors with light

but powerful sauces. We give the recipes for our favorite homemade sauces later in the book, but sometimes using a prepared sauce is best. The four bottled sauces we use most frequently are fish sauce, hoisin sauce, soy sauce, and Sriracha. They can be found online and at groceries and retailers nationwide (even Target sells fish sauce).

Fish Sauce

If fish sauce had a less ingredient-specific name, like Hanoi sauce or umami sauce, it would be as integral to American cooks as it is to Vietnamese. Case in point: Worcestershire sauce also contains fermented fish, but Caesar salad, beef stew, and Bloody Marys wouldn't be the same without it. The same goes for fish sauce—it is the secret ingredient that elevates our cooking to a magical place. Yes, it's fermented, but so are ketchup, wine, yogurt, sourdough bread, and sour cream. Yes, it has a particular smell, but so do vinegar and molasses. Fish sauce isn't meant to be inhaled or swigged from the bottle; it's a flavor booster that will add an extra dimension to almost any dish.

A little goes a long way, so if you're new to fish sauce, use it sparingly until you become accustomed to it. You can always add more, but it's impossible to remove excess. If you're hesitant, try using half the recommended amount in a recipe the first time. And not all brands are created equal, so purchasing a good one is important. Our favorite brands are listed in the Appendix on page 285.

To keep it from crystallizing, store fish sauce in a dark cabinet rather than in the refrigerator.

Hoisin Sauce

Hoisin sauce is a thick, dark sauce similar to American BBQ sauce and is used as a glaze for meat, a condiment, and a dipping sauce. It's typically made from a combination of soy sauce, red chiles, and garlic. Although hoisin comes from the Chinese word for seafood, it does not contain any fish. Hoisin sauce is sweet and salty and delicious warm or cold.

Once opened, hoisin sauce should be stored in the refrigerator.

Maggi Seasoning Sauce

Maggi is the brand name of the company that sells a number of ready-made sauces and noodles; it started in Switzerland and is now owned by Nestlé. Their Seasoning Sauce is very popular in Asian cooking because it offers a rich, concentrated flavor, like a cross between soy sauce and beef bouillon.

Even when opened, Maggi seasoning sauce can continue to be stored in the cabinet or another cool, dry place.

Oyster Sauce

Oyster sauce is an oyster-flavored sauce believed to have been invented in the late nineteenth century by a Cantonese chef. Savory with a hint of sweetness, it's made by caramelizing oyster juice along with other ingredients such as chicken broth, sugar, and a thickening agent to concentrate the flavor.

Oyster sauce should be refrigerated once opened.

Sambal

Sambal refers to a type of spicy, chile-based condiment. It can be made with ground or puréed chiles, along with other ingredients ranging from citrus juice to shrimp paste. Sambal can be found in powder, sauce, or relish form. Many brand names offer their proprietary version of sambal, or you can make your own.

Unless it is a powder, sambal should be stored in the refrigerator once opened.

Soy Sauce

Soy sauce is a brown liquid made by fermenting soybeans, salt, water, and wheat. It has a salty, earthy umami flavor that complements many Asian dishes. There are four main types of soy sauce. Light soy sauce is the most common, usually marketed as regular soy sauce. Dark soy sauce includes either molasses or caramel for thickening and a touch of sweetness. Low-sodium soy sauce has less salt, and tamari soy sauce is gluten-free.

Once opened, soy sauce can be stored in a cabinet, but putting it in the refrigerator will help prevent degradation of flavor.

Sriracha Sauce

A hot chili sauce named for the town of Si Racha in Thailand, sriracha is a rather new product that was created in the 1980s. It's like a ketchup that's sweet, tangy, and hot all at once and goes wonderfully with almost any food from soup to pizza. It can be used as a condiment or added to other sauces like marinara or hummus to give them a kick. It's hot but not unbearably so, since it's made primarily with jalapeños. In the United States, it's also known as "rooster sauce," since the bottle of the most common brand, California-based Huy Fong Foods, features a rooster on it.

Once opened, sriracha sauce will keep in the refrigerator for up to one year.

THE SECRET TO COOKING RICE

It seems like a simple process, but like making eggs, cooking rice can confound even the best cook. Rice is very important to most Vietnamese people because it is the foundation of the meal and must be able to stand up to and transfer flavors. Helene is very picky about her rice; it has to have just the right amount of moisture without being too sticky, too mushy, or too dry. Here is her recipe for making perfect rice every time.

STEP 1: Polish the Rice

Measure out the amount of rice you want to use into an empty pot. Fill the pot with cold water, raking your fingers through the rice to help wash it. Strain the rice in a fine-mesh colander. Do this about three times until the water runs clear to help remove any impurities from the rice.

NOTE: *Save the rice straining water for your garden or houseplants; it is full of vitamins.*

STEP 2: Use the Right Amount of Water

Start with the following ratio: 1 cup of rice to 1½ cups of water for long- or medium- grain rice and 1¼ cups of water for short-grain rice, and adjust the measurements until you find the perfect consistency for you. Do not add any salt or butter to the rice at this time. After it's cooked, you can add flavorings.

For an electric rice cooker, follow the manufacturer's directions for cooking. Skip to step 5.

For stovetop cooking, continue to step 3.

STEP 3: Boil Uncovered, Simmer Covered

Put the rice and water in a heavy pot over high heat and bring the water to a boil, uncovered. (Be sure to choose a pot with a tight-fitting lid, since steam is integral to cooking rice.) Once the water is boiling, turn the heat down to low, cover, and simmer until all of the water has been absorbed, about 15 minutes. Resist the urge to remove the lid and check on the rice more than once, and replace the lid promptly when you do.

STEP 4: Let Rice Rest

Turn the heat off and put the pot on a cold burner. Allow it to sit undisturbed, still covered, for 5 to 30 minutes. This will allow the moisture to redistribute evenly among the rice kernels.

STEP 5: Fluff and Enjoy

Remove the lid. Fluff the rice with a fork or wooden spatula. Serve.

Cornerstone Classics

You've been introduced to our family, our heritage, and our way of cooking. But before we continue with our story, we wanted to get you started on a few classic dishes that personify the An family's flavor profile.

Mama's Beef Phở

PHỞ IS A DEEPLY PERSONAL DISH *to many Vietnamese people and variations abound around the country. While phở is traditionally served in the North with only scallions and a little cilantro, in the South it's presented with a full herb platter. My mother's phở recipe is a more northern version, Hanoi-style, simpler and less complicated than southern versions. In the South, daikon is often used to add sweetness, but my mother omits it, preferring only charred onions and ginger for the same effect. She adds oxtail and knuckle bones to add more sweetness and depth.*

MAKES 8 SERVINGS

FOR THE PHO:

2 pounds (2-inch thick) beef brisket or sirloin steak, cut in half to fit into the pot

2 teaspoons salt, divided

3 quarts Phở Beef Broth (page 272)

3 whole star anise

1 large white onion, charred and then peeled (see note, page 55)

One 3-inch piece fresh ginger, charred and then peeled (see note, page 55)

1 teaspoon sugar

2 (14-ounce) packages flat rice stick (*bánh phở*) noodles, see note, page 54)

4 teaspoons fish sauce, or more or less depending on your personal preference

½ large red onion, thinly sliced

1 cup chopped scallions (from about 2 bunches)

1 cup chopped fresh cilantro leaves (from about 2 bunches)

1 teaspoon freshly ground black pepper

FOR THE HERB PLATTER:

Fresh Thai basil leaves

Fresh bean sprouts

Fresh culantro (*ngò gai*) leaves

2 limes, each cut into 8 pieces

4 serrano or jalapeño peppers, thinly sliced

Chili sauce (optional)

Hoisin sauce (optional)

1) Put the brisket in an extra large stockpot and add water until the meat is covered. Add 1 teaspoon of the salt and bring the water to a boil. Boil for 3 minutes, then strain the meat and rinse it well with cold water. Discard the liquid and rinse the pot.

2) Return the brisket to the clean pot and add the beef broth and 1 quart of water. Bring the liquid to a boil over medium heat, skimming the surface often to remove any fat, froth, and impurities. Continue to cook until most of the impurities are gone and the water is almost clear, 15 to 20 minutes.

3) Add the star anise, charred onion, and ginger to the pot and bring the mixture back to a boil. Boil for 15 minutes, reduce the heat to low, and simmer for 1 hour. Add the remaining teaspoon of salt and the sugar and cook for another 30 minutes to meld the flavors.

4) Remove the brisket from the pot and transfer it to a plate to cool. Once it is cool to the touch, cover the brisket and place it in the refrigerator.

(Continued)

NOTE: *To store the brisket at this point for use later in the day or the next day, place it in a large airtight container. Let the broth come to room temperature, pour it over the brisket, then cover the container and store it in the refrigerator. This will infuse the brisket with flavor and keep it from drying out.*

5〕 Remove and discard the star anise, charred onion, and ginger from the broth. Strain the broth through a fine-mesh sieve to remove any impurities. The phở broth should be clear. (If it is not, strain it again.)

6〕 About 30 minutes before you are ready to serve the phở, soak the rice noodles in warm water for 15 to 20 minutes, then drain. Meanwhile, slice the brisket paper thin against the grain (into about ⅛-inch slices), and set aside.

7〕 When you are ready to serve, bring a large pot of salted water to a boil over high heat. Add the noodles and cook them until al dente, 20 to 30 seconds. Drain and rinse the noodles very well with cold water, quickly rinse them with warm water to remove any remaining starch, and then strain the noodles. Divide the noodles evenly among eight serving bowls. Place the brisket slices on top of the noodles. Add the red onion slices on top of the brisket.

8〕 Bring the broth back to a boil and stir in the fish sauce. Ladle the boiling broth over top of the sliced meat to fill each bowl. Top each serving with scallions, cilantro, and a pinch of black pepper. Serve immediately with the herb platter on the side.

BUYING PHỞ NOODLES

Phở noodles—*bánh phở*—are similar to Italian pasta, except for the fact that they are made from white rice flour rather than wheat flour, which makes them naturally gluten-free. Rice noodles have a similar calorie, carbohydrate, fat, and fiber content to wheat noodles, but rice noodles don't get soggy and are therefore perfect for soups and leftovers.

Like pasta, rice noodles come in varying widths, from extra-small (similar to angel hair) to extra-large (similar to pappardelle). The wider noodles are preferable for stir-fries, while thinner noodles are best in soups. For phở, choose small-width (3-mm or ⅛-inch) or medium-width (6-mm or ¼-inch) rice noodles. While round rice noodles, also called rice vermicelli, are used in other recipes, traditionally the noodles for phở are flat.

Bánh phở, also known as rice stick noodles, can be purchased at Asian specialty markets, in addition to Trader Joe's, Whole Foods, and in the international aisles of many large grocery stores.

CHARRING ONIONS AND GINGER

Charring brings a wonderfully smoky and sweet flavor to dishes, especially soups. Onions and ginger—and other vegetables, such as garlic—may be charred on the stovetop or in the oven. Once the vegetable is charred, peel and remove its blackened skins and rinse it before adding to your dish.

TO CHAR ON THE STOVETOP: Turn a gas or electric burner to medium-high heat. Using tongs, hold an onion or piece of ginger directly over the burner for about 5 minutes, rotating until all sides are blackened. Repeat for each onion and/or piece of ginger. You can also set the onions and/or ginger on a rack set directly on top of the gas or electric burner to cook more of them at once. Just be sure to keep rotating the vegetables for even charring.

TO CHAR IN THE OVEN: Move a rack up to the highest position in the oven and preheat the oven to 450°F. Cut the onions in half. Put the onions and the ginger on a baking sheet on the top rack. Cook until the tops of the vegetables turn slightly black, about 5 minutes. Turn the onions and ginger over and repeat.

HOW TO EAT PHỞ: A CRASH COURSE

True appreciation of the delicate flavors of phở, the perfect mixture of sweet and spicy broth, aromatic spices, and chewy noodles, requires two hands and a bit of know-how.

1] Although phở is usually served with accompanying herbs and sauces, your first taste should be of nothing but the unadulterated broth. Savor a sip of the crystal-clear broth before adding anything to it or even tasting the meat and noodles.

2] You can now add condiments to your phở, although it's not required. While phở is generally served with some greens on top of the meat in the bowl, it should also be presented with a side dish that resembles a fresh salad—piled high with basil, bean sprouts, culantro (ngò gai), or even chiles—and homemade or bottled sauces for extra bite. Add any or all at your discretion.

3] To get the perfect mouthful of noodles and broth, you'll need both hands. Use a soup spoon in your left hand and chopsticks (or a fork) in your right hand. Fill the spoon with broth and hold it steady while you retrieve the noodles or meat with the chopsticks. Place the noodles or meat in your mouth and follow immediately with a slurp of the broth before chewing.

Oven-Roasted Lemongrass Chicken

IN OUR LARGE FAMILY—FIVE KIDS, ELEVEN GRANDCHILDREN, AND COUNTING!—this is a dish that always goes over well with everyone. The younger ones love the fragrant and moist chicken, while my mother loves that she can do most of the preparation the night before and then just relax and play with her grandchildren when they visit for a meal. This is an easy and delicious introduction to my mother's favorite flavors: basil and thyme, Vietnamese parilla (tía tô), lemongrass, and fish sauce. At our home we eat this with rice, spooning the pan juice over top, with a side of sliced tomatoes and butter lettuce with Helene's Lemon-Sugar Dressing (page 280).

MAKES 4 SERVINGS

6 garlic cloves, smashed

6 sprigs fresh cilantro, chopped

½ bunch (about 1 handful) fresh Vietnamese balm (kinh giới) or lemon balm leaves, chopped

½ bunch (about 1 handful) Vietnamese perilla (tía tô) leaves

½ bunch (about 1 handful) fresh Vietnamese coriander (rau răm) leaves

5 kaffir lime leaves, very finely chopped

2 fresh lemongrass stalks, tender inner white bulb only, finely chopped

1 tablespoon white peppercorns

1 teaspoon coriander seeds, toasted

2 tablespoons fish sauce

1 tablespoon low-sodium soy sauce

1 tablespoon freshly squeezed lemon juice

3 tablespoons palm sugar, coconut sugar, or lightly packed light brown sugar

1 teaspoon sea salt

1 whole (2½-pound) chicken, quartered, backbone removed

2 tablespoons unsalted butter, melted

1 tablespoon honey

1) **TO MAKE THE MARINADE:** With a mortar and pestle or in a food processor, process the garlic, cilantro, all leaves, lemongrass, peppercorns, and coriander into a paste. Transfer the paste to a medium bowl and stir in the fish sauce, soy sauce, lemon juice, sugar, and salt.

2) Put the chicken in a resealable plastic bag. Add the marinade and seal the bag. Turn the chicken to coat well. Refrigerate for at least 4 hours or overnight.

3) Preheat the oven to 350°F.

4) Remove the chicken from the refrigerator and allow it to come to room temperature, about 20 minutes. Reduce the oven temperature to 300°F. Place a 2½-foot-long piece of aluminum foil in a 13 x 9-inch baking pan. Coat the top of the foil with nonstick cooking spray. Place the chicken in the center of the foil, skin-side up, and fold the foil over it to make a packet. Transfer the pan to the oven and bake for 30 minutes.

5) Increase the oven temperature to 450°F. Carefully peel back the foil and bake the chicken uncovered for 5 minutes longer so the skin is lightly golden browned. The sugar in the marinade might make the juice in the foil look burned, but it won't affect the chicken. Remove the pan from the oven and brush the chicken skin with the melted butter. Then brush with honey. Return the pan to the oven and roast the chicken uncovered for another 5-10 minutes until golden browned. The chicken is done when it shows no sign of pink when pierced in the center with a sharp knife. Serve hot.

Vietnamese Chicken Coriander Cabbage Salad

MY MOTHER RECENTLY MADE THIS FOR MY SON ELIAN'S FIRST BIRTHDAY PARTY. *It's so simple yet packs so much flavor that it is always a top request from my friends. It is important to cut the cabbage into very thin strips. My mother's secret is the grapeseed oil. She uses it to lighten the fish sauce, which makes the entire dish more refreshing.*

MAKES 4 SERVINGS

3 cups Homemade Chicken Broth (page 273) or store-bought low-sodium chicken broth

1 large (8-ounce) boneless, skinless chicken breast

1 head green cabbage

3 tablespoons plus 1 teaspoon sugar, divided

3 tablespoons freshly squeezed lemon juice

1 tablespoon finely chopped roasted garlic

1 teaspoon fish sauce

1 teaspoon sambal chili paste

1 cup coarsely chopped fresh Vietnamese coriander (*rau răm*) leaves (about 1 bunch or 2½ ounces), divided

1 cup coarsely chopped fresh basil (about 1 bunch or 2½ ounces), divided

3 teaspoons grapeseed oil

1 tablespoon Fried Shallots, optional (page 281)

1 tablespoon Roasted Peanuts, optional (page 281)

Cooked shrimp or sesame puff crisps, prepackaged or homemade (page 219), for serving

1) Add the chicken stock to a medium pot and bring it to a boil over high heat. Reduce the heat to medium and add the chicken breast. Cook for 10 minutes. Turn the heat off, cover the pot, and let it sit for 10 minutes. Remove the chicken from the broth and set it aside in a large mixing bowl. Once the chicken is cool enough to handle, shred it by hand in the bowl. Set aside.

2) Meanwhile, prepare the salad. Remove and discard any discolored or wilted leaves from the cabbage head, keeping just the nicest, greenest ones. Using a cabbage slicer or large chef's knife, shred the cabbage leaves and place them in a large serving bowl.

3) To the large mixing bowl with the shredded chicken, add 1 teaspoon of the sugar, along with the roast garlic, fish sauce, and chili paste, and mix well. Add half of the coriander and half of the basil and toss lightly. Set aside to marinate at room temperature for 30 minutes.

4] Meanwhile, in a small bowl, whisk the remaining 3 tablespoons of sugar with the lemon juice until the sugar dissolves, about 2 minutes. Set aside.

5] When ready to serve, drizzle the lemon sugar over the cabbage. Add the grapeseed oil and toss well. Add the seasoned shredded chicken to the top of the cabbage and sprinkle with the remaining coriander and basil. Top with fried shallots and roasted peanuts, if desired, and serve immediately with crisps.

MAKING SESAME CRISPS

Sesame rice crisps, also called Asian shrimp crisps, shrimp puffs, or prawn crackers, can be bought inflated and ready-to-eat, or compressed and in need of cooking. If you have the latter, to get them to expand, heat 1 cup of canola oil in a large, deep skillet or wok over medium heat, add the crisps a few at a time so they have room to expand, and then cook slowly until they inflate. When they are fully puffed, scoop them out with a slotted spoon or spider strainer and place them on a paper towel–lined baking sheet to absorb the oil.

You can also make your own using sesame rice paper. Sesame crisps can be made by grilling or baking the wrappers, but we prefer to achieve the perfect puff by frying. Here's how:

MAKES 16 CRISPS

2 (8-inch) sesame rice paper wrappers

2 cups canola oil

1] Cut each wrapper into 8 pieces, for a total of 16 pieces.

2] Heat the oil in a large, deep skillet or wok over medium heat until it reaches 350°F on a candy or deep-frying thermometer. Once the oil is hot, reduce the heat to medium-low or low. Working in batches (because the pieces will expand in size as they cook), add three rice wrapper pieces to the pan. Fry the crisps until they puff, turn lightly golden, and float up to the top, about 15 seconds. Using a skimmer or slotted spoon, scoop out the crisps and drain them on paper towels before using.

NOTE: *To test if the oil is hot enough to use, drop in one small piece of onion. If it turns golden and floats to the top in 5 seconds, then the oil is ready.*

Caramelized Black Cod

LIKE MANY DISHES IN VIETNAM, THIS CLASSIC COMFORT FOOD VARIES BY REGION *(in the North it's saltier and drier; in the South it's sweeter and juicier), but one thing is always constant: the incredible harmony of otherwise contradictory flavors—sweet caramel and savory fish sauce. You can vary the amount of sugar or fish sauce depending upon your personal preference, but here's how my family likes it best. The secret is to let the fish soak in the caramel fish sauce long enough for the umami flavor to arrive. While we use buttery and delicate black cod in our restaurants, you can also use catfish if you want a more rustic, slightly meatier tasting fish.*

Serve with jasmine rice and a side of steamed or Pickled Vegetables (page 237).

MAKES 2 TO 3 SERVINGS

6 tablespoons fish sauce, divided

6 shallots, minced (about 6 tablespoons)

1 bunch scallions (6 to 8 bulbs), white part only, pounded

1 dried bird's eye chile, pounded

4 teaspoons sugar

1 teaspoon sea salt

1 (1-pound) black cod fillet, skin on, cut in half

2 tablespoons canola oil

3 garlic cloves, minced

2 tablespoons Caramel Sauce (page 275)

2 tablespoons coconut water

1) In a large bowl, mix 4 tablespoons of the fish sauce with the shallots, scallions, chile, sugar, and salt. Add the fish and turn to coat. Set aside and let the fish marinate for 30 minutes to 1 hour.

2) Heat the oil in a large saucepan over high heat. Add the garlic and sauté until it is lightly browned and fragrant, about 2 minutes. Add the marinated fish, sear each side for 1 minute, then spoon the caramel sauce over the top of the fish and gently move around, shifting the pan or using a spatula so the sauce drips down the sides of the fish. Cover the pan, reduce the heat to medium, and cook the fish for 3 minutes allowing the fish to absorb the sauce. Remove the lid and add 2 tablespoons of the coconut water; lower the heat to a simmer cook for 10 more minutes allowing the fish to again absorb the sauce and for the sauce to thicken.

3) Serve the fish hot over rice with extra sauce from the pan spooned on top.

Fried Rice with Shrimp, Chicken, and Chinese Sausage

EASY AND QUICK, THIS DISH IS A WEEKNIGHT FAVORITE AT OUR HOUSE *because it's the perfect vehicle for reinventing leftovers. Roast meat from last night's dinner stir-fried with rice turns into something new and equally delicious.*

Fried rice was my father's specialty, although he and my mother still debate who taught whom how to make it and whose is the best. My father likes to use ham and add a fried egg on top for an extra level of homey decadence, while my mother always adds fried shallots and garlic for a fragrant kick.

Aside from the endless ingredient combinations, the secret to perfect fried rice is to use day-old rice. Before adding it the pan, massage the rice with some good butter or olive oil for extra flavor. This keeps the rice moist, and prevents it from charring or clumping together when you cook it.

MAKES 6 TO 8 SERVINGS

1 cup long grain rice, cooked

2 tablespoons extra-virgin olive oil

1 teaspoon sea salt

1 teaspoon freshly ground black pepper

2 teaspoons sugar, divided

3 egg yolks, beaten

4 tablespoons canola oil, divided

1 large white onion, diced

4 garlic cloves, minced

½ medium boneless, skinless chicken breast (about 3 ounces), cut into ¼ inch slices

3 ounces Chinese sausage

¼ pound large shrimp (size 31/35; about 8 pieces), peeled, deveined, and halved

1 tablespoon Maggi seasoning sauce

¼ cup cooked carrots, diced

¼ cup diced celery

¼ cup English peas

¼ cup cooked greens beans, diced

1 tablespoon Homemade Chicken Broth (page 273) or store-bought low-sodium chicken broth (optional)

2 tablespoons fish sauce, divided

4 tablespoons chopped scallions

1] Spread the cooked rice on a sheet pan and refrigerate uncovered for 2 hours to overnight.

2] Place the chilled rice in a large bowl, add the olive oil, salt, pepper, and 1 teaspoon of the sugar and massage the mixture together, breaking up the clumps with your fingertips. Mix in the egg yolks.

3] Heat 1 tablespoon of the canola oil in a large skillet or wok over medium-high heat. Add the diced onion and garlic and sauté until softened and fragrant, about 2 minutes. Add the chicken and sausage, and sauté for about 5 mintues until nicely browned, then add the shrimp and sauté for 3 minutes until the shrimp becomes opaque. Sprinkle the meat with the Maggi seasoning, then transfer the mixture to a plate; set aside.

4] In the same pan, heat 1 tablespoon of the canola oil. Add the carrots, celery, peas, and green beans. Stir in the chicken broth (if using) or 1 tablespoon of water and sauté the vegetables until they are slightly tender, about 2 minutes. Scoop the vegetables out of the pan and into a large bowl. Set aside.

5] Still using the same pan, place it over high heat and add the remaining 2 tablespoons of canola oil. Add half of the rice and sauté over medium heat until it is dry, fragrant and no longer clumped together, 4 to 5 minutes. Stir in 1 tablespoon of the fish sauce, half of the meat mixture, and half of the vegetable mixture. Cook, stirring frequently, until everything is heated through, about 5 minutes. Repeat this process with the remaining rice, fish sauce, meat, and vegetables. Stir in the scallions just before serving.

FRIED VEGGIE RICE

I personally love to add as many fresh vegetables to my fried rice as possible: celery, carrots, asparagus—the crunchier the better. In fact, I recently discovered that, when sliced thinly, the hard kale stems I usually throw away make a wonderful addition to fried rice. The heat makes them tender but crisp and maintains their delicious tanginess.

Filet Mignon Shaken Beef

MANY PEOPLE THINK SHAKEN OR SHAKING BEEF IS NAMED FOR A PLACE IN ASIA *(like Peking duck, perhaps), but it really refers to the cooking technique used to make it: we shake the wok to make sure all sides of the beef are seared and the flavor is locked in. The secret to tender, flavorful, and juicy shaken beef is to not only use a good cut of meat, but to also have a very hot wok or pan and include just a touch of cornstarch in the marinade to seal the flavors to the meat.*

This is a great dish to start with if you are trying to introduce someone to fish sauce, since the combination of Maggi seasoning sauce and Worcestershire sauce (which is made of fermented anchovies), is a close approximation of the flavor. At Crustacean, we serve this with roasted potatoes, while at Tiato, we serve it on a bed of lettuce with Helene's Lemon-Sugar Dressing (page 280).

MAKES 2 SERVINGS

2 tablespoons canola oil, divided

½ teaspoon cornstarch

1 teaspoon sea salt

½ teaspoon freshly ground black pepper

1 tablespoon oyster sauce (optional)

1 pound filet mignon, cut into 1-inch cubes

1 cup red wine

¼ cup Maggi seasoning sauce

¼ cup Worcestershire sauce

¼ cup sugar

6 garlic cloves, minced (about 4 teaspoons)

1 large red onion, sliced

2 large tomatoes, peeled and cut into 6 wedges each, for garnish

1) In a large bowl, combine 1 tablespoon of the oil with the cornstarch, salt, pepper, and oyster sauce (if using). Mix well. Add the steak and toss well to coat. Cover the bowl and set it aside for 30 minutes.

2) Meanwhile, make the red wine sauce: In a medium bowl, combine the red wine, Maggi sauce, Worcestershire sauce, and sugar. Cover the bowl and set aside. Note: As we only use 2 tablespoons for each serving, you can save the extra wine sauce for future meals or increase the amount of meat.

3) Heat the remaining tablespoon of oil in a large skillet or wok over high heat. When the oil is hot (a small piece of garlic dropped in it will sizzle instantly), reduce the heat to medium. Add half of the marinated steak and sear for 3 minutes on one side, then flip and sear for 1 minute on the other side. Add 2 teaspoons of the minced garlic, and shake the pan for 30 seconds. Then add 2 tablespoons of the red wine sauce and cook for 2 minutes, shaking the pan continuously. The meat will be nicely browned and medium rare. Cook longer for more well-done meat. Spoon the steak onto a serving plate. Repeat the process with the other half of the steak and the remaining garlic. Note: You don't want to overcrowd the pan, as it is important to keep the wok very hot for tender and flavorful steak.

4) Return the pan to medium heat and add the onion. Sauté for 1 to 2 minutes, until the onion is soft and fragrant. Spoon the onion over the meat, and serve hot with the tomato wedges.

Spicy Chicken & Shrimp Ramen in Cognac XO Sauce

THIS DISH IS ONE OF OUR NEWEST MENU ADDITIONS AT CRUSTACEAN.

When my mother left Vietnam, she never had a chance to say goodbye to her parents. This still saddens her to this day, and to help make up for it, she's created many dishes over the years in remembrance of them. This one was inspired by her mother. I never met my maternal grandmother, but my mother often talks about her. One of the things my grandmother loved was spicy food. She often used dried scallops in her cooking because their salty sweetness adds an amazing umami flavor. She also loved quail and would mince its meat with dried scallops and sprinkle it over many dishes for added flavor, or wrap it with herbs and lettuce for a light snack. We use chicken instead of quail here, and top the noodles with a literal twist on homemade XO sauce (see the note on next page).

MAKES 4 SERVINGS

5 dried bird's eye or Thai chiles
(or 2 chiles for a milder taste)

1½ ounces (just less than ¼ cup)
dried shrimp

1½ ounces (just less than ¼ cup)
dried scallops

3 tablespoons minced shallots, divided

2 tablespoons chopped
coriander root

1 tablespoon minced garlic cloves

¼ cup chili or hot chili oil

4 ounces ground chicken

2½ ounces fresh small shrimp,
peeled and deveined, then minced
(about ⅓ cup)

2 tablespoons sugar

1 teaspoon sea salt

1 teaspoon fish sauce

1 teaspoon cognac

6 ounces fresh ramen noodles

2 tablespoons canola oil, divided

1] Submerge the chiles in a small bowl of hot water and soak until they are soft and dark red, about 20 minutes. Drain the chiles and pat them dry with a paper towel. Remove the stems, cut the chiles open, then scrape out and discard the seeds and mince the flesh. Set aside.

2] In a medium bowl, soak the dried shrimp and scallops in hot water until they plump up and are soft, about 20 minutes. Drain and dry the shrimp and scallops, and then mince them. Set aside.

3] Using a mortar and pestle or food processor, process the chiles, 2 tablespoons of the shallots, the coriander root, and the garlic into a paste.

(Continued)

4] Heat the chili oil in a large skillet over medium heat. Add the spicy paste mixture to the skillet, stirring until fragrant, about 5 minutes. Add the ground chicken and stir to combine. Cook for 5 minutes to brown the chicken. Stir in the dried shrimp and scallops and cook for 5-7 minutes and add sugar, salt, and fish sauce and simmer for 10 minutes to meld the flavors. Increase the heat to medium. Add the fresh shrimp and cook for 5 minutes until fresh shrimp becomes opaque. Stir in the cognac and remove the skillet from the heat.

5] Bring a medium pot of salted water to a boil over high heat. Cook the noodles according the package directions until al dente. Strain the noodles, rinse them in cold water, and then shake well to remove any excess water.

6] Add 1 tablespoon of the canola oil to a clean large skillet or wok over high heat. Add the remaining tablespoon of shallots and cook until soft and fragrant, about 5 minutes. Add the noodles and toss a couple of times, then add the spicy meat sauce. Toss well and cook for 5 minutes to heat the noodles and meld flavors into the noodles. Serve hot.

XO SAUCE

Invented in Hong Kong in the 1980s, XO sauce is a spicy condiment made of premium dried seafood, including dried scallops, mixed with chiles, onions, and garlic. Since the ingredients are expensive (dried scallops can sell for $100/pound), XO sauce was named for another luxury item, extra-old cognac, although it doesn't have any alcohol in it. At Crustacean however, we take the name literally and add a splash of brandy at the end.

2

indochine reverie

resurrecting old world elegance

From the mid-eighteenth century until World War II, Vietnam, then called Indochina, was a dynamic mix of cultures. The French, who had helped establish the Nguyễn Dynasty, brought European glamour to the already elegant Asian society. East met West in a heady marriage of romance, beauty, and refinement.

My mother was born into this fairy tale world of wealth, privilege, and power. Her family, the Trầns, were well-known scholars and counselors with a family history that traces back over 500 years through twenty-two generations of high achievers. The first of her family, Trần Xỉ, assisted warlord Nguyễn Hoàng to lay the foundation for the Nguyễn Dynasty and expand the territories of Vietnam. Our most well-known ancestor was my great-great grandfather, Trần Lưu Huệ. In 1886, the Emperor Đồng Khánh bestowed my great-great grandfather Trần Lưu Huệ with a title and position of *Kinh Lược Bạc Kỳ Đại Sứ*, or Viceroy of Tonkin. As such, Trần Lưu Huệ governed the northern province of Vietnam as the Emperor's ambassador with responsibilities to conduct diplomatic negotiations both domestic and international. In 1902, Emperor Thành Thái bestowed upon my great-grandfather the noble title *Đông Các Đại Học Sĩ*. This was the highest position that a dignitary in Tonkin could receive at that time.

ABOVE: Helene's mother in royal court garb ; **OPPOSITE:** Helene's father, Trần Lưu Mậu, at his country estate, with Helene's sister and three older brothers. A servant is holding Helene's brother.

In ancient Asian monarchies, it was customary to bestow an honorary name on sovereigns after their death to commemorate their virtue and service to their country. When my great-great-grandfather passed away, the Emperor Duy Tân, who succeeded Emperor Thành Thái, gave him the court title of *Thái Tử Thiếu Bảo*—the highest possible honorary title, equivalent to the level of authority of the exclusive six Supreme Councilors of the Imperial Court. This posthumous honor raised the status of his entire family.

ANCIENT RESPECT

When the Communists took over my mother's family's land in northern Vietnam, we weren't able to return for many years to visit it, and in the interim, after decades of war, many of our family's burial sites were lost. It was my maternal grandmother's dying wish that we find our ancestors' tombs, and my uncle Trần Lưu Cung, my mother's brother, made it his mission to do so. He returned to our ancestral lands in the North many times, and in 1999 he found the tomb of our esteemed great-great-grandfather Trần Lưu Huệ in the middle of a small island. Although the tomb was covered in foliage, the honorary inscriptions from the Emperor were still clear.

Not all of our ancestors' gravesites were lost to war; some were threatened by progress, such as the burial place of my great-great-great-grandfather Trần Gia Chiếu who died in 1867. His gravesite is significant because it's located on a prime piece of property right in the middle of Hanoi—on the shores of Lake Trúc Bạch right in front of the Buddhist temple Châu Long. My uncle learned from local villagers that the government had realized how valuable of an asset our land was and therefore broke it up into several smaller plots and parceled it out for development. The government had planned to build a retail supercenter right over the tomb, but every time they tried to excavate, the workers would get mysteriously ill. The villagers are very superstitious and refused to help demolish it. Eventually the government gave up and the locals built a market around the tomb, leaving the monument untouched.

Many of the villagers believe that my great-great-great-grandfather still walks the land at night. They tell stories of seeing an old man with a long, white beard. They believe he protects them, and in thanks they still leave fruit and tokens at his burial site.

Helene's great grandfather, Trần Lưu Huệ, also the Viceroy of Tonkin.

As a descendant of generations of mandarins, my mother enjoyed a noble childhood of pampering and prominence. As the baby of the family, the youngest of seventeen children, she was coddled and cared for by everyone in the house, siblings and servants alike. Her education was a top priority, and she was sent to a prestigious French school at the age of five.

As head of a large province, my mother's father, Trần Lưu Mậu, regularly entertained dignitaries from around the world and hosted opulent dinners, the men wearing formal attire and the women dressed up in heavy gold and jade jewelry. In Vietnamese society, especially in the aristocratic class, a family's worth was often measured by the events they hosted. Every meal was carefully orchestrated. No detail, no matter how small, was left to chance. The food had to be the freshest available,

Since the family's reputation hinged upon the success of their events, everyone involved was highly trained in the art of entertaining: from the women of the household, who were ultimately responsible for the planning, managing, and outcome of the meal, to the chefs, who employed centuries-old secrets in preparing the dishes.

HELENE: *Despite having household help, Vietnamese women believed in being hands-on in the cooking process. Wealthy women in Vietnam took pride in having the best kitchen and were extensively schooled by their mothers and aunts. Cooking secrets and technique were not passed on via written recipes but through cooking together.*

My mother came from one of the most prominent families in Vietnam and had eaten well all her life. She was extensively schooled in the art of cooking by her mother and had likewise trained her staff and made it her mission to have my

> Since the family's reputation hinged upon the success of their events, everyone involved was highly trained in the art of entertaining.

prepared in the most delicious manner possible by the most talented chefs in the land. The dinners lasted four or five hours as the guests talked politics or debated about how they could improve the country. Typically up to ten courses were served, including multiple soups, multiple meats, and lots of smaller dishes in between. Nothing was cooked in advance; instead, the chefs prepared each course in order. The guests were happy to wait, talking and exchanging ideas while live music—a violin or *dan tranh* (long zither)—played in the background or they were entertained by *co dao*, Vietnamese traditional singing. A chef personally introduced each course, explaining the significance of the dish and how it was cooked, while servers made their way around the table with platters, serving each person individually.

sisters educated in cooking and hospitality. For every gathering—holidays, dinner parties, and banquets—my sisters not only supervised the cooking but also pitched in themselves.

As such, from a very young age my mother spent hours in the family's expansive kitchens learning from her sisters and the chefs.

HELENE: *I talked to the chefs almost every day and asked them, "Why are you making it this way?" and "How do you make that?" I became enamored with the entire process.*

I learned not just about our own local ingredients but also about international ingredients, because when foreign diplomats would visit, which was often, our chefs would prepare food from their country. For instance, when a dignitary came from India, our chefs made goat curry. They encouraged the goat to run so it would sweat out toxins and provide

Growing up we had a formal dinner once a month. My mother and grandmother planned the menu, and everyone came together dressed in their finest. — HELENE AN

sweeter meat. I learned how the French chef used saffron to complement the meat but added Vietnamese turmeric to it as well because the saffron, while delicious, wasn't strong enough to cut the pungency of the goat.

The chefs soon discovered that I had a very good palate, just like my mother, and they had me taste test everything. If I liked it, the guests would like it.

Even ordinary dinners at the Trần house were six courses long and precisely planned. My mother became the family taste tester for all food before it was even served to her parents.

HELENE: *My mother was very meticulous. She didn't just want the chefs to use chicken bones for broth, she* had them find special birds native to Vietnam that made a sweeter stock. She was very particular about water spinach; she would only keep the best parts, discarding any wilted or tough patches. And while the Japanese had a machine that could roll water spinach, my mother believed in the traditional method of rolling it by hand.

The beauty of a dish was very important to her, and she made sure a lot of time was spent plating everything so that it sat evenly or looked as good as possible. Even after the Communists invaded the North and we lost everything and were living in the forest without any money, my mother still insisted that we have elegant family dinners, and that the food look perfect.

A TEST OF INTELLIGENCE

Although my grandfather's family, the Trầns, were well-established nobility, my maternal grandmother's family, the Dươngs, were even wealthier and more well-known, due to their academic achievements. My grandmother's grandfather was very famous in Vietnam for being a scholar of the highest honor.

To find the best and brightest citizens and employ them as councilors to the king, the realm would periodically hold a competition that included written and oral examinations in two areas: academics and military strategy. The men with the highest scores in each were appointed to the royal court and their families received lifelong privileges that came with their rank. My great-great-grandfather's name can still be seen etched on a stone plaque in the imperial city in Huế, to commemorate his victory in this competition; he was one of the winners of the academic contest, while his brother won the military strategy test. Still to this day, school children have to learn some of the teachings of my great-great-grandfather.

My grandfather Trần Lưu Mậu loved food, all different kinds of food, and while he didn't participate in the meal planning or preparation, he was intimately involved in the production of crops on his lands. He owned several plantations as well as land in the neighboring villages, and he took special care to plant different varieties of rice and experiment to find the best outcome for the soil. To honor my grandmother's interest in Eastern medicine, he had lemongrass and peonies planted with the other vegetables, mustard greens, fava beans, zucchini, melons, and onions. He oversaw the orchards and made sure they produced a wide variety of fruit. He set aside certain fields for seasonal crops. He enlarged the fish ponds and brought in new species. He loved the land and treasured his role as its caretaker.

HELENE: *One of my earliest memories is of going to the Harvest Festival in the local village. Every year when the crop was brought in, we would travel from our big house in Kiến An out to the countryside for the ceremony and celebration. There were games and parades. The children would wear papier-mâché masks and carry colorful shadow lanterns. There were seesaws, with the women on one side and the men on the other. We would bring grasshoppers home to sauté and eat. These were not just normal grasshoppers but ones from the rice fields. They were fatty and fragrant. I still remember how much I liked them!*

My sisters and I grew up listening to and loving the stories of this refined and gracious era. In many ways, my mother made sure it didn't die out. She recreated the same experience in our home and in our restaurants. In fact, it was always the driving force of our businesses. We naturally incorporate that kind of hospitality into everything we do because our mother taught us to; she doesn't know how to do it any other way.

Elegance is a state of mind. You can add it to any event, however big or small, and it doesn't require money; we managed it even when we had none. To plan an elegant feast, there's no need for fancy plates or serving platters, either. In fact, some of my favorite pieces for entertaining are mismatched dishes I found at flea markets. You can incorporate an old world aesthetic anywhere. My husband and I used to throw elaborate dinner parties in our tiny New York City apartment. If people are dressed up and you have fresh flowers and good wine, it doesn't matter where you are. The atmosphere is what you make it.

EVERYDAY ELEGANCE

Here are a few tips for bringing glamour to any gala.

1) **Dress up for dinner.**
It's an honor to spend time and enjoy fine food and wine with those you love. Dress accordingly and ask your guests to dress up, too.

2) **Set a theme.**
Need to give your guests a nudge to don party clothes? Choose a historical theme and ask everyone to match it. Great ideas: 1940s pre-World War II or French Colonial Indochina.

3) **Use cloth napkins.**
Even if you forgo a tablecloth, the addition of cloth napkins can up the elegance factor of any table. Inexpensive and eye-catching, cloth napkins can complement your theme, the time of year, and even your menu.

4) **Fill the table with flowers.**
Go all out and hire a florist to decorate your space sumptuously, or do it yourself. Fresh-cut flowers can be purchased inexpensively at farmers' markets. Simply snip the stems short and place low-profile bouquets everywhere. Almost anything can serve as a vase: old teacups, water glasses, small outdoor planters . . .

5) **Add a ritual.**
Whether you open your dinner party with a prayer or a celebratory toast or close it with a traditional tea ceremony, adding a ritual can help elevate the occasion.

THE SECRET TO SUMPTUOUS MEALS:
FRESHNESS & BALANCE

I was very lucky to grow up in the unspoiled beauty of Vietnam, before war and the use of pesticides scarred our land. My father was very smart with agriculture. He knew there were no shortcuts. He grew everything organically with no chemicals. He treated the land with respect and in return it gave him great soil.

Food tasted better back then. Lychee seeds used to be small and very juicy; now they have big seeds and very little flesh. Rice was naturally sweeter. I find that food raised with chemicals is much blander than that which is raised organically.

I grew up with kitchen gardens, orchards, a chicken farm, a fish farm, a shrimp pond—all right in my backyard. Using our natural resources wasn't a trend back then, it was a part of our culture. Fresh food that you grew yourself in good soil made you feel healthy. Today, modern food can make you feel bloated or weighted down. This is very against my philosophy: food should never make you feel bad, it should always make you feel good. The key is to use the freshest ingredients possible. Fresh food makes you feel light and gives you energy.

I grow everything I can in my own kitchen garden now. The thyme I grow at home is so much better than the thyme in the supermarket. You don't need a lot of room, especially for herbs. You can plant them in a container outside or inside on a windowsill. Plant what you know you will use frequently. I have a small kaffir lime tree since I use the leaves and the fruit in a lot of my cooking; the dwarf citrus trees will grow extremely well in containers and indoors. To grow the best food you must respect the cycle; you must feed the soil with compost, and it will produce more beautiful food for you. When I polish and rinse rice, I always save the soaking water and pour it over my plants.

Freshness is also very important in proteins. Find the freshest protein you can: fish, meat, and eggs. If you can't produce it yourself, find a local farmer or farmers' market. Then add other fresh ingredients that will enhance the natural flavor of the protein rather than smother it. I find traditional French cooking to be very beautiful, but the sauces they use can sometimes overpower the natural flavors of the food. Let the food itself shine.

To me, the best dishes have restraint, subtlety, and a balance of flavors. The more you get to know your ingredients, the more you work with them, the easier it will be to put them together. Just remember to balance each of them out. For instance, sage brings out the deep flavor of a milder fish like tilapia, but the sage itself must be paired with something so it doesn't overpower the dish, such as essence of lemon or ginger. The mark of a great dish is that no one thing overwhelms your senses. Instead, everything works together in harmony on the plate and on your palate. — HELENE AN

The following recipes are inspired by the meals prepared for my mother's family when she was a young child in French Colonial Vietnam. The dishes equally honor our country's Vietnamese, French, and Chinese heritages, along with my mother's personal culinary philosophy. Some recipes have been passed down for generations, and we are sharing them here for the first time as we welcome you to our table.

Cognac Crab and Asparagus Soup

AS CHILDREN, WE ALWAYS CONSIDERED THIS FRENCH COLONIAL SOUP A DELICACY. *It's similar to Chinese egg drop soup but with fresh asparagus, tender crab, and extra flavor. The secret is a splash of cognac that adds a hint of sharp sweetness just before serving.*

MAKES 4 TO 6 SERVINGS

2 tablespoons canola oil

1 tablespoon finely chopped shallots

4 ounces (¼ pound) fresh blue crab meat

½ teaspoon sea salt

½ teaspoon freshly ground black pepper

1 teaspoon sugar

1 pound fresh white asparagus, trimmed and peeled, or 1 jar white asparagus in water, cut into 1-inch pieces

4 cups Homemade Chicken Broth (page 273) or store-bought low-sodium chicken broth, divided

1 egg white, beaten

1 tablespoon cornstarch

Chopped fresh cilantro, for garnish

½ to 1 teaspoon cognac

1) In a large saucepan over medium heat, combine the oil and shallots and cook, stirring often, until the shallots have softened, about 2 minutes. Add the crab, salt, pepper, and sugar and cook until fragrant, about 3 minutes. Remove the crab meat from the pan and set it aside.

2) Increase the heat to medium-high. To the same saucepan, add the asparagus, 3½ cups of the chicken broth, and 2 cups of water. Bring the mixture to a boil, then add the seasoned crab meat. Reduce the heat to medium and continue to cook at a slow boil for 3 to 5 minutes until the asparagus is cooked.

3) In a small bowl, stir the cornstarch into the remaining ½ cup of chicken broth to make a slurry. Mix well until the cornstarch is dissolved, then pour the mixture into the saucepan, stirring constantly.

4) Slowly drizzle the beaten egg white into the soup, stirring vigorously so the egg doesn't cloud but instead splits into tiny ribbons.

5) Ladle the soup into bowls and top each serving with a garnish of chopped cilantro. Before enjoying, have each guest add ½ to 1 teaspoon of cognac (or as much as desired) to his or her own soup bowl. Lightly stir once or twice and eat immediately.

Red Snapper Tamarind Soup

A CROSS BETWEEN FRENCH BOUILLABAISSE AND THAI HOT AND SOUR SOUP, *this sweet and slightly tangy soup is one of my favorites. Tamarind juice, gives this recipe a punch of flavor, and the use of the whole fish— including the fish head—makes for a sweeter, more robust broth. While you can eat the soup by itself, in my family, we pour it over a small bowl of rice and dip the delicate fish in nước chấm, or Garlic Lemon Sauce (page 274). We use the whole fish in this recipe because the fish head is the key to giving the soup lots of flavor, but if you prefer to use only the body, replace the water in this recipe with 8 cups of really good fish or chicken broth to make up for not having the head.*

MAKES 4 TO 6 SERVINGS

1 (1½ to 2-pound) whole red snapper, head separated, skin on

4 teaspoons sea salt, divided

3 teaspoons fish sauce, divided

1 tablespoon canola oil

3 garlic cloves, minced

3 tablespoons sugar

4 tablespoons tamarind juice, home-made (page 283) or store-bought

2 medium sized tomatoes, quartered

¼ pineapple, peeled, cored, and chopped, or 3 canned pineapple rings, chopped

6 fresh okra pods, sliced ⅓-inch thick on an angle

1 cup mung bean sprouts

3 taro stems (dọc mùng), thinly sliced on an angle

1 red chile or jalapeño pepper, thinly sliced

2 tablespoons chopped fresh rice paddy herb (ngò ôm)

1] Fillet the body of the fish, cutting it in half to fit in the pot. Wash the fish with salt by rubbing 1 teaspoon salt all over including inside fish head and then rinse with water.

2] In a medium bowl, mix together 1 teaspoon of the salt and 1 teaspoon of the fish sauce. Add the fish and coat it with the sauce. Set the fish aside to marinate for 15 minutes.

3] Meanwhile, heat the oil in a small skillet over medium heat. Add the garlic and cook until it is golden brown, about 3 minutes. Remove the skillet from the heat. Spoon the garlic into a fine mesh strainer over a small bowl. Set the fried garlic aside.

4] In a large stockpot, combine the sugar, tamarind, remaining 2 teaspoons of salt, and remaining teaspoon of fish sauce, and 8 cups of water. Bring the mixture to a boil over high heat, then reduce the heat to medium and add the tomatoes, pineapple, marinated fish fillet, and fish head. Cook for 5 to 7 minutes, then remove the fish body so it doesn't get too soft and transfer it to a large serving bowl. Set aside.

5] Continue cooking the broth over medium heat for 10 minutes for the sweet-ness from fishhead to come into the broth. Remove the fish head and add the okra, bean sprouts, and taro stems to the pot. Taste the broth and season with more fish sauce, sugar, and or salt as preferred. When you are ready to serve, add the fried garlic, 3 to 4 sliced of chile or jalapeño, and the rice paddy herb to the pot. Bring the broth just back to a boil, then remove the pot from the heat. To serve, pour the hot broth over the fish in the serving bowl.

NOTE: *Taro stems should not be eaten raw as they contain a toxin that can cause throat irritation.*

Crispy Chicken Spring Rolls

LIKE OUR SUMMER ROLL, THIS IS ONE OF OUR MOST POPULAR APPETIZERS *and has been on our menu from the beginning. Since it is fried, we like to serve it with our Garlic Lemon Sauce (page 274), pickled vegetables, and a Vietnamese herb salad to cut the oil, balancing the heavy with the light.*

MAKES 30 ROLLS

FOR THE SPRING ROLLS:

4½ pounds ground dark meat chicken

4½ pounds white onion, minced and squeezed to remove excess juice

2 pounds carrots, finely chopped

2 pounds jicama, julienned into long strips

2½ ounces fresh shiitake mushrooms, minced

2½ ounces fresh wood ear mushrooms, minced

3½ ounces transparent vermicelli cellophane noodles (miến), cooked

2 tablespoons oyster sauce

1 tablespoon fish sauce

2 teaspoons sugar

1 teaspoon sesame oil

1 teaspoon sea salt

1 teaspoon freshly ground black pepper

30 sheets rice paper, dampened and stacked (see note, page 86)

3 cups canola oil

FOR THE HERB PLATTER:

Fresh butter lettuce

Fresh basil leaves

Fresh cilantro

Fresh Vietnamese perilla (tía tô) leaves

Pickled Carrots (page 238)

Pickled Cucumbers (page 240)

Garlic Lemon Sauce (page 274)

1) In a large bowl, mix the chicken with the onions, carrots, jicama, and mushrooms. Add the noodles and mix well. Mix in the oyster sauce, fish sauce, sugar, oil, salt, and pepper.

2) Place one rice paper wrapper in front of you on a hard surface or cutting board. Put 1 tablespoon of the meat mixture in a horizontal line about one-third of the way up the wrapper from the bottom, leaving a finger-width border on either side. Fold the bottom of the wrapper over the meat and start rolling upward, making sure to tuck in the sides as you go. Don't roll too tightly or the wrapper might tear. Place the roll on a plate and repeat with the remaining wrappers and meat filling.

3) Heat the oil in a deep skillet or wok over medium heat. Line a baking sheet with paper towels. Once the oil is hot, place 5 rolls at time in the pan and cook them until their outsides turn golden brown, about 7 to 10 minutes. Using a slotted spoon or skimmer, transfer the cooked rolls to the prepared baking sheet to drain. Repeat the process with the remaining rolls.

4) Serve the spring rolls hot along with the herb platter and Garlic Lemon Sauce.

THE SECRET TO PREPARING RICE PAPER
FOR CRISPY ROLLS

To make perfectly crispy spring rolls, you'll need to use several different towels at once and stack them so the rice paper doesn't dry out. The perfect towel for the job is a small, clean, lint-free kitchen towel that will hold moisture. (Paper towels will break and washcloths hold too much water.) We usually have about ten kitchen towels on hand for this purpose.

TO PREPARE THE RICE PAPER:

1] Fill a large bowl with warm water and soak the towels all together. Remove the towels one-by-one and squeeze all of the water out of each towel. Lay the cloths flat on a hard surface or wooden cutting board, one on top of the other.

2] Take the top cloth off and place it on a hard surface or cutting board. Place one rice paper wrapper on top of the cloth, and then place another cloth on top of it. Continue making a new stack, alternately layering cloths and rice wrappers until you have covered all of your wrappers.

3] Now flip the stack over so that the rice wrapper on the bottom is now on the top, and use that one first, as it will be the wettest and ready to go.

Lotus, Chicken & Shrimp Salad

THIS LIGHT AND REFRESHING SALAD IS EXTREMELY POPULAR *during the hot and humid summer months in Vietnam, because lotus is widely believed to improve circulation and have a cooling effect on the body. The secret to getting the lotus nice and crunchy with the right semi-pickled flavor is to squeeze all of the water out of it before marinating it in vinegar and sugar. Serve this salad with shrimp chips.*

MAKES 4 SERVINGS

1 cup Homemade Chicken Broth (page 273) or store-bought low-sodium chicken broth

4 fresh lemon leaves, crushed

1 large (8-ounce) boneless, skinless chicken breast

1 tablespoon white wine

1 teaspoon sesame oil

⅓ pound jumbo shrimp (size ²¹/₂₅; about 6 pieces), peeled and deveined

1 tablespoon fish sauce

2 tablespoons sugar

1 tablespoon white vinegar

8 ounces canned lotus stem, rinsed, drained, and cut into 2-inch pieces

2 celery stalks, cut into 2-inch long, thin strips

½ carrot, cut into 2-inch long, thin strips

4 tablespoons chopped fresh Vietnamese coriander (rau răm) leaves

1 teaspoon chopped roasted garlic

1 tablespoon crushed roasted peanuts, for garnish

1 teaspoon chopped shallots, for garnish

1] In a medium pot, combine 1 cup of water, the chicken broth, and the crushed lemon leaves. Bring the mixture to a boil over high heat, then reduce the heat to medium and add the chicken breast. Continue to low boil for 10 minutes, making sure to skim off the froth. Turn off the heat, cover the pot, and let it sit for 10 minutes. Remove the chicken from the broth and transfer it to a large bowl to cool. Once the chicken has cooled down, shred it by hand into the bowl. Set aside.

2] Meanwhile, in a second medium pot, bring 1 cup of water, the wine, and the sesame oil to a boil over high heat. Fill a medium bowl with ice water and set it nearby. Blanch the shrimp by adding them to the boiling pot of water for 1 minute. Strain the shrimp through a colander, discarding the cooking liquid, and then transfer the shrimp to the ice water for 2 minutes. Remove the shrimp from the water and set them aside.

3] Warm the fish sauce in a medium saucepan over low heat, and stir in 1 tablespoon of the sugar; cook, stirring, until the sugar has completely dissolved, about 2 minutes. Remove the pan from the heat. Once the sauce has cooled, add the shrimp and chicken and turn to coat them in the marinade.

4] Meanwhile, in a medium bowl, stir together the vinegar, the remaining tablespoon of sugar, and 2 tablespoons of water. Squeeze out any excess water from the lotus stems, then add them to the bowl; set them aside to marinate for 30 minutes. Remove the lotus stems from the marinade and squeeze slightly, but not too much; you only want to remove excess marinade.

5] In a large bowl, toss the marinated shrimp and chicken with the lotus, celery, carrots, Vietnamese coriander, and roasted garlic. After tossing, place the salad on a serving plate, arranging the shrimp and chicken on top. Garnish with peanuts and shallots before serving.

Shrimp Summer Rolls

WHEN MY GRANDMOTHER DIANA WANTED TO SUPPLEMENT THE MENU *at our old Italian deli with Vietnamese-inspired dishes, one of the first items she chose was a summer roll. She saw that Americans liked salad and bet that they would like it even more if they could hold it in their hands in a neat rice paper package. Of course she was right, and the light and flavorful summer roll was an instant hit. This popular item is still on our menus today.*

While it is not a traditional Vietnamese condiment, we've added an optional aioli sauce to give these summer rolls a richer, creamier flavor.

MAKES 16 ROLLS

FOR THE SUMMER ROLLS:

8 ounces dried thin rice noodles

1 tablespoon rice wine, such as Michiu

1 tablespoon sesame oil

½ pound medium shrimp
(size $^{41}/_{50}$; about 25 pieces), peeled
and deveined

16 sheets rice paper

16 butter lettuce leaves

1 cup Pickled Carrots (page 238)

½ cup (about 1 bunch) fresh Vietnamese perilla (tía tô) leaves

¼ cup (about ½ bunch) fresh cilantro leaves

¼ cup (about ½ bunch) fresh mint leaves

1 bunch fresh chives

FOR THE AIOLI SAUCE (optional):

2 tablespoons mayonnaise

1 teaspoon Fried Shallots (page 281)

1 teaspoon Fried Garlic (page 282)

½ teaspoon sea salt

½ teaspoon freshly ground black pepper

Bean Sauce, for serving (page 279)

Garlic Lemon Sauce, for serving
(page 274)

1] Soak the dried noodles in warm water for 10 minutes.

2] Meanwhile, bring a large pot of salted water to a boil over high heat. Drain the noodles from the soaking liquid and add them to the boiling water. Cook for 5 to 7 minutes until soft. Drain the noodles, rinse them well under cold water, and then rinse them under warm water. Transfer the noodles to a large serving bowl. Set aside.

3] TO COOK THE SHRIMP: Bring 2 cups water to a boil with the wine and sesame oil in a medium saucepan over high heat. Fill a medium bowl with ice water and set it nearby. Add the shrimp to the boiling liquid and cook just until they are opaque, about 1 minute. Drain the shrimp and transfer them to the ice water to cool completely. Drain again and pat the shrimp dry with paper towels. Cut the shrimp in half.

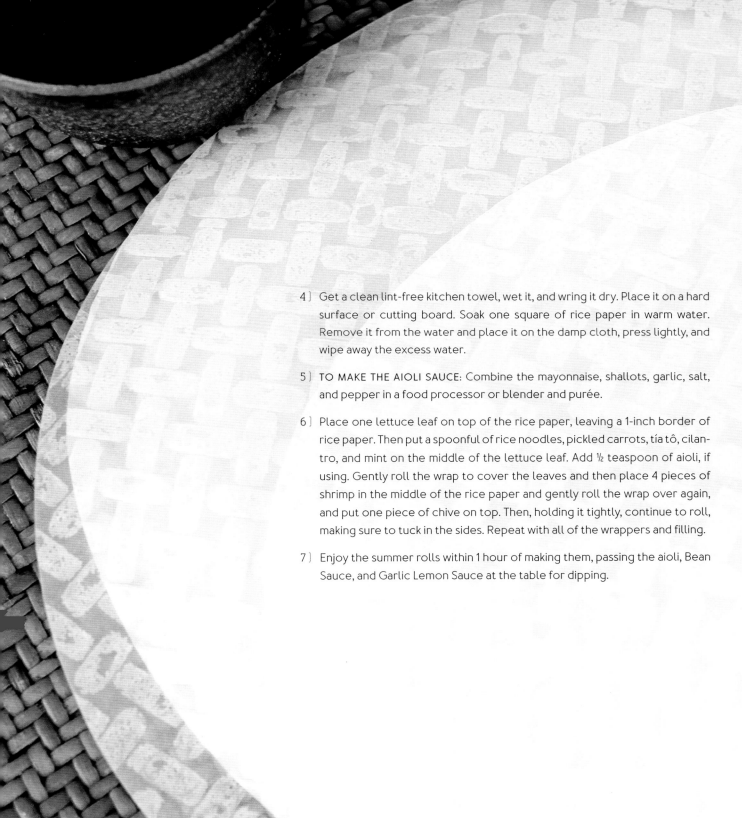

4] Get a clean lint-free kitchen towel, wet it, and wring it dry. Place it on a hard surface or cutting board. Soak one square of rice paper in warm water. Remove it from the water and place it on the damp cloth, press lightly, and wipe away the excess water.

5] **TO MAKE THE AIOLI SAUCE:** Combine the mayonnaise, shallots, garlic, salt, and pepper in a food processor or blender and purée.

6] Place one lettuce leaf on top of the rice paper, leaving a 1-inch border of rice paper. Then put a spoonful of rice noodles, pickled carrots, tía tô, cilantro, and mint on the middle of the lettuce leaf. Add ½ teaspoon of aioli, if using. Gently roll the wrap to cover the leaves and then place 4 pieces of shrimp in the middle of the rice paper and gently roll the wrap over again, and put one piece of chive on top. Then, holding it tightly, continue to roll, making sure to tuck in the sides. Repeat with all of the wrappers and filling.

7] Enjoy the summer rolls within 1 hour of making them, passing the aioli, Bean Sauce, and Garlic Lemon Sauce at the table for dipping.

Sizzling Shrimp Crêpes

THE GREAT THING ABOUT THIS DISH, *called bánh xèo in Vietnam, is that you can essentially use any type of vegetable or meat that you like to fill the crêpes. It's traditionally made with shrimp, pork, and mung beans, but we wanted a lighter, crunchier version, so we swapped out the mung beans for mung bean sprouts and added zucchini and snow peas. The secret to a perfectly crispy crêpe is to add beer to the batter.*

MAKES 7 SERVINGS

FOR THE CRÊPES:

6 ounces (about 1½ cups) white rice flour

½ teaspoon ground turmeric

¼ teaspoon sea salt

½ cup (8 ounces) lager-style beer

½ cup (8 ounces) coconut milk

¼ cup (4 ounces) coconut water

5 tablespoons canola oil, divided

1 teaspoon chopped shallots

¾ pound jumbo shrimp (size ²¹/₂₅; about 16 pieces), peeled, deveined, and chopped

1 zucchini, julienned into 2-inch long, thin strips

10 fresh snow pea pods, julienned into long, thin strips

1 tablespoon Michiu rice cooking wine or white wine

1 cup mung bean sprouts

FOR SERVING:

Fresh butter lettuce leaves

Fresh mint leaves

Fresh Vietnamese perilla (tía tô) leaves

Bean Sauce (page 279)

Garlic Lemon Sauce (page 274)

Pickled Carrots (page 238)

Pickled Cucumbers (page 240)

1] TO MAKE THE BATTER: In a large bowl, whisk together the rice flour, turmeric, and salt. Stir in the beer, coconut milk, and coconut water. Mix well, then set aside.

2] Heat 1 tablespoon of the oil in a large skillet over medium heat. Add the shallots and sauté until fragrant, about 2 minutes. Add the shrimp and sauté until it becomes opaque, about 2 to 3 minutes. Transfer the shrimp to a plate and set aside.

3] Add the zucchini and snow peas to the same pan over medium heat. Add the wine, being conscious of a possible flame-up. Add the bean sprouts and cooked shrimp and sauté for 1 minute to meld the flavors.

4] Brush the inside of a clean, medium nonstick pan with 1 tablespoon of the oil and place the pan over medium heat. Once the pan is hot, reduce the heat to medium-low and pour one ladle of batter into the middle of the pan. Spread the batter slowly around the pan, and cook until the edges of the crêpe turn golden brown.

5] Spoon about 3 tablespoons of filling onto half of the crêpe and, using a thin spatula, flip the other half over to cover the filling. Cook for 2 minutes, then use the spatula to flip the crêpe over. Continue to cook until the crêpe turns golden brown and crispy. Slide the crêpe onto a serving plate and repeat this process with the remaining batter and filling.

6] Serve the crêpes hot with the lettuce, herbs, sauces, and pickled vegetables.

Hot Pastry Pies (Pâté Chaud)

MY GRANDMOTHER USED TO MAKE HOT PASTRY PIES FOR US ALL THE TIME, *and they were my favorite snack. She would make several dozen at once and freeze them, then pop them in the oven to reheat for a special after-school treat.*

Savory meat wrapped in a puff pastry crust was a French dish that the Vietnamese made their own by using different flavor profiles in the stuffing. While it traditionally consisted of ground pork (the word "pâté" referring to the pastry), we use ground chicken and add pork liver pâté as well for its decadent taste and creamy, buttery texture.

MAKES 7 PIES

4 tablespoons Homemade Chicken Broth (page 273) or store-bought low-sodium chicken broth

2 teaspoons cornstarch

1 pound ground dark meat chicken

1 (3 to 4-ounce) can pork liver pâté

1 medium white onion, chopped

3 shallots, chopped

½ teaspoon fish sauce

1 tablespoon freshly ground black pepper

1 teaspoon sea salt

1 teaspoon sugar

1 (14 to 17-ounce) package frozen puff pastry phyllo dough, thawed

1 egg yolk

1) Preheat the oven to 350°F.

2) In a small bowl, whisk together the chicken broth and cornstarch. Set aside.

3) In a large bowl, combine the ground chicken with the pâté. Add the onion, shallots, fish sauce, pepper, salt, and sugar. Add the chicken broth mixture from the small bowl and mix well.

4) Make the egg wash: In a small bowl, mix the egg yolk with 2 tablespoons of water. Set aside.

5) Cut the dough into four 7 x 7-inch squares. Spoon some of the filling mixture into one corner of each dough square, leaving room for the dough to be sealed around it. Divide the filling evenly among the squares. Fold each dough square in half over the filling to create a rectangle, completely enclosing the filling. Press the edges to seal.

6) Put the pastries on a parchment-lined baking sheet and brush each one all over with the egg wash. Using the point of a sharp knife, cut a small slit into the top of each pastry. Transfer the baking sheet to the oven and bake the pastries for 15 to 20 minutes or until the crust is golden brown. Serve hot.

Slow-Roasted Pork with Ginger Balsamic Glaze

WE ALWAYS KNEW WHEN MY GRANDMOTHER WAS MAKING THIS FRENCH COUNTRY-STYLE PORK *because it filled the house with such an amazing aroma that our mouths would start watering instantly. It's one of my favorites because it's an easy, everyday dish that you just throw in the oven, and it makes fantastic leftovers—my father loves to eat it the next day in sandwiches.*

Traditionally, thịt heo rôti is made with pork tenderloin, but my grandmother preferred to use the pork shoulder because the extra fat will render and make the meat all the more moist.

MAKES 6 SERVINGS

FOR THE PORK:

1 (3½-pound) pork shoulder

10 whole garlic cloves

2 tablespoons sambal chili sauce

2 tablespoons lightly packed brown sugar

2 tablespoons sea salt

1 tablespoon garlic powder

2 fresh lemongrass stalks

3 carrots, oblique cut [see note, page 127]

1 white onion, cut into ¾-inch dice

6 bay leaves

10 sprigs fresh thyme

3 cups pineapple juice

2 cups freshly squeezed orange juice

FOR THE GLAZE:

4 tablespoons unsalted butter

4 tablespoons fresh ginger, peeled and julienned into 2-inch long, thin strips

4 tablespoons lightly packed brown sugar

1 cup balsamic vinegar

½ cup soy sauce

1] Preheat the oven to 500°F.

2] Cut ten slits in the pork shoulder big enough to fit a garlic clove, and insert a clove into each one.

3] In a small bowl, stir together the sambal, brown sugar, salt, and garlic powder. Massage this mixture into the pork.

4] Cut a slit into the middle of the pork and insert the lemongrass stalks.

5] Layer the carrots, onion, bay leaves, and thyme sprigs on the bottom of a roasting pan. Pour the pineapple and orange juices over top. Place the pork on top of the vegetables. Transfer the roasting pan to the oven and cook the pork uncovered for 30 minutes until caramelized and charred golden brown

[Continued]

6] Remove the roasting pan from the oven and cover the top with foil. Reduce the oven temperature to 250°F, return the roasting pan to the oven, and cook the pork for 3 hours until charred brown and meat is fork tender.

7] About 30 minutes before the roast has finished cooking, prepare the glaze. Melt the butter in a medium saucepan over medium heat. Add the ginger and sauté just until it is aromatic, 15 to 20 seconds. Whisk in the brown sugar, balsamic vinegar, and soy sauce. Reduce the heat to low and cook, stirring occasionally, until the glaze thickens, about 20 minutes.

8] Take the pork out of the oven and allow it to rest for at least 15 minutes before slicing. Drizzle the glaze over the pork when you are ready to serve. Slice the pork and serve it with white rice on the side, being sure to spoon the pan juices over all.

DON'T THROW OUT THE JUICE!

When I first got married and my husband was making dinner for me, I was shocked when he put the pan right into the sink still full of brown juices. "What are you doing?" I asked. "Throwing away the waste," he said. "It's not waste!" I practically screamed. "It's pan juices!"

In Vietnamese households, we don't waste anything. We use every part of the animal, we find ways to soften otherwise inedible hard stems (like kale in my stir-fry), and we definitely save the pan juices. This brown juice studded with flavorful bits of whatever you've just cooked is a wonderful condiment to serve with just about anything. We spoon it over rice, use it to season sandwiches, and even substitute it as salad dressing in a pinch. If you don't need them for your current meal because you've just made a separate sauce or glaze, save the pan juices in a small covered container in your refrigerator for up to 5 days. They will moisten and brighten any leftovers.

MY GRANDMOTHER DIANA AN—"BÀ NỘI"

My paternal grandmother, "Bà Nội" as we children called her, is an amazing chef. My grandfather was so proud of her cooking that after every dinner she prepared he would say, "There is no better chef!" He didn't say it to be polite, it was true to him as it was true to all of us kids and anyone else who was fortunate enough to have her cook for them. It always amazed me how fast she was able to pull a meal together. Even when we stopped by without any notice, within minutes she would have a whole dinner prepared.

In many ways she epitomized Vietnamese cooking, since it is incredibly forgiving. She tasted her food rather than following any recipes, so sometimes the end result was slightly different from her earlier attempt, but it was always just as delicious. She had an inquisitive mind and loved going out to eat, learning and tasting other cuisine and figuring out how to make other people's specialties. There wasn't any dish that she couldn't recreate.

Whatever recipe she did have, she kept in her head. No matter if the recipe was Vietnamese or French, savory or sweet, I never saw her crack open a cookbook. I remember as a child I used to help her make the choux pastry for *choux a la crème*. We didn't have a mixer, so we did everything back then by hand. I would squat on the floor, put the large, heavy steel pot between my legs for leverage, and mix until my grandmother said the dough was ready. I would ask her, "How many more minutes?" I wanted an exact answer.

"I can't tell you that," she'd smile. "Nothing is exact. You know when it's done because you taste, feel, observe, and fix." That was her style of cooking.

From her I learned that recipes are meant to be a base for your imagination. I hope that with the recipes in this book, you too will take license as my grandmother did, adding your own flavor and twists, and being just as fearless with your cooking.

Snapper Baked in Banana Leaf

UNLIKE MY MOTHER'S MOTHER, WHO LIKED EVERYTHING WITH A SPICY KICK, *my mother's father had a very clean palate and liked his dishes steamed or baked. Baked snapper was my grandfather's favorite dish in Vietnam. He had a huge clay oven at his house, almost like an Italian brick oven. His chef would pick the freshest fish, just off the hook, season it, wrap it in banana leaves, and bake it in the outdoor oven.*

Banana leaves are wonderful for cooking because they're eco-friendly, they seal in moisture and help steam bake, and they infuse a delicious aroma and taste into foods, especially fish. For instructions on how to buy, store, and cut banana leaves, see page 36.

MAKES 4 SERVINGS

4 tablespoons mayonnaise

4 (6-ounce) skinless red snapper or tilapia fillets

4 large banana leaves, each cut into a 12-inch square (see note)

4 ounces (about 1½ cups) fresh Hon Shimeji mushrooms (also called brown clamshell or beech mush-rooms), coarsely chopped

2 ounces fresh ginger, peeled and julienned into 2-inch long, thin strips

2 teaspoons low-sodium soy sauce

1) Preheat the oven to 350°F.

2) Brush 1 tablespoon of mayonnaise over each fillet.

3) Place each fillet in the middle of a banana leaf. Sprinkle ginger pieces evenly over each fillet, then sprinkle mushrooms evenly over each fillet. Pour ½ tea-spoon of soy sauce over the top of each fillet. Fold the sides of the banana leaf over the fish, then fold the opposite sides of the leaf up as well to create a package. Flip the entire packet over to keep the seams closed.

4) Place the packets in a baking dish, seam-sides down, and bake for 30 minutes until fish flakes easily with a fork. Serve with rice.

NOTE: *If you can't find banana leaves, parchment paper or foil squares will work just fine.*

PAPA'S SECRET SAUCE

For additional flavor, my father makes a Dijon Sriracha dipping sauce that goes great with this dish. Feel free to driz-zle a little of the dipping sauce over the cooked fish or spoon some in a little bowl for dipping. Just mix the following ingredients in a small bowl.

1 teaspoon Dijon mustard

1 teaspoon Maggi seasoning sauce

¼ teaspoon sriracha sauce

Crispy Turmeric Fish with Fresh Dill

A SIGNATURE DISH OF NORTHERN VIETNAM *called chả cá thăng long, this dish was traditionally made by grilling the fish on a three-legged grill made of clay. When we first moved to America we didn't have a grill, so my grandmother improvised by using the oven, as we still do today at home and in our restaurants. The delicious sizzling of hot oil on fresh dill was achieved with pork belly fat in Vietnam, but today we use canola oil.*

Catfish was always my grandmother's go-to choice for this dish, but feel free to experiment with other types of firm fish if you like.

MAKES 4 SERVINGS

FOR THE FISH:

2 tablespoons fish sauce

1 teaspoon oyster sauce

1 tablespoon Tamarind Juice (page 283)

1 tablespoon sugar

1 tablespoon dried dill

1 teaspoon ground turmeric

1 (½-inch) piece freshly peeled galangal, firmly pounded, or 1 teaspoon galangal powder (see note, page 103)

1 tablespoon minced shallots

1 tablespoon chopped scallion bulbs (white parts only)

1 pound snapper, tilapia, or catfish, filleted and skinned, cut into 2-inch pieces

1 (14-ounce) package dried rice vermicelli noodles

1 bunch scallions, green parts only, cut into 2-inch pieces (⅓ cup)

1 bunch fresh dill, cut into 2-inch pieces (⅓ cup)

2 tablespoons canola oil

FOR SERVING:

Garlic Lemon Sauce (see page 274)

Fresh butter lettuce leaves

Fresh mint leaves

Fresh Vietnamese balm (kinh giới) or lemon balm leaves

Fresh Vietnamese perilla (tía tô) leaves

Roasted Peanuts (page 281)

1) In a medium bowl, combine the fish sauce, oyster sauce, tamarind, sugar, dried dill, and turmeric. Mix well. Stir in the galangal, shallots, and chopped white scallion bulbs. Add the fish and toss to coat. Cover the bowl and refrigerate for 2 hours.

2) Ten minutes before the fish is done marinating, preheat the oven to 400°F.

3) Soak the dried noodles in warm water for 10 minutes.

4) Meanwhile, bring a large pot of salted water to a boil over high heat. Drain the noodles from the soaking liquid and add them to the pot of boiling water. Cook the noodles for 7 minutes. Drain the noodles, rinse them well under cold water, then rinse them under warm water and transfer them to a large serving bowl. Set aside.

(Continued)

5] While the noodles are cooking, spray non-stick oil on a baking sheet. Place the fish on the baking sheet and bake for 3 minutes on each side, until golden brown. Remove the baking sheet from the oven and gently transfer the fish to a serving plate. Top the fish with the scallion stalks and fresh dill.

6] Heat the oil in a heavy skillet over high heat until it begins to sizzle. Remove the skillet from the heat and pour the oil over the fresh dill, scallions, and fish. Serve the fish immediately with the noodles, Garlic Lemon sauce, herb platter, and peanuts.

NOTE: *A chunk of dried galangal can also be used in place of fresh galangal—just be sure to rehydrate it first by soaking it in hot water for 30 minutes. And remember that galangal is used as a dye and its juice will stain fingers and clothing. Take care when handling it.*

COOKING WITH WINE

While wine won't generally ignite like a high-proof liqueur will, if the pan is hot enough the alcohol vapors can catch fire and cause a brief (but exciting) flare up. It's a common sight for restaurant cooks, but it can cause some initial alarm if you've never experienced it in your own kitchen. While the flames can rise a foot out of the pan, the ignition of the vapors is quick and should subside almost instantly. However, it doesn't hurt to take some safety precautions. Never cook with alcohol near loose fabric such as curtains. Stand back from the pan when adding alcohol. And pour the measure of alcohol into a separate container before adding it to the pan; never pour directly from the bottle.

3
new home comfort

from riches to rags

Helene, about 5 years old, in her family's garden in Hanoi.

T hroughout our lives, most of us will move to a different home at least once. We grow up and move out, establish our own family, relocate for a new job or career change, seek a different climate, and sometimes, unfortunately, we are forced to move when we really would like to stay. For all of the stories I've heard of other people being shipped out or displaced, none compares to the saga my mother endured. She was born into a time of war: the French, Japanese, Communists, and Americans forever fighting on her native soil. Bombs were falling the day she born—my grandmother had to hide in the hospital's bomb shelter before she gave birth—and in a terrible full-circle moment, bombs were falling the day she had her own daughter, my sister Elizabeth. My mother was uprooted not once, not twice, but three separate times—each instance more dramatic, violent, and earth-shattering than the last. And yet through it all, she always bloomed where she was transplanted.

Although she was born into an aristocratic family, wealth and power only provide security when the status quo is maintained. In the face of political change, it can turn one into a target overnight. And there was a lot of change in Vietnam in the mid-twentieth century. Communist forces frequently traveled the countryside and terrorized local leaders. Just after my mother was born, a band of Communists arrived in the province where her father was the governor, pulled him out of bed, and tied him to a tree. The local townspeople rallied to his defense and he was freed. Fortunately, my grandfather was ordered to leave Kiến An to assume new responsibilities in Hanoi. This was a great relief for our family, as a revolution was about to explode. Much later, the family found out that the person who replaced my grandfather as interim Province Mandarin in Kiến An was killed by revolutionaries. This could have been my grandfather's fate had he not been transferred back to Hanoi.

Yet, sadly, my family fared no better with the patrolling French troops who were quick to condemn all Vietnamese as enemy collaborators during this time of turmoil. My aunt remembers one such invasion when she and the other women were sent to hide in the woods just before my grandfather was tied up by French forces. The women were discovered and threatened, only to be saved at the last minute by a horn that called the soldiers away.

In 1955, when North Vietnam fell to Hồ Chí Minh's revolution, time was up. My mother was just eleven years old

LIFE-SAVING HERBS

After having so many children, my mother, Nguyệt Dương Thường , was frequently sick. She was very suscepti-ble to viruses and caught them frequently. Her father was very knowledgeable in Eastern medicine and taught her about herbs. Especially when she was ill, she had our chefs prepare her meals with herbs chosen specifically to heal her ailments.

When my mother was six months pregnant with me, she started bleeding. My father was very worried. The French doctors told him that she had a very dangerous condition. At seven months, they determined that she needed an operation to remove me. Medicine was not so advanced back then. They told my father he must choose whom to save: my mother or me. He chose to save my mother.

When they took me out of her womb, they set me to the side because they didn't think they could save me—I was too premature. As they worked on saving my mother, someone turned and saw that my heart was beating. I was alive. Nobody could believe that I survived. I've been fighting since the day I was born. — HELENE AN

when she was woken up in the middle of the night and told that they would have to make an immediate escape. There were only three Trần children left at home at that time, my mother and her two brothers; the rest had already married and moved down to Saigon.

The family quickly ran to the river, where small basket-boats *(thuyền thúng)* were waiting for them. They had very little cash and only a few of the smallest family heirlooms they could carry. Everything else was left behind. In the confusion of piling people and possessions into the basket-boats, many things were lost and broken.

HELENE: *We were in complete darkness. My brother heard a splash, looked over the side of the raft, and saw a large fish. He called everyone over. "We have a big fish here!" he said. But it wasn't a fish, it was me! I had fallen overboard! My brother immediately jumped in and saved me, but I still dislike swimming to this day.*

The trip south took over a week, my mother's immediate family sleeping in the basket-boats. They eventually settled in Saigon, where my grandfather fell into a deep despair. He had not only been displaced, but he had also lost everything: everything that had been in his family for

generations, everything he had worked for, everything he believed in and loved. His family's source of wealth had been in land they could not replace; his family's source of pride had been in serving a country they were forced to leave behind. The burden of loss was so great that he was hospitalized for two months and never fully recovered his formerly vibrant constitution.

Since they had no money, my grandparents were forced to rent a house in the forest, where it was cooler and better for my grandfather's health. My mother's siblings joined the army or went to work, and she was left alone with her parents. She grew up very quickly and learned from her mother how to take care of her father. My grandmother taught her all about the healing power of herbs: how to grow them, where to buy them, and how to prepare them.

My grandfather became too ill to leave his bed, and his skin took on a green hue. They believed he was anemic and needed iron from fresh meat, but they could not afford it. To provide for her father, my mother hiked through the woods to a nearby Catholic church and bartered for the meat her father needed.

HELENE: *There were wild animals in the forest—mountain lions and bears. I was very scared. I saw them, but they never saw me. I got a rod and sharpened it into a sort of homemade spear that I carried with me for protection. Other times, I would carry a large metal pot and spoon and just ring, ring, ring it to chase the animals away.*

While the Trầns had always been a very traditional family, the loss and devastation surrounding them changed the way they viewed the world. Education was always a top priority for the Trần family, but women only needed so much schooling before they became wives. As such, my mother's older sisters had gotten married without much formal schooling, but my grandfather began to

ful training for how to entertain and how to interact with customers. I generally liked it until I did something wrong, because for punishment we had to kneel on the stone floor until the incense stick finished burning.

My mother found that she could handle the school well, however. The first loss of the family fortune and subsequent exile into a life of poverty in the woods had taught her how to be strong.

HELENE: *My mother would counsel me every day. She would tell me: "Life is difficult, you have to learn to deal with the difficulties. Instead, you must be strong and patient. You have to use your brain and learn to adapt and the best way to do that is to keep involved in culture and education."*

> There were wild animals in the forest—mountain lions and bears. I was very scared. I saw them, but they never saw me. — HELENE AN

regret it because it left them vulnerable in the new environment of war and chaos. He didn't want the same fate for his youngest, so he insisted that my mother continue her education. A good education was the best insurance he could give my mother in this new world.

My grandfather enrolled my mother in an all-girls Catholic school; her older brother paid the tuition. The family didn't have a car and they were in such a remote location that my mother had to walk to school. It took her an hour each way. At the school with the children of other aristocrats, she learned science, math, literature, and how to be an elegant woman.

HELENE: *They taught me how to look, how to sit, how to eat, and how to have proper manners. We learned how to talk and carry conversations. Looking back, it was wonder-*

Mama took her mother's advice to heart and transformed herself into an independent, determined teenager. She didn't want to be like her housewife sisters, intelligent minds absorbed with only managing a household. She wanted more for herself and her country. She wanted to do something modern, something with politics. Her dream was to get a position that would help her country, to be a patriot like her father. She emulated her older brothers and uncles who got involved in the new government; her brother Trần Lưu Cung became the Vice Minister of Education. At just 16 years old, she joined a youth movement called the Children of Buddha to help those oppressed in their religious freedoms. Her political aspirations and family connections even put her in the path of the infamous "first lady" of Vietnam, Madame Nhu.

OPPOSITE, FROM TOP LEFT, CLOCKWISE: Helene at age 13; Helene at age 16; Helene at age 18 with older brother in Danang; Helene with relatives in Dalat, age 19.

A women's revolution was taking hold in Vietnam, and my mother was thrilled to be a part of it. Instead of staying home, women around the country were stepping out and speaking up for the first time. Mama wanted to be part of the change, part of the new Vietnam. She attended meetings, put on plays, and even sang on the radio to raise money and spread the message. She had to do a lot of her political activity in secret, however, because both her mother and father opposed it. Still very traditional, her mother didn't believe it was becoming of a well-bred young lady; she wasn't even allowed to sing because at the time it was considered a profession for the lower classes. To get around this, my mother told her mother that her weekend job to make extra pocket money tutoring young children took eight hours a day, when really it took only four. Her father wanted her to have a modern education and to be a modern woman, but he dreamed of her becoming a doctor or a chemist, not a politician. After a lifetime of proudly serving his country despite the constant danger, he had still lost everything. He didn't want his daughter to have such a life. He wanted better for her.

Despite all of her modern yearnings, my mother was still part of a patriarchal Vietnamese society. Her parents arranged a promising match for her with Danny An, a handsome, worldly Air Force pilot who had been educated in France. In 1965, at the age of 20, she married Danny, the only son of wealthy industrialists John and Diana An. My mother was thrilled to discover that the An family was progressive, especially her spunky mother-in-law Diana.

ENTERPRISING WOMEN

Although traditional gender roles in Vietnam are patriarchal, the women in my family have never been content with sitting on the sidelines or standing still. We have always had a passion for work, even when it wasn't proper. We believe it comes from the legacy of enterprising An women, and that it got into our own mother Helene's blood as well.

In Indochina, when aristocrats were known for being scholarly and merchants were looked down upon, my great-grandmother An, John An's mother, could not quiet her business mind. When the French arrived, she saw an opportunity and started a wine import-export business between Vietnam, France, and China. She became famous for being one of the first Vietnamese female entrepreneurs and real estate developers and went on to own a lot of property in her own right. Her business ventures were so successful that she ran out of places to put her profits, eventually settling for the roof of her house. It was well known that the people who worked for her collecting rents were soon very rich themselves, perhaps from their not-so-honest dealings, but she had more money than she knew what to do with, so she turned a blind eye.

The benefits of my great-grandmother's business acumen were felt well into the future, as she helped keep the family afloat in difficult times and passed along her progressive ideas.

from rags to riches

While, traditionally, daughters became their new family's property when they were married and catered to their mothers-in-law, Diana An didn't view things that way. She treated my mother like the daughter she never had, and insisted that Helene keep her independence, as she had.

HELENE: *My mother-in-law was not like the other mothers-in-law. She was very modern for her time. She told me, "We don't need you to take care of us. We want you to continue your education."*

While most women stopped their schooling when they got married, Diana believed that a woman who continued her education was far more valuable than one who was locked away from the world.

HELENE: *My mother-in-law wanted me to be an active part of society, to be learning every day. "How can you throw a great dinner party if you don't have an education?" she would ask. "You must be able to join the men when they talk about important things, when they talk about our country."*

Even when my mother got pregnant, the Ans didn't want her to stop her schooling, so they did everything they could to accommodate her. Though she didn't need to do it herself, my grandmother loved to cook and would prepare special meals for my mother. My grandfather would drive around town getting fresh ingredients to make sure his daughter-in-law was happy and well cared for.

HELENE: *Back then, I never cooked, never held a knife, never touched anything in the kitchen. My brothers and sisters all laugh to this day that I was the one who opened famous restaurants. Nobody would believe it!*

With her new family doting on her and her future secure, my mother thrived in her new environment and gave birth to three beautiful daughters—Hannah, Elizabeth, and Monique—each of whom had their own personal servant. Despite the war, life was good. My father's career flourished. He became a colonel in the Vietnamese Army with 100 men under his command. He was frequently away on missions, but Mama was never alone. Her father-in-law John An was a renowned real estate developer who owned many different businesses in banking, construction, and trade and a lot of property throughout southern Vietnam. Like Helene's own father, he was influential, interested in politics, and loved to be surrounded by progressive thinkers. He hosted nightly dinner parties that were more like salons, the ever-changing guest list including the most prominent people of the day. With the country engaged in war, the Ans provided a place for the exchange of ideas between otherwise disparate groups, from powerful politicians and fellow businessmen to philosophers and poets. Diana reveled in her role as hostess, and my mother was once again mentored in the art of elaborate entertaining.

With her only son grown and settled, Diana found that she had an itch for adventure. In 1968, she took a trip around the world and fell in love with America. While in San Francisco visiting a cousin, Diana was determined to visit the beach for a picnic, the way she'd heard the American women did it. As they were walking, they passed

a small Italian deli that had two signs in the window: "picnic baskets to go" and "hot dogs." She'd never heard of a hot dog, so she said to her cousin, "We're going to do this right, the American way, so let's go in and see about these hot dogs." She never made it to the beach. Instead, she ended up talking with the owner for hours, and by the end of the day, on a whim, she offered to buy his place for $44,000. She had no intention of running a restaurant empire, but she thought that owning a business would give her a better chance of securing visas in the future to return for longer periods of time. Her plan worked and she settled into a happy routine: six months in Saigon and six in California every year. No one could guess that the little diner with just one counter and twenty stools would eventually become the family's lifeline.

Life was wonderful once again for my mother and her family. They had love and prosperity, a purpose, intellectual stimulation, and even though the country was at war, they had hope . . . until early one morning in 1975 when there was a knock at the door.

. . . and back again

While the war was raging throughout most of Vietnam, the south was very quiet. Officials worked hard to quell any distressing news in order to keep people from panicking. Danny was off on a mission, and my mother had a feeling that something was wrong. A friend of my father's delivered the shocking news: Saigon was going to fall. North Vietnamese troops were on their way to the city, and the Ans needed to leave immediately. My father's friend promised to get the family on an American plane if they could depart in less than an hour.

Everything was so quiet and normal in Saigon, my mother wasn't sure she could believe the news. But the friend was reliable and she had no way to contact her husband, no idea that he was stranded in Manila, his plane confiscated. She decided she couldn't risk her children's safety, so she prepared to leave. Her plan was to take my sisters to the base and then go back and check on her house and her parents.

My sisters were playing peacefully in the backyard when she called them in and told them they needed to

OPPOSITE, TOP ROW, FROM LEFT: Diana and Danny, Eiffel Tower, Paris, in 1955; John and Diana An. **MIDDLE ROW, FROM LEFT:** Diana An; Danny in T-6 Texan Japan Zero. **BOTTOM ROW, FROM LEFT:** Helene back row left, Diana back row center, Danny seated with Hannah at her 1st birthday celebration; Monique, Grandpa John, Hannah, Elizabeth, Helene in Vietnam before fall of Saigon, 1973.

leave immediately, that they were going to visit their grandparents in California. My mother was terrified, but she tried to hide it. My mother packed snacks for Monique, the youngest, comforted Elizabeth, who started crying because she couldn't find her favorite doll, and they ran to the airport, leaving everything behind once again. Mama thought it was a false alarm and that they would be gone for two days at the most and would be able to come back and resume their life. She was wrong. Once they were let into the airbase, no one was allowed back out. She didn't even get to say goodbye to her parents.

At the local airbase, the family friend showed some paperwork to the Military Police and my mother and sisters were shoved into the back of a cargo plane, forced to hang on to each other for support as there weren't even any seatbelts. They flew to Clark Air Base in the Philippines, where the vast hangar was crammed with too many people.

They found a spot on the floor and waited for two weeks until they were finally reunited with my father. From there they were flown to Guam where they lived in a makeshift tent city with thousands of other refugees waiting for permission to leave. They finally arrived in Camp Pendleton in Oceanside, California. My grandparents' deli in San Francisco, Diana's impulse purchase from a few years earlier, proved to be the magic ticket out.

When the family arrived in the Bay Area, they had nothing except the one-bedroom holiday apartment the Ans were renting and the tiny Italian deli. The Vietnamese government confiscated everything they had been forced to leave behind: another trove of family heirlooms, memories, and hard-earned wealth, lost forever.

The An men were hit hard by the reversal of family fortune because they were not able to provide for their families as they had done their whole lives. John An's businesses were gone; everything he had built was taken over by strangers. Danny's pilot career was grounded as he was deemed too old to work for the American airlines. He went from having an entire base of men under his command to working the night shift at an hourly job. But of course, no one would give up. They had each other and they had a fighting spirit. They needed little else.

The An women had been taught from an early age that behind every great man is a great woman, and they got right to work. My grandparents encouraged my mother to continue her education, so she quickly learned English and enrolled in college classes, earning an accounting diploma while tutoring school children in French in the morning and math in the afternoon. She then got a job as a full-time accountant at the University of California San Francisco's Langley Porter Psychiatric Hospital. My father took computer classes and helped care for the children, while everyone pitched in at Diana's deli.

Life settled into a routine of hard work, my mother and grandmother putting in sixteen-hour days, seven days a week. After preparing breakfast, Mama took the bus to work at 7:30 a.m., got home at 6 p.m., made dinner, and went to work at the restaurant until long after closing. Her father-in-law was not a huge fan of the restaurant business, believing it owned its owners and wouldn't make any money. "But at least we will have food together," he conceded.

They didn't make any money . . . at first. Initially, to keep the current customer base happy, they kept the menu of the Italian deli untouched, but eventually my mother began to experiment. She noticed that the creamy, sauce-laden noodles were a top-seller, but since such heavy cooking wasn't her specialty, she slowly changed the menu. Inspired by the meals she grew up with, she started with her take on spaghetti—a simple garlic sauce on a lighter noodle—and her famous garlic noodles were born. Customers loved this new dish, so she added more flavors from home to the menu: shiitake mushrooms and tía tô leaves. She purposefully added them to classic dishes like spring rolls and barbecue that she knew Americans would be willing to try. Before long, the Ans were operating the first Vietnamese restaurant in San Francisco.

the birth of thanh long

The time had come to change the name and claim the new restaurant as their own. Diana chose Thang Long, *the ancient name of Hanoi when it was the capital of Indochina. The name meant "soaring" or "ascending dragon" and was to represent the family's rise from the ashes. However, when the first new menus arrived from the printer, the name was misspelled as Thang Long, or "green dragon." Undeterred, Diana decided that it was an omen of prosperity, since green was the color of wealth. Who could argue?*

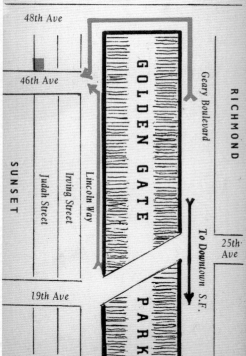

QUOTATIONS

1. "Authentic Vietnamese food is tasteful and delicious at Thang Long — Vietnam Restaurant.
It's truly a gourmet delight and please don't confuse Vietnamese food with Chinese cuisine . . . they are difinitely different." (Syd Goldie)
(San Francisco Progress, July 23, 1971)

2. . . . "Oh the crab! Never in our lives have we tasted anything so delicious. This dish could serve to kings, presidents and emperors!"
(Share The Wealth, Vol. 1, No. 5, Sept. 1971)

3. "Our dinner at the Thang Long Vietnam Restaurant has alerted so many of our gourments, that we see ourselves obliged again to arange for a second evening."
(U.E.A.C., Gourmet Group News, Oct. 12, 1971)

Pacific Ocean

48th Ave

46th Ave

GOLDEN GATE PARK

Geary Boulevard

RICHMOND

Lincoln Way

Irving Street

Judah Street

SUNSET

25th Ave

To Downtown S.F.

19th Ave

VIETNAM Thăng Long RESTAURANT

Member
San Francisco Convention
and Visitors Bureau

PHONE 665-1146
664-9983

4101 JUDAH ST.
AT 46th AVE.

SAN FRANCISCO

& IMPORTED WINE & BEER

LA CARTE

. . . . $ $ .50

. 50

(i Vitamins Roll)   .50

(rk, Chicken or Beef)   .50

m Style   .60

am, egg, green peas)   .35

.15

) with Vietnam noodle)   .85

soup with Vietnam noodle) .85

Bouillabaisse)   .75

(5) with salad   1.95

salad & rice   1.85

LUNCH

e with egg   1.10

Sauté with vegetable   1.50

é with vegetable   1.50

auté with vegetable   1.95

Sauté with noodle   1.50

é with noodle   1.50

auté with noodle   1.50

JR WORLD FAMOUS
ROAST CRAB
and
ient Multi Vitamins Roll
to experience the fantastic food
of Vietnam!

Open Noon to 9 p. m.

CLOSED ON MONDAY

SPECIAL DINNERS
$5.00 — 7.50 — 9.95
on request

For Reservation, call 665-1146 or 664-9983
ALL FOOD PREPARED TO TAKE OUT

Slowly, slowly, they expanded. They removed the deli counter and added seating for twenty-two. Customers loved the changes and the exotic yet somehow familiar food. My mother got her accounting work done early and then spent the remainder of the day planning new entrées. She would call my father on the phone and tell him what she envisioned. When she came home from work, he would have a test dish ready for her.

Back then, the only place Asian ingredients could be found was in Chinatown, and they made frequent visits, getting to know the locals and spreading the word about their restaurant. What they couldn't buy, they made from scratch. Soon, the small restaurant in Outer Sunset was the talk of the Asian community. Good reviews spread around the city and the restaurant grew. They expanded to forty seats, then sixty. When the space next door became available, they took their first big risk: they bought it and then closed for two months to renovate both spaces. My mother's vision was to create an environment that replicated the gracious atmosphere surrounding her parents' and in-laws' dinner tables. She wanted guests of the restaurant to feel as though they were in her home.

They reopened Thanh Long with eighty seats and a line of customers out the door.

The new success meant that they were able to move from the cramped apartment across the street to a house five blocks away, slightly bigger and still within walking distance. Any extra money, though, was reinvested back into their business or saved for their daughters' educations.

"We didn't want to be rich," my mother remembers. "We just wanted to make sure we could feed our family."

Everyone worked at Thanh Long, even the An girls. We went straight to the restaurant after school, charged with making dumplings or rolling rice paper. My sister Elizabeth recalls less glamorous jobs. "In the early days, Mom had me working as a dishwasher, and I spent a lot of time cutting vegetables. Just because you're the boss's daughter, you don't get it any easier."

The following recipes reflect the dishes from this time of transition: special meals that traveled from my mother's youth in Vietnam to our kitchen table in America to our first restaurant. It's a mix of classic flavors and comfort food—a fusion of cultures old and new that we hope will warm your heart as it has ours.

Chicken Phở with Kaffir Lime

THE SECRET TO MY MOTHER'S INFINITE ENERGY? *It might be her daily breakfast of chicken phở (phở ga). The flavorful protein- and antioxidant-packed broth is to Vietnam as chicken noodle soup is to America—classic, comforting, and healthy. We eat phở ga regularly for breakfast and it's a staple meal during flu season, but the rice noodle soup is great any time of day or year. What makes my mother's phở ga unique is the addition of kaffir lime leaves for extra fragrance and a lighter taste.*

MAKES 8 SERVINGS

FOR THE BROTH:

1 whole (about 3 pound) organic, free-range roasting chicken, giblets removed

3 quarts Homemade Chicken Broth (page 273) or store-bought low-sodium chicken broth

2 large white onions, charred and peeled (see note, page 55)

2 ounces fresh ginger, unpeeled and smashed (see note, page 55)

2 garlic cloves, peeled

2 whole star anise

1 tablespoon rock sugar, to taste

1 tablespoon sea salt, to taste

2 (14-ounce) packages flat rice stick (banh phở) noodles

5 fresh kaffir lime leaves

½ large red onion, thinly sliced

1 cup chopped scallions, white and green parts (about 2 bunches)

1 cup chopped fresh cilantro leaves (about 2 bunches)

4 teaspoons fish sauce, or to taste

FOR SERVING:

Fresh Thai basil leaves

2 limes, quartered

4 serrano chiles or jalapeños, thinly sliced

Chili sauce

Hoisin sauce

1) Place the chicken, breast-side up, in a large stockpot. Put the onion, ginger, garlic, and star anise in the pot around the chicken. Add the chicken broth and about 1 quart of water to cover the chicken and set the pot over high heat. Bring the liquid to a boil and boil for 20 minutes, making sure to skim off the excess fat and froth on top, until the broth is clear with no bubbles. Cover the pot and remove it from the heat. Let it sit at room temperature for 15 minutes.

2) Remove the chicken from the pot and transfer it to a cutting board. When the chicken is cool enough to handle, carve all the meat off the bones and return the bones to the broth. Rub the kaffir lime leaves between the palms of your hands to slightly bruise them, then add them to the broth. Bring the broth back to a boil over high heat, then reduce the heat to low and simmer, uncovered, for 30 minutes. Stir in the sugar and salt and cook until the sugar dissolves, about 5 more minutes.

(continued)

3] Remove and discard the bones, vegetables, spices, and lime leaves from the pot. Strain the broth through a fine-mesh strainer to remove any impurities. The broth should be clear. (If it is not, strain it again.) Slice the chicken meat, separating the white and dark meat, and set it aside.

4] Soak the rice noodles in warm water until they are softened, about 10 minutes, then drain them.

5] Bring a large pot of salted water to a boil over high heat. Add the noodles and cook them for 20 to 30 seconds or until al dente, stirring constantly. Drain the noodles, rinse them very well under cold water, and then rinse them quickly with warm water to remove any excess starch. Strain well.

6] Bring the broth back to a boil over high heat. Divide the noodles evenly among eight serving bowls. Place the chicken on top of the noodles, giving each person light or dark meat as they prefer. Add some fish sauce (more or less as desired) to the broth, then ladle the boiling broth over the chicken to fill each bowl. Top each serving with red onions, scallions, cilantro, and a pinch of black pepper. Serve immediately with the herb platter and condiments.

NOTE: *It's important to rinse the remaining starch off your noodles after cooking them, as starch will make the broth taste bland.*

NOTE: *Use the side of a butcher's knife or the bottom of a pot to smash the fresh ginger to release its flavor.*

THE BEST CHICKEN PHỞ I EVER HAD

Phở originally came from the North, and because cattle were hard to raise there, chicken phở was and is more common and popular in the North than beef. Like most Vietnamese food, phở ga is extremely versatile and easy to personalize. Some people (my sister Hannah) like the white meat of the chicken in their soup, and some people (the rest of my family) prefer the dark meat. My mother adds kaffir lime leaves; others add coriander or fish sauce. Vietnamese chefs pride themselves on their personalized versions, and phở enthusiasts are happy to indulge.

The dish is served everywhere in Vietnam, from street vendors who cook it in pots on the sidewalk to gourmet restaurants. It's hard to know before you taste it whose phở is going to be great and whose isn't. The first time I visited Vietnam, I was by myself and stumbled into a tourist trap in Hanoi where the phở was terrible. When I returned with my parents a few years later, one of their friends led us to a hole in the wall on a side street.

He happened to be one of the wealthiest men in Vietnam, so it was a surprise to end up in a dingy little restaurant like this one with only one item on the menu: Chicken Phở. The whole place seemed rather rickety and had a bare cement floor. Child-sized plastic chairs were set up in front of low wooden tables covered in cheap plastic tablecloths. It definitely didn't seem like the kind of place that catered to the rich, yet when I looked around I noticed the customers were very well-to-do. Impeccably dressed women had their Louis Vuitton purses on the floor next to them, while I was told that top "out-of-uniform" Communist leaders were squatting throughout the restaurant enjoying their phở. One spoonful, though, and I understood why: this hole-in-the-wall served the best chicken phở (besides my mother's) that I had ever tasted. It just goes to show that you can only judge a phở by its flavor.

EATING WITH YOUR NOSE

There's a saying that "you eat with your eyes," but in our household, our sense of smell takes precedence. My mother is always experimenting with ingredients to get not just the best taste, but also the best aroma out of her creations. Although chicken phở is not traditionally made with kaffir lime leaves, my mother added them to her recipe because she was inspired when wrapping chicken in lemon leaves for the grill. She wanted to infuse the same citrusy accents in her chicken broth, but she chose lime leaves since they release a stronger flavor and more fragrance when cooked.

Green Papaya, Long Bean, and Tomato Steak Salad with Tamarind Dressing

IN VIETNAM, TEXTURE IS VERY IMPORTANT TO A DISH, *which is why the crunchy green papaya is a popular choice for salads. However, papaya can be a bit bland, so my mother created a sweet-and-sour tamarind dressing to liven it up. The secret to perfectly crisp yet tender papaya? Soak the slices in an ice water bath and lightly scrunch the papaya strips.*

If you can't find green papaya, slightly yellow papaya, still firm, will work great for this salad as well. If you want a vegetarian salad, simply omit the steak.

MAKES 4 TO 6 SERVINGS

2 ounces filet mignon, cut into thin strips

1 teaspoon freshly ground black pepper

1 tablespoon canola oil

1 garlic clove, minced

5 whole garlic cloves, peeled

1 tablespoon chili paste

3 tablespoons fish sauce

2 tablespoons palm sugar

1 tablespoon Tamarind Juice (page 283)

1 pound fresh Chinese long beans, trimmed and cut into 1½-inch pieces

4 cherry tomatoes, quartered

1 green papaya, peeled, seeded, and julienned into thin strips

Roasted Peanuts, crushed (page 281) or hazelnuts, crushed, for serving

1] Season the steak all over with the pepper.

2] Heat the oil in a medium skillet over medium heat. Add the minced garlic and sauté until fragrant, about 1 minute. Add the steak and cook, stirring constantly, until it is cooked through but still pink in the center, about 3 minutes. Remove the skillet from the heat and set it aside.

3] Using a mortar and pestle, pound the whole garlic cloves and chili paste until smooth and uniform in color.

4] In a small bowl, combine the fish sauce, palm sugar, and tamarind juice, and then stir this mixture into the garlic-chili paste.

5] Place the long beans and tomatoes in a large bowl and pound them lightly with a wooden mallet to release the flavors and juices, being careful not to bruise the vegetables. Add the papaya and tamarind dressing to the bowl and lightly crush the papaya, beans, and tomatoes with your hands. Add the steak on top of the salad, and serve garnished with nuts.

NOTE: *Papaya salad is usually spicy. Using 1 tablespoon of chili paste will give it a spicy kick. For a milder taste, decrease the amount of chili paste.*

Spicy Beef & Lemongrass Soup

KNOWN AS BÚN BÒ HUẾ, *this soup originated in the central Vietnamese city of Huế, a onetime capital of the country and home to some of my favorite Vietnamese dishes. Huế is well known for its spicy cuisine, but our version of bún bò huế has a softer kick so everyone in our family can enjoy it. My mother finds the traditional annatto seeds bitter, so instead she uses more mellow paprika for heat and color and coconut water to add a mild sweetness and extra depth of flavor to the broth. If you want to eat it the way my father, who eats raw chiles whole, does, then you can dip the meat in Papa's Chile, Salt & Pepper Lime Sauce (page 126).*

We serve this with citrus wedges, fresh herbs, and banana flower to cool the tongue.

MAKES 8 SERVINGS

FOR THE SOUP:

1 teaspoon sea salt

1 teaspoon whole black or white peppercorns, crushed

1 tablespoon fish sauce

1 teaspoon shrimp paste

2 pounds beef shank or beef round, blanched (see note, page 127)

2 to 3 fresh lemongrass stalks

7 whole shallots, divided

5 cups homemade chicken broth (page 273) or store-bought low-sodium chicken broth

¼ cup rock sugar

1 tablespoon canola oil

3 whole dried bird's eye chiles, finely chopped

2 teaspoons paprika

1 tablespoon white wine

1 (14-ounce) package dried thick rice noodles, medium or large width

2 cups coconut water

1 white onion, cut into paper-thin slices

½ cup chopped scallions (about 1 bunch)

½ cup chopped fresh Vietnamese coriander (*rau răm*) leaves (about 1 bunch)

FOR SERVING:

1 tablespoon fish sauce, or to taste

Fresh Thai basil leaves

Fresh Vietnamese perilla (*tía tô*) leaves 2 limes, quartered

Mung bean sprouts

2 bird's eye chiles or jalapeños, deseeded and thinly sliced

1 banana flower (optional)

1] In a small bowl, whisk together the salt, crushed peppercorns, fish sauce, and shrimp paste. Place the beef in a large airtight container and rub the beef all over with the marinade, then seal the container and let the beef marinate in refrigerator for 2 hours.

2] Cut the lemongrass to separate the white bulbs from the stalks. Tie the stalks into a bunch with cooking twine. Mince the white bulbs. Cut two of the shallots into thin slices. Set aside.

3] Put the marinated meat and the remaining five whole shallots in a large stockpot and add chicken broth and about 7 cups of water. Bring the water to a boil over medium heat, skimming out the impurities and froth. Reduce the heat to low. Add the rock sugar and the bundled lemongrass stalks, cover, and simmer until the meat is soft, about 2 hours, regularly skimming the surface of fat and froth.

4] Transfer the meat to a clean airtight container and place it in the refrigerator. Strain the broth through a fine-mesh strainer into a new pot.

5] Heat the oil in a medium skillet over medium heat. Add the minced lemongrass, sliced shallots, chiles, and paprika and sauté until fragrant, about 1 to 2 minutes. Add the wine, being conscious of a possible flame-up. Add the seasoned lemongrass and shallots to the broth and cook for 5 minutes to meld the flavors.

6] About 30 minutes before serving, soak the rice noodles in warm water for 10 minutes.

7] Meanwhile, bring a large pot of salted water to a boil over high heat. Drain the noodles and add them to the pot of boiling water. Cook the noodles for 7 minutes, or until al dente, then drain them, rinse them under cold water, and finally rinse them under warm water to remove excess starch. Divide the noodles among individual bowls.

8] Add the coconut water to the broth, then bring the broth to a boil over high heat. Sample the broth and add fish sauce as desired to taste. Remove the meat from the refrigerator, cut it into thin slices, and divide it evenly among the serving bowls on top of the noodles. Ladle the boiling broth over the sliced meat to fill each bowl. Top with the white onion, scallions, and coriander (rau răm) leaves. Serve with the herb platter.

NOTE: *You can decrease the amount of chiles if you want a milder soup, but the broth won't be as red.*

PAPA'S CHILE, SALT & PEPPER LIME SAUCE

MAKES 1 SERVING

½ **teaspoon sea salt**

½ **teaspoon freshly ground black pepper**

1 **fresh bird's eye chile, minced**

1 **teaspoon freshly squeezed lime juice (about 1 lime wedge)**

Mix all the ingredients in a small saucer. Enjoy.

NOTE: HOW TO BLANCH BEEF

Asian cooks frequently blanch raw meat, because it helps remove impurities that would otherwise make broth cloudy and it slightly cooks the meat, helping eliminate the possibility of cross-contamination with other raw foods like vegetables. It's a relatively easy and quick process. All you need is a large stockpot, a large bowl, and a pair of tongs.

1) Bring a large stockpot of water to a boil over high heat. (Be sure to leave enough room to add the beef, which should be fully submerged.) Fill a large bowl with ice water and set it aside. Trim the beef of any excess fat.

2) Use tongs to carefully lower the beef into the boiling water. Boil the beef for 5 minutes, skimming the surface of froth and fat.

3) With the tongs, remove the beef from the water and submerge into the ice water bath until it is no longer hot and can be safely stored in refrigerator.

4) Rinse the meat well. It is now ready to cook.

OBLIQUE CUTS

Oblique cutting is popular in Asian cuisine, not just because it produces beautiful shapes but also because it exposes more of the surface area of a vegetable, allowing for faster cooking. Also called roll-cutting because it's done while rolling the vegetable, oblique cutting is easily done as follows:

1) Cut the vegetable once at a 45-degree angle.

2) Keeping your knife raised over the vegetable at the same angle, use our free hand to roll the vegetable a quarter turn so that the newly cut diagonal side faces up toward the ceiling.

3) Now cut down at the same 45-degree angle, slicing through the middle of the cut face.

4) Quarter turn the vegetable again and repeat.

Beef Stew with Vietnamese Spices

ALTHOUGH IT'S HARD TO IMAGINE EATING SOMETHING SO HEARTY FOR BREAKFAST, *growing up in Vietnam, that's exactly how we often enjoyed this traditional stew, called bó kho. Stews and soups were generally considered day dishes, while stir-fries were reserved for evening meals.*

What makes this stew so special is the fragrant addition of anise and red peppercorns. You can use whatever cut of meat you prefer. I like fattier cuts, while Mama prefers leaner meat.

MAKES 6 SERVINGS

3 lemongrass stalks

4 tablespoons canola oil

2 shallots, chopped

1 tablespoon minced garlic

3 star anise

10 whole red peppercorns

2 pounds beef chuck or beef shank, blanched (see note, page 127)

2 tablespoons tomato paste

1 teaspoon sea salt

1 teaspoon freshly ground black pepper

1 tablespoon grated fresh ginger

3 cups Homemade Chicken Broth (page 273) or store-bought low-sodium chicken broth

½ cup rock sugar

2 bay leaves

1 cinnamon stick

2 carrots, cut into obliques (see note, page 127)

1 cup red wine

1 tablespoon fish sauce

1 tablespoon light soy sauce

1 tablespoon oyster sauce

1 white onion, finely chopped, for garnish

1 bunch fresh scallions, finely chopped, for garnish

½ cup finely chopped fresh basil leaves, for garnish

1) Remove the tough outer leaves of the lemongrass stalks and set aside. Finely chop the tender inner white bulbs.

2) Heat 1 tablespoon of oil in a large saucepan over medium heat. Add the shallots, garlic lemongrass bulbs, star anise, and red peppercorns and sauté for about 5 minutes until aromatic.

3) Cut the beef into 1½-inch squares. In a large bowl, mix the tomato paste with the salt, pepper, and ginger. Add the beef and the sautéed aromatics, and drizzle 2 tablespoons of oil over the top, and marinate for 15 minutes.

4) In the same saucepan, heat 1 tablespoon of oil over medium heat. Add the beef and cook, stirring frequently, until golden brown, about 3 minutes.

5) Add the chicken broth and enough water to cover the meat, about 4 cups. Stir in the rock sugar. Add the bay leaves, cinnamon stick, and the lemongrass stalks. Cover the pot and cook for 1½ hours.

6) Remove the meat and set it aside. Strain the broth through a fine-mesh strainer into a new pot. Add the meat and carrots to the broth. Stir in the red wine, fish sauce, soy sauce, and oyster sauce and cook over medium heat until the meat is tender, about 30 minutes. Serve hot garnished with the white onion, scallion, and basil.

Lotus Soup with Pork

THIS DISH IS A PERFECT EXAMPLE OF THE SIMPLICITY OF EVERYDAY VIETNAMESE COOKING. *The sweetness from the pork bones and the lotus root gives the soup a delicious depth of flavor.*

Lotus root is loaded with vitamins, including iron and vitamin C, and has antioxidants that are believed to fight cancer and help calm the nerves. Whenever my sisters or I had trouble sleeping, my mother would make this soup for us.

MAKES 4 TO 6 SERVINGS

2 lotus roots, peeled

1 teaspoon plus 1 tablespoon sea salt, divided

2 pounds pork spareribs, cut into 1-inch pieces

3 large shallots, peeled

1 ounce (about 2 tablespoons) rock sugar, or to taste

1 tablespoon fish sauce, to taste

2 tablespoons chopped scallions, white and green parts for garnish

2 tablespoons chopped fresh cilantro leaves, for garnish

1) Cut the lotus roots into ¼-inch slices and sprinkle them with 1 teaspoon of the salt. Put the lotus slices in a bowl of water to soak for 15 minutes, then drain and rinse them well.

2) Add 6 cups of water to a large stock pot. Add the spareribs to the pot and bring the water to a boil over medium heat, carefully skimming the fat and froth from the surface. Reduce the heat to low, add the whole shallots and lotus root, and cook for 30 minutes. Remove and discard the shallots.

3) Continue cooking the meat over low heat until the ribs are soft and the lotus root is tender-crisp, about 30 minutes.

4) Add the remaining tablespoon of salt, the sugar, and the fish sauce to the broth and cook for one minute. Transfer the soup to a large serving bowl and garnish with scallions and cilantro. Serve hot.

LOTUS: MOTHER'S MILK

Lotus soup is commonly used in Asia by new mothers as part of a postpartum diet because it's believed that lotus helps increase a mother's milk supply. When I became a new mother myself, I ate this soup several times a week. I'm not sure if it helped with breastfeeding or not, but it did help me sleep. I found that eating it relaxed my mind and soothed my nerves—both vital benefits for any new parent!

Eggplant Ragoût with Tofu & Vietnamese Herbs

INSPIRED BY THE CLASSIC VIETNAMESE DISH CÀ BUNG, *this dish features a tomato turmeric base, eggplant, and tía tô leaves. Though it is traditionally made with pork belly and spareribs, my mother opted for a vegetarian version with tofu and more vegetables; feel free to add whatever other vegetables you desire. Like a lot of my mother's recipes, this vegetarian ragoût is healthy and light, yet still full of flavor.*

MAKES 2 TO 4 SERVINGS

8 ounces firm tofu, cut into squares

8 ounces eggplant, cut into 16 angled pieces (a little more than ½ cup)

1 small carrot, cut into 5 pieces

½ chayote (optional), peeled and seeded

2 tablespoons extra-virgin olive oil

1 white onion, cut into quarters

4 tomatoes, cut into quarters

2 teaspoons fresh turmeric juice or ½ teaspoon ground turmeric

5-6 pieces jicama

8 pieces sweet pea (garden peas) or snap peas

2 tablespoons White Sauce (page 278)

2 tablespoons tomato juice

1 tablespoon soy sauce

1 teaspoon fish sauce

1 teaspoon sugar

Fresh Vietnamese perilla (tía tô) leaves, coarsely chopped, for garnish

1) Bring a large pot of salted water to a boil. Add the tofu, eggplant, carrots, and chayote (if using), blanch the tofu and vegetables for 5 to 6 minutes, and then immediately drain the water from the pot and set the tofu and vegetables aside.

2) Heat the oil in a large skillet over medium heat. Add the onions, tomatoes, and turmeric and sauté for 3 minutes or until the onions and tomatoes begin to soften. Add the jicama and the blanched chayote, carrots, eggplant, and tofu and sauté for 5 minutes longer, allowing the turmeric tomato sauce to infuse its flavors into the vegetables and tofu.

3) Meanwhile, heat a large clay or regular pot over medium heat, and transfer the items from the skillet into the pot, along with the peas. Stir in the white sauce, tomato juice, soy sauce, fish sauce, and sugar. Cook until the eggplant is soft, about 5 minutes. Serve hot, garnished with the tía tô leaves.

Lemongrass Beef Vermicelli

YOU CAN MAKE THIS WITH ALMOST ANY CUT OF BEEF, *but for our family, my mother always used filet mignon. The secret to cooking a good beef stir-fry using filet mignon is to make sure your pan is sizzling hot and to only cook the meat to a medium-rare level, then quickly transfer it to a plate. Don't wait until the meat looks fully cooked because it will continue to cook as it sits on the plate. There are two ways to enjoy this dish: over rice vermicelli noodles with a Vietnamese herb salad as we present here, or just over plain rice.*

MAKES 2 SERVINGS

FOR THE VERMICELLI:

1 teaspoon Maggi seasoning sauce

1 teaspoon fish sauce

1 teaspoon soy sauce

1 teaspoon oyster sauce

½ teaspoon sugar

8 ounces filet mignon, cut into thin (⅛-inch) slices

3 tablespoons canola oil, divided

2 tablespoons finely chopped fresh lemongrass, tender inner white bulb only

1 teaspoon chili paste

½ red onion, sliced

4 ounces dried rice vermicelli noodles

2 tablespoons coarsely chopped Roasted Peanuts (page 281), for garnish

FOR THE HERB SALAD:

2 cups (about 2 ounces) butter lettuce, coarsely chopped

1 ounce Pickled Carrots (page 278)

½ cup (about 3 ounces) seeded and julienned cucumber

¼ cup (about ½ bunch) chopped fresh Vietnamese perilla (tía tô) leaves

¼ cup (about ½ bunch) chopped fresh basil leaves

¼ cup (about ½ bunch) chopped fresh mint leaves

¼ cup coarsely chopped fresh Vietnamese coriander (rau răm) leaves (about ½ bunch)

3 fresh Vietnamese balm (kinh giới) or lemon balm leaves, chopped

1] In a large bowl, mix together the Maggi sauce, fish sauce, soy sauce, oyster sauce, and sugar. Add the steak and 1 tablespoon of the oil, cover the bowl, and set it aside to marinate for 15 minutes.

2] Meanwhile, bring a medium pot of water to a boil over high heat. Cook the noodles according the package directions until al dente, usually about 6 minutes. Strain the noodles, rinse them in cold water, and then shake them well to remove any excess water.

3] TO MAKE THE HERB SALAD: In a large bowl, toss together the butter lettuce, carrots, cucumber, tía tô, basil, mint, coriander, and balm leaves. Set aside.

4] Heat the remaining 2 tablespoons of oil in a large skillet over medium heat. Add the lemongrass and chili paste and stir well. Add the marinated beef and red onion and cook for 5 minutes, stirring constantly. Serve hot on top of rice noodles and herb salad, sprinkled with peanuts, if desired.

Seared Steak Salad with Garlic Lemon Dressing

MY MOTHER CREATED THIS FAST AND EASY STEAK SALAD, PACKED FULL OF NUTRIENTS *and protein, for her health conscious customers. Daikon radish is a "superfood" containing enzymes that aid digestion, the sweet mango is packed with vitamin C, the tangy bell peppers can reduce bad cholesterol, and snow peas are rich in fiber and iron. This entrée salad is perfect for the summer, since the steak can also be grilled outdoors.*

MAKES 4 TO 6 SERVINGS

FOR THE MEAT:

8 tablespoons Garlic Lemon Sauce (nước chấm) (page 274)

1 tablespoon lightly packed brown sugar

1 tablespoon light soy sauce

1 tablespoon freshly squeezed lime juice (from ½ lime)

1 tablespoon peeled, finely chopped fresh ginger

1 tablespoon chopped garlic cloves

2 teaspoons chili paste

½ teaspoon freshly ground black pepper

¼ fresh pineapple, peeled, cored, and chopped, or 3 canned pineapple rings, chopped

12 ounces beef tenderloin, cut in half

2 tablespoons canola oil

FOR THE DRESSING:

4 tablespoons Garlic Lemon Sauce (nước chấm) (page 274)

2 tablespoons freshly squeezed lime juice (from 1 lime)

2 tablespoons lightly packed brown sugar

1 teaspoon chili paste

½ teaspoon freshly ground black pepper

FOR THE SALAD:

½ cup chopped daikon

½ cup julienned shallots

½ cup julienned red bell peppers

½ cup julienned mango

12 fresh snow peas, blanched and julienned

FOR SERVING:

½ cup chopped fresh cilantro (about 1 bunch), for garnish

½ cup chopped fresh Vietnamese coriander (rau răm) leaves (about 1 bunch), for garnish

¼ cup chopped fresh mint (about ½ bunch), for garnish

1) In a medium bowl, mix together the nước chấm, brown sugar, soy sauce, lime juice, ginger, garlic, chili paste, black pepper, and pineapple. Put the steak in a resealable plastic bag. Add the marinade to the bag and seal. Turn the steak to coat it well in the marinade, and refrigerate it for 2 hours.

2) After the steak is done marinating, remove it from refrigerator and set it aside to allow it to come to room temperature, about 20 minutes.

3) Meanwhile, make the dressing: In a medium bowl, whisk the together the nước chấm, lime juice, brown sugar, chili paste, and black pepper. Set aside.

4) To cook the meat, heat the oil in a large skillet over medium-high heat. Add the marinated steak and sear it on all sides until golden brown, about 2 minutes on each side for medium-rare. Remove the steak to a plate and allow it to cool. Cut the steak lengthwise into 3-inch long, ¼-inch thick slices. Note: Depending on the size of the pan, you may want to cut the steak in half and sear it in batches, as it's important that the pan is not overcrowded.

5) TO MAKE THE SALAD: Mix together the daikon, shallots, peppers, mango, and snow peas in a large serving bowl. Add the dressing and toss to coat the salad evenly. Drain any excess dressing from the salad, then add the steak and toss well.

6) Sprinkle the cilantro, rau răm, and mint over top of the salad and serve.

Turkey Stuffed with Sticky Rice

MY GRANDMOTHER ALWAYS STUFFED ROASTED GAME HEN WITH STICKY RICE AND WE LOVED IT. *To celebrate Thanksgiving in our new country, my mother wanted to create a dish that would merge both our cultures and help us make new memories. She knew Americans stuffed turkeys with dressing, so she decided to do with the same with sticky rice. It was always such a hit with our friends that, when we started An Catering, this dish became an instant classic on our holiday menu. We have customers who order it from us year after year for their Thanksgiving dinner.*

MAKES 8 SERVINGS

FOR THE STICKY RICE:

2 cups long grain sweet or glutinous rice

1½ teaspoons sea salt

1 teaspoon sugar

1 teaspoon coconut oil

1 tablespoon canola oil

½ onion, diced

2 shallots, diced

¼ pound (about ½ cup) ground chicken or turkey

2 links Chinese or Italian sausage, diced

½ cup roasted chestnuts, chopped

2 tablespoons diced fresh shiitake mushrooms

½ carrot, cut into thin slices

1 tablespoon Maggi seasoning sauce

1 teaspoon fish sauce

1 teaspoon freshly ground black pepper

FOR THE TURKEY:

1 whole (10-pound) turkey, giblets removed and discarded

1 cup mayonnaise

Zest and juice of 1 lime

1 bunch fresh thyme

1 bunch fresh rosemary

1 bunch fresh sage

1 orange, halved

1 white onion, cut into large dice

10 garlic cloves, peeled

1] TO MAKE THE RICE: Put the rice in a small bowl and cover it with water. Set the rice aside to soak overnight. After it has soaked, drain the water from the rice. Add the salt, sugar, and coconut oil and mix well. Steam the rice until it is soft, or cook it in an electric rice cooker with 1½ cups of water. Set aside.

2] Heat the canola oil in a medium skillet or wok over medium heat. Sauté the onion and shallots until they are lightly golden and fragrant, about 2 minutes. Add the ground poultry and cook for 2 minutes, stirring frequently. Add the sausage and cook for 2 minutes, stirring frequently to brown evenly. Stir in the chestnuts, mushrooms, carrots, salt, pepper, fish sauce, and Maggi sauce and continue sautéing for 2 to 3 minutes. Add the sticky rice and mix well. Remove the skillet from the heat.

(Continued)

3] Preheat the oven to 350°F.

4] In a small bowl, mix the lime juice and zest with the mayonnaise. Set aside.

5] Place the turkey breast-side up in a large roasting pan. Stuff the cavity with the sticky rice. Rub the mayonnaise mixture evenly over the turkey's skin, then season the turkey liberally with salt and pepper. Arrange the thyme, rosemary, sage, orange, onion, and garlic cloves around the turkey in the roasting pan. Roast for 2½ hours or until the juices run clear and an instant-read thermometer registers 160°F when inserted into the meatiest part of the breast. (The temperature will continue to rise after the turkey is removed from the oven. The final safe temperature should be 180°F.) For a crispier skin, raise the oven temperature to 500°F and watch the turkey closely to prevent the skin from burning. Once the skin reaches a golden brown color, immediately remove the turkey from the oven. Allow the turkey to rest for 30 minutes before slicing.

NOTE: *Save the turkey bones and any leftover meat for Leftover Turkey Porridge (opposite page).*

VARIATION: *You can use the thyme, rosemary, sage, orange, onion, and garlic cloves as a stuffing instead of the sticky rice. Simply stuff them all into the turkey cavity after seasoning the skin with salt and pepper.*

Leftover Turkey Porridge

GROWING UP IN SAN FRANCISCO, PORRIDGE WAS A STAPLE COMFORT FOOD *in our house because it was inexpensive, made good use of leftovers, and, most importantly, was delicious. Now and then, we made family trips to Chinatown for fish porridge, but nothing beat my mother's or grandmother's homemade porridge. My sisters and I were treated to it any time we felt sick or just needed a bowl to warm us up. Our favorite was turkey porridge, especially the day after Thanksgiving. After a long Black Friday shopping session, it was what all of us girls looked forward to coming home to. As usual, nothing went to waste in our house, as even the turkey bones were saved for this special next-day porridge.*

MAKES 6 SERVINGS

½ cup jasmine rice

Leftover bones from Turkey Stuffed with Sticky Rice (page 137)

4 cups Homemade Chicken Broth (page 273) or store-bought low-sodium chicken broth

1 white onion, peeled and quartered

2 ounces peeled fresh ginger, smashed

6 whole garlic cloves, peeled

Leftover turkey meat and sticky rice from Turkey Stuffed with Sticky Rice (page 137), optional

½ cup chopped scallions (about 1 bunch)

½ cup chopped fresh Vietnamese coriander (rau răm) leaves (about 1 bunch)

1) TO COOK THE RICE: Put 3 cups of water and the rice in a medium pot over medium heat. Bring the water to a boil, then reduce the heat to low and cook until the rice is watery and soft, about 20 minutes.

2) Put 6 cups of water in a large stockpot over medium heat. Add the chicken broth, turkey bones, onion, ginger, and garlic, and bring to a boil, then simmer for 15 minutes, removing the impurities and froth that float to the top. Decrease the heat to low, cover the pot, and simmer for 30 minutes to release the flavors. Remove and discard the bones, garlic, and ginger from the broth. Optional: Add about 1½ cups of shredded leftover turkey meat and sticky rice.

3) Stir in some of the cooked rice until the porridge reaches your desired consistency. Cook for about another 10 minutes at a simmer to soften the rice, stirring constantly. Porridge is ready when the rice looks smooth. Porridge made with unstuffed roasted turkey will require almost all of the cooked rice, while porridge made from our Turkey Stuffed with Sticky Rice (page 137) recipe will require less (assuming that you have leftover sticky rice).

4) Garnish with the scallions and rau răm leaves and serve hot.

Pork Chops with Caramel Marinade

CALLED SƯỜN NƯỚNG IN VIETNAM, *this dish is traditionally served over rice with pickled vegetables, although my father often adds a sunny-side-up egg, too, breaking it into the rice as he eats. While it's tradition-ally grilled until golden and then brushed with the roasting sauce toward the end of cooking—we prefer a slightly different method. Our secret to cooking a pork chop without drying the meat lies in the roasting and then searing method outlined below.*

MAKES 4 SERVINGS

3 pounds ½-inch-thick pork chops, preferably still on the bone

4 tablespoons canola oil

2 tablespoons honey

2 tablespoons finely chopped garlic

2 tablespoons finely chopped shallots

2 tablespoons oyster sauce

1 tablespoon hoisin sauce

1 tablespoon fish sauce

1 teaspoon freshly ground black pepper

1 tablespoon unsalted butter, optional

2 tablespoons Scallions in Hot Oil (page 282)

1) To make the marinade: In a large bowl, mix together the oil, honey, garlic, shallots, oyster sauce, hoisin sauce, fish sauce, black pepper, and 4 table-spoons of water. Add the pork chops, cover the bowl, and let the pork chops marinate in the refrigerator overnight.

2) Preheat the oven to 400°F.

3) Remove the pork chops from the bowl and discard the marinade. Place the pork chops in a roasting pan and cover the pan with foil. Transfer the pan to the oven and roast the pork for 15 to 20 minutes. Remove the pork chops from the oven but reserve the sauce in the pan.

4) Heat a large skillet over high heat. Add the roasted pork chops and sear them for 2 minutes on each side until golden. Pour 2 tablespoons of the roasting pan sauce (or more if you like more sauce) over the pork chops and cook for another 30 seconds, allowing the sauce to reduce. Stir in the butter, if desired. Serve hot.

Helene's Wok Noodles with Stir-Fried Vegetables

ONE OF OUR AT-HOME FAVORITES FOR ITS VERSATILITY, *this dish has also been on our restaurant menus for a long time. This preparation will work with any vegetable; feel free to try it with your favorites. We frequently make triple the amount of noodle sauce and pour the remainder in a glass jar, as it will keep in the refrigerator for a week and is great to use in other stir-fry dishes.*

MAKES 4 TO 6 SERVINGS

FOR THE VEGETABLES
AND NOODLES:

2 cups fresh vegetables such as
snow peas, broccoli florets,
 asparagus

½ cup sliced fresh shiitake or enoki
mushrooms

1 pound fresh Chinese egg noodles

1 tablespoon canola oil

½ teaspoon salt

FOR THE NOODLE SAUCE:

1 teaspoon salt

1 teaspoon chili paste

1 teaspoon Maggi seasoning sauce

1 teaspoon fish sauce

1 teaspoon soy sauce

1 teaspoon oyster sauce

1 teaspoon minced garlic

½ teaspoon sugar

FOR THE STIR-FRY:

2 tablespoons canola oil

1 tablespoon Michiu rice cooking wine
or white wine (optional)

1) Bring a large pot of water to boil over high heat. Fill a large bowl with ice water and set it nearby. Add the vegetables and mushrooms to the boiling water in batches, blanching them for just 1 to 2 minutes and then immediately transferring them to the ice water bath. When all the vegetables and mushrooms have been blanched and shocked in the ice water, drain the water from the bowl, pat the vegetables and mushrooms dry, and set them aside.

2) Rinse out the same pot, fill it with water, and bring to a boil over high heat. Separate the noodles so they don't stick together, then add into the boiling water. Stir in the oil and salt and cook the noodles for 6 to 7 minutes until al dente. Drain the noodles, rinse them under cold water, and then shake them well to remove any excess water. Put the cooked noodles in a large bowl.

3) TO MAKE THE NOODLE SAUCE: In a medium bowl, mix together the chili paste, Maggi sauce, fish sauce, soy sauce, oyster sauce, minced garlic, and sugar. Pour 1 tablespoon of the sauce over the noodles and toss to mix well.

4) TO MAKE THE STIR-FRY: Heat the oil in a wok over high heat. Add the vegetables and mushrooms and sauté for 2 minutes to soften and cook vegetables. Add the wine to the wok, if using, being conscious of a possible flame-up. Add 1 tablespoon of the noodle sauce, cook for 3 minutes to meld the flavors, and then add the noodles. Toss and stir well for 2 minutes to coat noodles. Serve hot.

Bánh Mì with Tropical Marinated Flank Steak

INFINITELY CUSTOMIZABLE, THE BÁNH MÌ SANDWICH HAS JUST ONE RULE: *the bread shouldn't over-shadow the flavors of its fillings. Generally, in Vietnam bánh mì sandwiches are made with inexpensive cuts of pork, but here we've made it our own with thin slices of grilled steak marinated in tropical fruits, lemongrass, and our special satay sauce.*

My mother often uses pineapple and kiwi in her meat marinade. Not only are they natural tenderizers, but they also add some sweetness that is great for grilled meat. In fact, the flank steak here is so flavorful and tender that it can also be enjoyed on its own for a low-carb meal.

MAKES 6 SERVINGS

FOR THE STEAK:

½ cup Spicy Satay Sauce for Grilled Meat (page 277)

2 tablespoons pineapple juice

1 ounce chopped fresh pineapple, or 1 canned pineapple ring, chopped

⅛ fresh kiwi, peeled and chopped

1 tablespoon chopped fresh lemongrass, tender inner white bulb only

1 pound flank steak, cut into ¼-inch-thick slices

FOR THE AIOLI:

1 cup mayonnaise

2 tablespoons sriracha sauce

2 tablespoons ponzu (citrus seasoned soy sauce)

1 teaspoon chili oil

FOR THE SANDWICHES:

2 soft baguettes, split lengthwise and then cut into thirds

Butter lettuce

Pickled Carrots (page 278)

Pickled Daikon (see variation, page 278)

12 jalapeños, julienned into long, thin strips (optional)

12 sprigs fresh cilantro

Maggi seasoning sauce

Freshly ground black pepper

Sea salt

1] In a medium bowl, mix the satay sauce with the pineapple juice. Stir in the pineapple, kiwi, and lemongrass. Put the steak into a resealable plastic bag. Add the marinade and seal. Turn the steak to coat it in the marinade and refrigerate for 2 hours.

2] TO MAKE THE AIOLI: In a medium bowl, mix together the mayonnaise, sriracha, ponzu, and chili oil. Set aside.

3] Preheat an outdoor grill or grill pan and cook the marinated flank steak for 3 minutes per side for medium doneness.

4] Assemble each sandwich as follows: Spread aioli on the baguette, then layer with butter lettuce, 2 slices of flank steak, pickled carrots, pickled daikon, 3 jalapeño strips (if using), 2 sprigs of cilantro, and Maggi, salt, and pepper as desired. Serve.

Vietnamese Chicken-Stuffed Cabbage

MY GRANDMOTHER MADE THIS FOR US ALL THE TIME WHEN I WAS GROWING UP, *and it's one of my favorite dishes to make today because it tastes great fresh and stores well for leftovers. Though this dish is traditionally made with ground pork, we lightened it up with ground chicken instead. You could also use ground turkey, but choose one with a regular fat content rather than lean or extra-lean so it doesn't dry out during the cooking process.*

MAKES 20 ROLLS

FOR THE FILLING:

1 pound ground chicken or turkey

2 celery stalks, minced

1 medium white onion, minced

1 tablespoon fish sauce

1 tablespoon canola oil

½ teaspoon cornstarch

½ teaspoon sugar

½ teaspoon salt

½ teaspoon freshly ground black pepper

FOR THE CABBAGE:

1 large head of cabbage

10 scallions, optional [see note, opposite page]

1 tablespoon canola oil, plus more as needed

FOR THE TOMATO SAUCE:

1 tablespoon canola oil

2 medium tomatoes, sliced

1 medium white onion, sliced

1 teaspoon sugar

1 teaspoon Maggi seasoning sauce

1] TO MAKE THE STUFFING: In a large bowl, mix the meat with the minced celery and onion. Stir in the fish sauce, oil, cornstarch, sugar, salt, and pepper. Mix well and set aside.

2] TO PREPARE THE CABBAGE: Bring a large stockpot of water to a boil over high heat. Score the bottom of the cabbage head and place it in the boiling water. Cook for 2 minutes for the leaves to soften, then remove the cabbage from the pot and set it aside to cool. Once it is cool enough to handle, separate the head of cabbage leaf by leaf. Choose the twenty best leaves for wrapping; reserve the rest of the cabbage for another use. Pat each of the twenty leaves dry with a paper towel, and then cut a small upside-down V into the base of each cabbage leaf to cut off the tough end.

3] TO MAKE THE CABBAGE ROLLS: Place one of the cabbage leaves on a cutting board so the edges of the leaf curl upward like a small bowl. Spoon 1 tablespoon of the seasoned meat mixture in a horizontal line on the leaf about ½ inch up from the bottom. Roll the bottom of the cabbage leaf up over the meat and continue rolling until only half of the leaf is left. Tuck in the sides and continue rolling until you reach the end of the leaf. Secure the cabbage roll with a toothpick or tie a softened scallion stem around it (see note, below). Repeat the process with the remaining leaves and filling.

4] Heat the oil in a large saucepan over medium-high heat. Add the cabbage rolls to the pan in batches, turning occasionally and adding more oil as needed until the rolls are lightly browned on all sides, about 5 minutes. Set the rolls aside on a plate.

5] TO MAKE THE TOMATO SAUCE: Heat the oil in a medium skillet over medium heat. Add the tomato and onion slices, sugar, and Maggi seasoning sauce, and cook until the vegetables have softened, about 10 minutes.

6] Place all the cabbage rolls back in their original pan over medium-low heat. Pour the tomato sauce over the rolls, cover, and cook for 20 to 25 minutes until the cabbage is soft and the meat is cooked through.

NOTE: *To use the scallion stems as ties, use the green parts only and cut each stem in half crosswise to make 20 pieces. Soak the stems in a bowl of hot water for 1 minute to soften them. Drain and pat the stems dry with paper towels.*

Cashew Chicken

THIS FLAVORFUL STIR-FRY IS AN EASY, HOME-STYLE DISH. *My mother supplements the sweet, buttery flavor of the cashews with ginkgo nuts and goji berries not only for their delicious taste, but also for their health benefits. Ginkgo nuts are believed to help sharpen the brain and ward off dementia, while the high number of antioxidants in goji berries are believed to benefit vision and many other age-related ailments. For these reasons, many people think of ginkgo nuts and goji berries as modern-day fountains of youth.*

MAKES 4 SERVINGS

1 pound boneless, skinless chicken breast or thighs, white or dark meat, cut into about ¼-inch-thick slices

3 tablespoons canola oil, divided

1 teaspoon minced garlic

1 teaspoon fish sauce

1 teaspoon cornstarch

½ teaspoon minced ginger

3 tablespoons House Sauce (page 276)

1½ teaspoons oyster sauce

1 teaspoon unsalted butter + more to taste

1 medium red onion, quartered

¼ cup red bell pepper, cut in diagonals

¼ cup diced jicama

2 whole dried bird's eye chiles

¼ cup cashews

1 teaspoon goji berries (see note, below)

8 shelled ginkgo nuts, precooked (see note, below)

1 tablespoon Michiu rice cooking wine or white wine

1) In a large bowl, combine the chicken, 1 tablespoon of the oil, the garlic, and the fish sauce. Mix well. Add the cornstarch and 1 teaspoon of water and mix again. Cover the bowl and set it aside to marinate for 15 minutes.

2) Heat the remaining 2 tablespoons of oil in a large saucepan or wok over medium heat. Add the ginger and stir quickly. Add the House Sauce, oyster sauce, and butter and stir well, then add the marinated chicken and cook for 2 to 3 minutes to brown the chicken. Add the onion, bell peppers, jicama, ginkgo, and chiles and cook for 2 more minutes, tossing well.

3) Add the cashews and goji berries to the pan and pour in the wine, being conscious of a possible flame-up. Stir in about ½ teaspoon butter before serving. Serve hot with a side of rice.

VARIATION: *For a slightly sweeter version, substitute the ginkgo nuts with 8 dried Chinese red dates. My sister Cathy actually prefers this version.*

NOTE: *Goji berries can interact with certain medications for blood thinning, blood pressure, and diabetes, so check with your doctor if you are on any of these medications.*

NOTE: *To pre-cook shelled ginkgo nuts, bring a small pot of water to a boil. Add the ginkgo nuts and cook for 5 minutes. Let them cool before handling.*

Chicken and Potatoes in Curry Lemongrass Sauce

VIETNAMESE CURRY IS LIGHTER AND MILDER THAN INDIAN OR THAI CURRY, *but just as flavorful. Almost stew- or soup-like in texture, it is one of those dishes that tastes even better the next day. We usually serve it with a French baguette or with steamed rice.*

MAKES 4 SERVINGS

1 tablespoon fish sauce

1 teaspoon chili paste

1 teaspoon sugar

2½ teaspoons salt, divided

2 pounds boneless, skinless chicken thighs or breasts, cut into 2-inch pieces

3 tablespoons canola oil, divided

1 medium white onion, sliced

1 tomato, cut into 8 pieces

3 (3-inch) pieces fresh ginger, peeled

1 teaspoon chopped garlic

1 teaspoon ground turmeric or 2 tablespoon fresh turmeric juice

1 tablespoon curry powder

1 teaspoon cornstarch

3 cups Homemade Chicken Broth (page 273) or store-bought low-sodium chicken broth

3 fresh lemongrass stalks, white bulbs only, cut into 2-inch pieces and smashed to release flavor

½ cup coconut milk

½ cup coconut water

1 tablespoon freshly squeezed lime juice

2 fresh kaffir lime leaves

6 red potatoes, cut in quarters

1] In a medium bowl, mix together the fish sauce, chili paste, sugar, and ½ teaspoon of the salt. Add the chicken pieces and coat well. Cover the bowl and set it aside to marinate for 15 minutes.

2] TO MAKE THE SAUCE: Heat 1 tablespoon of the oil in a large skillet or wok over medium heat. Add the onion, tomato, ginger, and garlic and sauté until the onions and tomatoes are soft, about 10 minutes. Stir in the turmeric, curry, and cornstarch and continue to cook for 5 minutes. Add the chicken broth and lemongrass and cook for 20 minutes. Strain the sauce through a fine-mesh strainer into a new, large saucepan, discarding the vegetables and herbs.

3] Place the saucepan over medium heat. Add the coconut milk, coconut water, lime juice, and kaffir lime leaves to the sauce, and cook for 10 minutes or until the sauce begins to thicken and the lime leaves release their flavor.

4] Heat the remaining 2 tablespoons of oil in a new large skillet over medium heat. Line a plate with paper towels. Add the marinated chicken and cook, stirring constantly, it until it is golden brown, about 5 minutes. Transfer the chicken to the prepared plate to drain; do not wipe out the skillet.

5] Fill a large bowl with cold water and stir in the remaining 2 teaspoons of salt. Soak the potatoes in in the salt water for 5 minutes, then drain the water and pat the potatoes dry with paper towels. Add the potatoes to the same skillet you used to cook the chicken and fry them over medium heat for about 10 minutes until golden.

6] Add the chicken and potatoes to the sauce and cook over medium-high heat for 10 minutes to meld the flavors. Serve hot.

MY DAD'S SALT-AND-PEPPER SEASONING

Like many Vietnamese, my father makes his own salt-and-pepper seasoning sauce and has it on a little plate next to his meals. He'll then dip meat in it, especially chicken. Called *muối tiêu chanh*, this seasoning is easy to make and customize to your liking. Just mix salt (kosher salt works especially well), freshly ground pepper, and a little lime juice, adjusting the quantity of each to suit your personal preference.

Caramelized Lemongrass Shrimp

WHEN I WAS IN SPAIN, I FELL IN LOVE WITH SPANISH GARLIC SHRIMP *that reminded me of my mother's traditional Vietnamese caramelized shrimp, tôm rang xả. My mother's secret to this dish is two-fold: first, buy the freshest shrimp you can find at your local seafood counter, and second, add paprika for color and flavor, giving this dish a Spanish flair that makes it all the more delicious. No wonder I felt at home in Spain!*

The salty sweetness of the caramelized shrimp is delicious with rice.

MAKES 4 SERVINGS

4 tablespoons canola oil

1 pound jumbo shrimp (size $^{21}/_{25}$; about 21 pieces), peeled and deveined

1 tablespoon chopped garlic

1 tablespoon chopped shallots

2 tablespoon chopped fresh lemongrass, tender inner white bulb only

1 tablespoon sugar

½ teaspoon salt

½ teaspoon freshly ground black pepper

1 teaspoon paprika

1 tablespoon chopped scallions

1 teaspoon fish sauce

1) Heat the oil in a wok or large skillet over high heat. Add the shrimp and stir quickly, cooking for just 3 to 5 seconds until pink. Transfer the shrimp to a plate and set aside.

2) Reduce the heat to medium, add the garlic, shallots, lemongrass, sugar, salt, pepper, and paprika to the wok, and sauté until the garlic and shallots are fragrant, about 5 minutes. Add the shrimp back to the wok and sauté for a few minutes, then add the fish sauce and cook, stirring constantly, for 1 to 2 minutes. Carefully add 1 tablespoon of water to the wok and give the mixture a good stir.

3) Serve the shrimp hot with the scallions sprinkled on top.

Coconut Spareribs

THE SECRET TO THIS DELICIOUS DISH—*hot and yet cool at the same time—is to braise the spareribs in coconut water and coconut soda. The use of coconut soda in cooking arose after many wars in Vietnam left locals without the resources, both fresh food and money, that they were used to using in the kitchen. Instead of fresh coconut milk and coconut water, they improvised with inexpensive and easy-to-find coconut-flavored soda, such as Coco-Rico (sold in a bright green aluminum can). The acid and carbonation in the soda helped tenderize meat during cooking while leaving behind a thick, caramelized sugar—perfect for braising pork. You can find coconut flavored soda at specialty or gourmet grocers. Like most things caramelized, we usually enjoy the ribs with rice and boiled or pickled vegetables.*

MAKES 4 SERVINGS

2 pounds pork spareribs, blanched (see note, page 127)

1 teaspoon freshly ground black pepper

1 teaspoon salt

3 tablespoons chopped shallots

1 (12-ounce) can coconut-flavored soda

1 tablespoon canola oil

3 teaspoons sugar

1 tablespoon minced ginger

2 tablespoons fish sauce

1 teaspoon chili sauce

1 teaspoon sesame oil

2 teaspoon soy sauce

½ cup coconut water

1] In a large glass bowl, add the spareribs, pepper, salt, and 1 tablespoon shallots, and set aside to marinate for 30 minutes.

2] Pour the coconut soda into a large pot. Add the spareribs and bring the soda to a boil over high heat, then reduce the heat to medium and cook for 20 minutes until the ribs are light brown.

3] Meanwhile, heat 1 tablespoon of the oil in a large skillet over medium heat. Add the sugar and cook, stirring frequently, until the sugar becomes light brown, about 5 to 10 minutes. Stir in the remaining shallots, ginger, fish sauce, chili sauce, sesame oil, and soy sauce. Pour this sugar mixture into the pot with the spareribs.

4] Continue to cook the spareribs for 5 minutes over medium heat, then stir in the coconut water, reduce the heat to low, and cook until the meat is tender and the sauce thickens, 15 to 20 minutes. Serve hot.

4

everyday
gourmet

upscale expansion: crustacean

By the time Thanh Long expanded to its current 240-seat capacity in the 1990s, much had changed for the An family. My mother had two more daughters, myself and my younger sister Catherine, the first Ans born in America. We moved from a one-bedroom apartment to a house we shared with my grandparents just down the street from the restaurant, and then finally we moved into our own house.

FIVE PRINCESSES

When my mother had her fifth girl, Catherine, the family officially had *ngũ long công chúa* which is a very lucky thing in Vietnamese culture. It means "five good luck daughters" or, literally, "five princesses of dragons." According to an old proverb, it is extremely lucky to have five daughters, especially if they are born in a row.

Much like our older sisters had years before, Catherine and I grew up in our family's restaurant kitchens. Even though we were regularly peeling carrots or cleaning crab after school, it never felt like work because we loved it. Miniature versions of our mother, we would pepper the chefs with questions about how and why they did things. We were encouraged to experiment with food: frying bananas, making different ice cream flavors. The atmosphere in the kitchen was always so happy.

The restaurants were our second home. If we were taking dance classes, we would perform for the guests. We would help the servers sing happy birthday. It was a wonderfully creative environment to grow up in.

My older sisters went to college, majored in computer engineering, and pursued careers in fashion, but the hospitality industry was in their blood. They came back home and convinced my mother to let them handle Thanh Long so my mother could open a second restaurant. It was a big risk because it required taking out a sizable loan. Thanh Long regularly had long lines outside the door, the customers happy to wait in the wind for a chance to eat my mother's cooking. My sisters believed that these lines were a "gold mine." The family just needed to invest and dig in.

They found the perfect location across town in upscale Nob Hill, left behind by a bankrupt restaurant. Since crab was one of my mother's most popular dishes, Elizabeth thought Crustacean was a suitable name for the new venture. Having worked for a high-fashion designer and having a wonderful eye herself, Elizabeth helped design the new space. When they opened, they were busy . . . but not busy enough. Six months in, Crustacean was losing $10,000 a month and my mother feared that she would have to close it.

Then *San Francisco Chronicle* food critic Michael Bauer made an unannounced visit—and hated everything. Bauer didn't understand why Mama "fused" different culinary cultures together. The sauce for her ravioli wasn't straight-up Italian; it had Asian elements in it. Why? Back then, Vietnamese restaurants were supposed to serve only Vietnamese food; European restaurants should be strictly European. But Helene broke all the rules. She worked with Americans every day and knew hat traditional Vietnamese flavors were too strong or too fishy for the typical American palate. She created her own style of cooking based on her unique background and feedback from her customers. Bauer didn't get it. He gave the restaurant just two stars.

Loyal fans came to my mother's defense, furious that Bauer was so "unfair" to her. A competing food critic from the *San Jose Mercury News* heard about the hubbub and came by to do his own review. He fell in love with my mother and her food. He proposed marriage on the spot, joking that he would divorce her as soon as the secret recipes were his. He gave Crustacean a glowing five-star review.

My mother saw the conflicting opinions as an opportunity. She took a risk and spent $15,000 to publish both critiques in a full-page ad along with the challenge: "Judge for yourself." The public did, and Crustacean became a bona fide success.

THE SECRET KITCHEN®

The new attention brought with it new risks. The restaurant world is a competitive business, and after seeing two family fortunes lost, Mama didn't want to take any chances. Her success was built on her special recipes, and she couldn't risk losing them. When local restaurants debuted dishes suspiciously similar to her famous roasted Dungeness crab, she knew she had to act.

Much in the same way other successful companies stored their proprietary formulas in a vault, Helene set about securing the integrity of her creations. To protect her culinary legacy, she had a completely enclosed second kitchen, dubbed "The Secret Kitchen," built within Thanh Long's main kitchen (we now have a secret kitchen in each of our restaurants). No one is allowed inside except members of the An family and trusted chefs who've been employed with us for almost a decade; even *Oprah*'s cameras were denied admittance when the show came to visit our restaurant. Inside, a handful of our signature dishes are prepared to this day and served through a sliding window.

Serving the Stars

Elizabeth married, moved to Los Angeles, and begged our mother to follow her. *"I meet so many people who fly up to San Francisco for your food. Why not give them what they want down here?"* she said.

Elizabeth had befriended a socialite named Jacqueline Furer who became instrumental in the opening of our third restaurant. She recommended a location in Beverly Hills that was surprisingly affordable: just $2 per square foot for rent. It was very quiet at the time, a "dead corner," possibly because getting permits in that city was next to impossible. Furer, however, had countless connections, including the owner of the *Beverly Courier* newspaper. In a record two months, Crustacean Beverly Hills was ready for business.

It was the biggest restaurant in Beverly Hills at the time, an anomaly since most restaurants were small and intimate. People said we were crazy, that it would be closed in a year, but Elizabeth had a vision about how to incorporate a feeling of warmth and familiarity into such a large space. She was inspired by our great-grandparents' country estate in northern Vietnam. To ensure that the restaurant didn't suffer the same fate as the two that had previously occupied the building, everything was fashioned to adhere to the ancient art of feng shui.

WELCOME TO CRUSTACEAN BEVERLY HILLS

What has become our flagship restaurant is also the most personal to our family, as it is a loving rec-reation of our great-great-grandparents' country estate in Ha Dong. When you enter Crustacean you literally walk on water over an 80-foot-long, 3-foot deep serpentine stream that flows through the middle of the restaurant, safely covered by glass. The 6,000-gallon in-floor aquarium is filled with rare koi and leads into an indoor courtyard decorated with silk-covered banquettes, swirling palm-leaf fans, and painted tropical backdrops. Across a dark, lacquered wooden bridge is the two-story dining room—a 45-foot sky-lit atrium with balconies, a bamboo garden, and giant, antique birdcages filled with flowers and candles. Vietnamese coins are encased in the marble floor, and the walls are draped with precious family photographs. Our goal is to immerse visitors in the grace, beauty, and peace of a bygone era, the Vietnam of our mother's memories, thereby preserving it forever.

When it opened in January, 1997, Crustacean Beverly Hills was an instant success. Five hundred people waited in line to attend the opening night festivities. "I'm very lucky they all came to eat my food," my mother recalls. "And once they came, they kept coming!"

Esquire magazine named Crustacean one of the country's Top Ten Restaurants, food critic John Mariani noted that the food was so good it "could make you cry," and it was featured on the Food Network show *The Best Thing I Ever Ate*. The restaurant became a favorite for Hollywood stars and became famous for hosting Academy Awards before and after parties.

The following recipes are derived from the core of our restaurant menus modified for the home kitchen, as well as fancier dishes we prepare personally on holidays and special occasions. If you have someone to impress or something to celebrate, these recipes will transport you and your guests from your kitchen to our restaurants.

French Onion Phở with Beef Ravioli

THIS IS ONE OF MY MOTHER'S NEWEST RECIPES *that she created for the James Beard House in New York City, and it was chosen as one of the "Favorite Dishes of 2015" by the James Beard editors. Her inspiration came from my father's childhood memories.*

When my father was a young boy, he found that French soldiers who came to Vietnam enjoyed their phở in a very strange way. Instead of eating the broth with rice noodles as everyone he knew did, the soldiers dipped French bread into the fragrant broth. My mother honors this memory by combining her beef phở with a Gruyère French bread crisp and caramelized onions to make a French onion phở. The recipe that follows is the one she made at the James Beard House, but we've also included an option to make it without the beef ravioli.

MAKES 8 SERVINGS

4 large white onions

1 pound (2-inch thick) beef brisket or sirloin steak

2 teaspoons kosher salt, divided

3 quarts Beef Phở Broth (page 272)

3 whole star anise

1 (3-inch) piece fresh ginger, charred and then peeled (see note, page 55)

1 teaspoon sugar

1 tablespoon canola oil

12 garlic cloves, smashed

4 (6-inch) marrow bones, cut in half lengthwise (see note, page 167)

¼ teaspoon sea salt, plus more for seasoning the marrow

Freshly ground black pepper

½ French baguette

Nonstick cooking spray

3 ounces finely grated Gruyère cheese

16 to 20 large fresh Thai basil leaves, plus more for garnish

Fresh rice noodle sheets, cut into sixteen 4 x 6-inch pieces

Fish sauce, to taste

4 ounces flat rice stick (bánh phở) noodles, cooked

3 sprigs fresh cilantro, julienned into thin strips, for garnish

2 limes, halved, for garnish

1] Char two of the onions (see note, page 55). Let the onions cool, then peel off and discard the charred skins. Set one charred onion aside for the broth.

2] TO MAKE THE ONION BRÛLÉE PETALS: Take the remaining charred onion and if you haven't already, slice the onion in half. Remove each petal one at a time, saving only the nice, large ones since they will serve as little bowls for the noodles. Set the onion petals aside.

3] TO MAKE THE BROTH: Put the brisket in a large stockpot and add water until the meat is covered. Add 1 teaspoon of the salt and bring the water to a boil over high heat. Boil for 3 minutes, then strain the meat and rinse it well under cold water. Transfer the meat to a plate, discard the liquid, and rinse out the pot.

(Continued)

4] Return the brisket to the clean pot and add the beef broth and 1 quart of water. Bring the liquid to a boil over medium heat, skimming the surface often to remove any fat, froth, and impurities. Continue to cook until most of the impurities are gone and the water is almost clear, 15 to 20 minutes.

5] Add the star anise, ginger, and reserved whole charred onion to the pot of beef broth. Bring the liquid back to a boil, cook for 15 minutes, and then reduce the heat to low and simmer for another 60 minutes to imbue the beef with the aromatics. Add the remaining teaspoon of salt and the sugar and cook for another 30 minutes until the beef is tender.

6] Transfer the brisket to a plate and set it aside to cool. Once the brisket is cool to the touch, cover the plate and place the brisket in the refrigerator. Note: To store the brisket for use later in the day or the next day, let the broth cool to room temperature, place the brisket in a large airtight container, and pour the cooled broth over top. This will infuse the brisket with flavor and keep it from drying out.

7] Remove and discard the star anise, charred onion, and ginger from the broth. Strain the broth through a fine-mesh strainer to remove any impurities. The pho broth should be clear. (If it is not, strain it again.) Slice the brisket paper thin against the grain (into ⅛-inch slices), and set aside.

8] Meanwhile, caramelize the onions: Cut the 2 remaining uncharred onions into long, thin strips (a julienne cut). Heat the oil in a medium skillet over low heat. Add the julienned onions and cook them, stirring occasionally, for about 1 hour or until the onions are soft, translucent, and buttery.

9] TO PREPARE THE MARROW: Preheat the oven to 400°F. Rub 3 smashed garlic cloves onto each marrow bone piece and sprinkle with salt and pepper. Roast the bones cut-side up topped with the garlic cloves until the marrow is golden and bubbly, about 10 to 15 minutes. Remove the marrow bones from the oven and discard any garlic pieces.

10] TO MAKE THE GRUYÈRE CRISPS: Preheat the oven to 350°F. Cut the baguette into 6-inch-long, ¼-inch-thick slices. Place the slices cut-sides up on a baking sheet, spray them with cooking spray, and sprinkle each one with ¼ teaspoon salt. Bake until crispy, about 4 to 5 minutes. Remove the baking sheet from the oven and allow the crisps to cool. Preheat the broiler. Sprinkle the crisps evenly with cheese and place them under the broiler for 30 seconds or just until the cheese has melted.

11] TO ASSEMBLE THE RAVIOLI: Put one piece of brisket and one piece of basil on a rice noodle square, fold the top and bottom over the filling, then fold the sides in to make a smaller square package. Repeat until you have 16 to 20 ravioli. Set aside.

12] When you're ready to serve, pour the beef broth into a large pot and bring it to a boil over medium heat, adding some fish sauce to taste if it needs more seasoning.

13] TO SERVE: Place one large onion petal in the bottom of each serving bowl. Place a spoonful of cooked noodles (no more than ½ ounce) on the onion petal and top with some caramelized onions. Place 2 to 3 raviolis in the bowl next to the onion cup. Ladle the boiling broth over the onions and top with basil and cilantro. Serve with one length of marrow bone across each bowl. Garnish with a Gruyère crisp and lime wedges. Serve hot.

VARIATION: FRENCH ONION PHỞ (without beef ravioli)

If you can't find fresh rice noodle sheets or wish to omit the beef ravioli, the Gruyère French bread crisp and fragrant broth will still retain the spirit of the dish.

3 large white onions

1 tablespoon canola oil

12 garlic cloves, smashed

Four 6-inch marrow bones, cut in half lengthwise (see note, below)

¼ teaspoon sea salt, plus more for seasoning the marrow

Freshly ground black pepper

½ French baguette

Nonstick cooking spray

3 ounces finely grated Gruyère cheese

3 quarts Homemade Beef Broth (page 272)

Fish sauce, to taste

4 ounces flat rice stick (*bánh phở*) noodles, cooked

3 sprigs fresh cilantro, julienned into thin strips, for garnish

Fresh Thai basil leaves, for garnish

4 limes, halved, for garnish

1] Follow steps 1 and 2 above but only char 1 onion.

2] Skip to step 8. Proceed with steps 8, 9, and 10.

3] Skip to step 12, omitting the ravioli.

NOTE: *Beef marrow bones can be purchased from your local butcher. If you can, ask them to cut the bones for you to save yourself the trouble at home.*

Baked Tofu with Julienned Snow Peas

MY MOTHER SAYS THAT THE MOST ADDICTIVE KIND OF FOOD *is one that not only tastes good but also makes your body feel good. This is one of those dishes. When we did the photoshoot for this cookbook, it was quickly gobbled up as soon as the photographs were taken.*

In Vietnam, tofu isn't viewed as simply a meat replacement for vegetarians. Instead, it's prized as a highly versatile, healthy, and inexpensive protein that absorbs and then shines with the flavors of other ingredients. Tofu is frequently included in dishes with meat because it adds another layer of texture—incredibly important to the Vietnamese palate. Trumpet mushrooms are known for their "unami" flavor, and, combined with the onion roux, they give the sauce a buttery texture and add a healthy, earthy richness to the normally plain tofu.

MAKES 2 TO 3 SERVINGS

8 ounces firm tofu

1 teaspoon sea salt

1 tablespoon canola oil

1 tablespoon chopped shallots

4 trumpet mushrooms, julienned and blanched

1 cup snow peas, julienned and blanched

1 tablespoon Michiu rice cooking wine or white wine

2 tablespoons White Sauce (page 278)

2 tablespoons soy sauce

1 teaspoon sesame oil

1 teaspoon sugar

1 teaspoon sambal chili sauce

1) Preheat the oven to 350°F. Grease a baking pan with oil or butter.

2) Cut the tofu in half horizontally. Place the tofu in the prepared baking pan, sprinkle all sides with salt, and bake until the surface is light gold, about 10 to 15 minutes. Remove from oven and set aside to cool.

3) Cut the tofu lengthwise into ½-inch-wide strips (the size of your index finger).

4) Heat the canola oil in a large saucepan or wok over medium heat. Add the shallots and sauté until they are soft and fragrant, about 1 minute. Add the tofu and cook for 3 minutes, stirring regularly. Add the mushrooms and snow peas and sauté, tossing well. Add the wine, being conscious of a possible flame-up. Stir in the white sauce, soy sauce, sesame oil, sugar, and sambal chili sauce. Serve hot.

THE ART OF TOFU

Unlike the tasteless, white blocks sold at many American supermarkets, the tofu made in Vietnam, handcrafted by families who've been doing it for generations, is fragrant with a decadent, nutty flavor. It might be due to the care they take in crafting their sole product, or perhaps it's because they make tofu with only three ingredients: soybeans, water, and salt. Instead of using lemon juice, vinegar, or a chemical coagulant, they simply use the soy whey from the previous batch of tofu, which means that nothing gets in the way of the earthy taste.

Drunken Crab

MY MOTHER'S FATHER IS THE INSPIRATION BEHIND THIS DISH. *She always regretted not being able to say goodbye to him and that my younger sister and I could not meet him, so she passed his spirit to us through cooking his favorite meals. My grandfather loved fresh crabs cooked in beer and wine; the wine gives the dish a nice fragrance, while the beer imparts a sweet taste. In Vietnam, the crabs used are smaller freshwater varieties, but my mother chose Dungeness for this recipe because it's native to our first American hometown, San Francisco.*

MAKES 2 TO 4 SERVINGS

1 (2½-pound) whole fresh Dungeness crab

1 cup Homemade Chicken Broth or Homemade Fish Broth (page 273) or store-bought low-sodium chicken or fish broth, divided

½ ounce fresh ginger, peeled and sliced

1 teaspoon chopped garlic

½ teaspoon fish sauce

1 teaspoon oyster sauce

¼ teaspoon sugar

¼ teaspoon salt

½ cup white wine, Gray Riesling or Trousseau Gris preferred

½ cup pale lager beer

1 teaspoon freshly ground black pepper

½ cup scallions, cut into 1½-inch pieces

1] CLEAN THE CRAB: Scrub the crab with a brush under cold running water. Remove and dry the top shell and set it aside. Remove and discard the gills and clean any dirt and hair from this area. Cut the crab in half and then in quarters.

2] In a large pot over medium heat, combine the broth, ginger, garlic, fish sauce, oyster sauce, sugar, and salt and bring the mixture to a boil. Add the crab pieces, cover the pot, and cook for 3 minutes until the shells turn red. Stir in the wine, beer, and black pepper. Cover the pot again and reduce the heat to medium-low. Simmer for 2 minutes, then remove and discard the ginger and add the scallions to the pot.

3] Remove the crab pieces from the pot and reassemble them on a deep serving dish. Place the top shell back on top and pour the wine sauce over the crab. Serve hot.

Grilled Turmeric Calamari

TURMERIC GIVES CALAMARI NOT JUST A GREAT GOLDEN COLOR BUT ALSO A DELICIOUS TARTNESS. *The secret to soft calamari that doesn't have the texture of a rubber band is to marinate it first. It can be less expensive to buy calamari that hasn't already been cleaned, but if you buy uncleaned calamari, just be sure to remove the cartilage inside and rinse calamari well with cold water—the more rinsing the better. Clean calamari can make all the difference between a good and a great dish!*

MAKES 4 APPETIZER-SIZED SERVINGS

FOR THE CALAMARI:

2 tablespoons sugar

2 tablespoons canola oil

1 tablespoon oyster sauce

2 teaspoons chili paste

1 teaspoon ground turmeric

1 teaspoon freshly ground black pepper

½ pound cleaned calamari, bodies only (tentacles reserved for another use)

FOR THE DIPPING SAUCE:

2 cups Garlic Lemon Sauce (nước chấm) (page 274)

1 cup Homemade Chicken Broth (page 273) or store-bought low-sodium chicken broth, divided

4 tablespoons smooth natural peanut butter

1 tablespoon honey

1 teaspoon chili paste

Orange segments, for garnish

1) **TO COOK THE CALAMARI:** In a large bowl, mix together the sugar, canola oil, oyster sauce, chili paste, turmeric, and pepper. Add the calamari and turn well to coat. Cover the bowl and refrigerate for 1 hour.

2) **TO MAKE THE DIPPING SAUCE:** In a large bowl, mix together the nước chấm and chicken broth. Add the peanut butter, honey, and chili paste and mix well.

3) Preheat an outdoor grill or grill pan on medium heat.

4) Remove the squid from the marinade and grill it until it turns golden brown, about 2 minutes on each side. Remove the squid from the grill and cut it into 1½-inch rings.

5) Arrange the calamari rings on a serving platter and drizzle them with a little of the dipping sauce. Serve hot with the dipping sauce and orange segments.

Five-Spice Duck Salad

DUCK HAS DARKER AND JUICIER MEAT THAN CHICKEN *because it has more fat and a higher concentration of oil in the skin. Don't worry about that fat and oil being unhealthy, however, because we're going to cook most of it away. Cooking duck meat on low heat gives the fat a chance to melt out, or render, making for a healthier cut—up to 70 percent of the fat is lost—and leaving behind delicious crispy skin. If you wish, you can strain and save the leftover liquid fat. Duck fat is wonderful for searing meat and sautéing vegetables; just use it the same way you would use cooking oil or butter.*

MAKES 4 SERVINGS

FOR THE DUCK:

Four (8 to 10-ounce) skin-on duck breasts

1 tablespoon five-spice powder (see note, opposite page)

⅛ teaspoon kosher salt

⅛ teaspoon freshly ground pepper

FOR THE DRESSING:

3 tablespoons rice wine vinegar

2 tablespoons freshly squeezed orange juice

2 tablespoons pure maple syrup

2½ teaspoons Dijon mustard

1 teaspoon freshly grated orange zest

⅛ teaspoon kosher salt

½ teaspoon freshly ground black pepper

⅔ cup extra-virgin olive oil

FOR THE SALAD:

4 cups (½ pound, about 1 head) French curly endive (frisée) leaves

3 cups mixed greens

1 cup fresh mung bean sprouts

2 large navel oranges, supremed

½ cup cashews, toasted

1] TO COOK THE DUCK: With a sharp knife, score the duck skin by cutting lines ¼ inch apart in a criss-cross pattern, being careful not to cut into the meat. Sprinkle the five spice powder, salt, and pepper over the duck breasts.

2] Place the duck breasts skin-side down in a large skillet over low heat. Cook for 20 minutes or until the fat has rendered and the skin is crispy. Turn the breasts over, increase the heat to medium, and cook for 2 minutes or until an instant-read thermometer inserted into the thickest parts of the duck breasts registers at least 155°F (it will rise another 10°F to the recommended 165°F while it sets). Remove the skillet from the heat, transfer the duck to a platter, and let it rest for 5 minutes.

3] **TO MAKE THE DRESSING:** In a medium bowl, whisk together the vinegar, orange juice, maple syrup, mustard, orange zest, salt, and pepper. Slowly stream in the olive oil, whisking constantly, until it is fully incorporated in the dressing.

4] **TO MAKE THE SALAD:** In a large bowl, toss together the French curly endive, mixed greens, and bean sprouts.

5] Cut the duck into thin slices and place them on top of the salad. Garnish with the orange supremes and cashews, and serve with the dressing alongside.

FIVE-SPICE POWDER

Five-spice powder, also called Chinese five-spice, can be purchased at most gourmet grocery stores and online. If you can, get one without added salt. If salt is listed in the ingredients, omit the extra salt from this recipe.

You can also easily make five-spice powder yourself by mixing the five spices: anise, cinnamon, black pepper, fennel seed, and cloves. The following amounts will make about 1 tablespoon of seasoning, perfect for this recipe.

- 1 teaspoon crushed anise seed or 1 whole star anise, ground

- 1 teaspoon ground cinnamon

- ¼ teaspoon freshly ground black pepper

- ¼ teaspoon crushed fennel seed

- ⅛ teaspoon ground cloves

Mongolian Fried Chicken

FOR THIS DISH, A FAVORITE AT ANQI, *we married the spicy flavors of Mongolian Beef with deliciously juicy fried chicken. The secret is to brine the chicken in buttermilk and hot sauce overnight to allow the flavors to meld and work their way deep into the meat. The accompanying BBQ sauce can be used as both a glaze and a dip. Store any extra sauce in the refrigerator for up to 2 weeks. It's great for almost any meat and makes a wonderful sauce for a quick stir-fry.*

MAKES 6 SERVINGS

FOR THE CHICKEN:

2 whole, organic, free-range chickens, giblets removed

1 gallon buttermilk

1 (5-ounce) bottle Tabasco hot pepper sauce

4 cups self-rising flour

¼ cup garlic powder

¼ cup salt

¼ cup freshly ground black pepper

Peanut oil, for frying

Fresh chopped chives, for garnish

FOR THE BBQ SAUCE:

1 cup low-sodium soy sauce

1 cup hoisin sauce

¾ cup sugar

¼ cup minced garlic

¼ cup minced fresh ginger

3 tablespoons sambal oelek chili sauce

3 scallions, thinly sliced

1] Cut the chickens apart into wing, thigh, breast, and leg pieces.

2] TO MAKE THE BRINE: Combine the buttermilk and Tabasco in a large bowl. Divide the brine between two large resealable plastic bags. Add one chicken to each bag, seal, and turn well to coat. Refrigerate for at least 24 hours.

3] TO MAKE THE BBQ SAUCE: In a medium saucepan, combine the soy sauce, hoisin sauce, sugar, garlic, ginger, sambal oelek, and scallions. Simmer over low heat for 45 minutes until it thickens. Remove the pan from the heat and pour the sauce into a glass bowl or container. Cover the bowl and place it in the refrigerator to chill.

4] In a large bowl, whisk together the flour, garlic powder, salt, and pepper. Remove the chicken from the brine, discard the brine, and arrange the chicken on a baking rack set over a baking pan to catch the drips. Dredge the chicken in the flour mixture, shake off the excess, and return the pieces to the baking rack.

5] Preheat the oven to 350°F.

6] Line a baking sheet with paper towels and set it nearby. In a deep skillet or wok, heat enough oil for deep-frying over medium-high heat until it reaches 350°F on a candy or deep-frying thermometer. Working in batches, add as many chicken pieces as you can without overcrowding the pan. Fry the chicken until the outside turns golden brown, about 6 to 8 minutes. Remove the chicken pieces as they are finished cooking and place them on the paper towel–lined baking sheet to drain. Repeat the process with all of the chicken.

[Continued]

7] Remove the paper towels from the baking sheet, return the chicken to the baking sheet, and transfer it to the oven. Bake until an instant-read thermometer inserted in the thickest part of a chicken breast registers 165°F, about 8 to 10 minutes depending on the size of the chickens.

8] Remove the chicken from the oven and serve hot, drizzled with the BBQ sauce and garnished with chives.

THE SECRET TO QUICKER MEAT: PRE-BAKING

One of the ways we manage to serve meat dishes so quickly in our restaurants and still have them come out perfectly is by pre-cooking them first in the oven. Before putting meat on the grill, we'll throw it in the oven for a few minutes to start the cooking process. It cuts down on grilling time, allows the meat to be cooked faster and come out juicier, and even keeps the meat from sticking to the grill. We then finish the meat on the grill for the flavor and score marks.

SUGAR CANE SKEWERS

Sugar cane skewers are a wonderful carrier for food as they are environmentally friendly, they impart a slight sweetness to the food they hold, especially when heated, and they are completely edible (especially delicious with butter). They are great for the grill (and don't need to be soaked like bamboo skewers), but they can also be used for holding cold appetizers, or as swizzle sticks in drinks.

You can buy pre-made sugar cane skewers in the canned food or frozen aisle of many specialty grocery stores: just be sure to wash them well before using them. Or you can simply make them yourself. Here's how: Get one 12-inch length of fresh sugar cane. Stand the sugar cane on one end. Very carefully, use a heavy knife to cut the cane vertically into slabs about ½ inch thick. Cut the slabs lengthwise into ½-inch-wide pieces, and then cut them crosswise into 3-inch-long sticks.

Kobe Beef Meatballs on Sugar Cane

FOR A MODERN TWIST ON THE TRADITIONAL VIETNAMESE BEEF KEBOBS *(chả bò với mía), we took our Kobe burger, one of our popular lunch dishes at Crustacean, wrapped it around a sugar cane skewer, and grilled it to add a sweet fragrance and a touch of juiciness. It makes a great appetizer or an amazing entrée eaten over bún, thin rice noodles, with lettuce, pickled vegetables, and Vietnamese herbs. You can add a little Garlic Lemon Sauce (nước chấm) (page 274), but as this dish already packs a lot of flavor, we usually just drizzle the sauce that comes out of the beef and find that is more than enough.*

MAKES 4 SERVINGS

FOR THE MEATBALLS:

1 pound ground Kobe or wagyu beef

⅓ cup chopped red onion

⅔ cup chopped portobello mushrooms

1 tablespoon minced Fried Garlic (page 282)

1 tablespoon minced Fried Shallots (page 281)

2 tablespoons light soy sauce

1 teaspoon Worcestershire sauce

3 teaspoons sweet chili paste

½ teaspoon salt

½ teaspoon freshly ground black pepper

1 teaspoon canola oil, plus more for oiling your fingers

2 tablespoons Spicy Satay Sauce (page 277)

1 tablespoon hoisin sauce

8 sugar cane skewers (see Note, opposite page)

FOR THE HERB PLATTER:

Fresh butter lettuce

Fresh Vietnamese perilla (tía tô) leaves

Fresh Vietnamese balm (kinh giới) or lemon balm leaves

Fresh mint leaves

Pickled Carrots (page 238)

Pickled Cucumbers (page 240)

1] Preheat the oven to 350°F.

2] In a large bowl, mix together the ground beef, onion, mushrooms, garlic, shallots, soy sauce, Worcestershire sauce, chili paste, salt, pepper, canola oil, satay sauce, and hoisin sauce. Now oil your fingers and hands to prevent the mixture from sticking and scoop out 1 tablespoon's worth. Press the ground meat mixture onto one end of a sugarcane skewer, shaping it into a flat strip about 2 inches long and ½ inch thick. Repeat this step until all the meat and skewers are used.

3] Place the beef skewers on a baking sheet and bake them for 5 minutes. Remove the baking sheet from the oven and set aside.

4] Preheat an outdoor grill or grill pan to medium high (about 450°F). Lightly oil the grill grate or pan and lay the sugarcane skewers on the grill, running perpendicular to the grate. Cover and cook over medium-high heat, turning once with a metal spatula, until the meat is browned, about 3-4 minutes.

5] Transfer the skewers to a serving dish. Serve hot with the herb platter.

Sweet Shoyu Short Ribs

ONE OF OUR SIGNATURE DISHES AT ANQI, *this recipe can be made with boneless ribs, but we prefer to keep the bone in during the entire cooking process for a juicier result. Braising the ribs in sake and fruit-infused wine first and then slow cooking them at a low temperature in the oven is the secret to these slightly sweet and super tender ribs. Serve them with jasmine rice and roasted vegetables, such as baby squash, cipollini onions, or marble potatoes.*

MAKES 6 SERVINGS

3 pounds bone-in beef short ribs

Salt

Freshly ground black pepper

4 tablespoons canola oil, divided

1 medium white onion, cut into ½-inch dice

4 scallions

6 garlic cloves

6 tablespoons minced fresh ginger (about 1 knob)

2½ cups sake

2½ cups Homemade Chicken Broth (page 273) or store-bought low-sodium chicken broth, divided

2 cups black raspberry wine

1 cup low-sodium soy sauce

¾ cup sugar

½ cup dark corn syrup

2 limes, halved

½ Asian pear, cut into ½-inch dice with skin

1] Preheat the oven to 275°F.

2] Season the ribs with salt and pepper.

3] Heat 2 tablespoons of the oil in a large skillet over medium-high heat. Add the ribs and sear them until golden brown, about 3 to 4 minutes on each side. Remove the skillet from the heat and set it aside.

4] Heat the remaining 2 tablespoons of oil in a deep, oven-proof saucepan, Dutch oven, or rondeau over medium-high heat. Add the onion, scallions, garlic, and ginger. Sauté until fragrant, about 10 minutes.

5] Add the seared ribs to the pan, along with the sake, chicken broth, wine, soy sauce, sugar, corn syrup, lime halves, and pear pieces. Bring the mixture to a boil, then turn off the heat, cover the pan, and place it in the oven. Braise the ribs until they reach your desired tenderness, about 2 to 3 hours.

6] Remove the ribs from the oven and transfer them to a serving platter, reserving the pan juices. Strain the pan juices through a fine-mesh strainer into a small saucepan. Set the saucepan over medium heat and cook until the sauce thickens, about 10 to 12 minutes, constantly stirring.

7] Serve the short ribs hot with the sauce drizzled overtop.

NOTE: *This pan-juice sauce is also wonderful with vegetables. Simply sauté it with your vegetables of choice over medium-high heat until aromatic, about 8 to 10 minutes.*

NOTE: *Black raspberry wine can be found at Asian markets or online. A popular choice is Bohae Bokbunjajoo from Korea.*

Grilled Mongolian Lamb Lollipops

WHEN LAMB RIB CHOPS ARE FRENCHED *to leave some of the bone exposed as a built-in "handle," they are called lollipop chops. Using our Mongolian BBQ sauce as a marinade cuts the gaminess of the lamb and makes this dish one that everyone will enjoy, even those who are not normally partial to lamb's unique flavor. We typically serve this with Swiss chard, shiitake mushroom caps, new potatoes, and roasted red peppers.*

MAKES 6 SERVINGS

FOR THE BBQ SAUCE:

1 cup low-sodium soy sauce

1 cup hoisin sauce

¾ cup sugar

¼ cup minced garlic

¼ cup minced fresh ginger

3 tablespoons sambal oelek chili sauce

3 scallions, thinly sliced

2 New Zealand or Australian lamb racks, cut into single chops or 12 lamb rib chops

1 bunch chopped fresh chives, for garnish

1) With a sharp boning knife, trim the chops to leave about 2 inches of rib bone bare at the top.

2) TO MAKE THE BBQ SAUCE: In a medium saucepan, combine the soy sauce, hoisin sauce, sugar, garlic, ginger, sambal oelek, and scallions. Simmer over low heat for 45 minutes until sauce thickens. Remove the pan from the heat and pour the sauce into a glass bowl or container. Cover the bowl and place it in the refrigerator to chill.

3) Put the lamb chops in a large glass bowl. Add 2 cups of the cooled BBQ sauce, reserving the rest to drizzle over the cooked lamb. Turn the lamb chops to coat, cover the bowl, and refrigerate for at least 3 hours to overnight.

4) Preheat an outdoor grill or grill pan to medium (about 350°F). Lightly oil the grill grate or pan. Remove the lamb chops from the bowl and discard the marinade. Place the marinated lamb chops on the grill, running perpendicular to the grate. Cover the grill or pan and cook over medium heat, turning once with a metal spatula, until the meat is done to your preference, about 3 minutes per side for medium doneness.

5) Just before the lamb is done cooking, brush the chops with some of the reserved BBQ sauce.

6) Serve the lamb chops hot, drizzled with more reserved BBQ sauce and garnished with the chives.

Note: To get perfect diamond grill marks, place the lamb at the direction of 10:00, then rotate to 2:00 and repeat on the opposite side.

Steamed Filet of Sole with Miso Sauce

THE SECRET TO THIS HEAVENLY DISH *is that rather than just putting aromatics on top of the fish, my mother rolls the fillets around in the ginger and scallions before steaming. This imparts more of a herbaceous flavor during the steaming process. This dish is a veritable feast of fermented sauces, from the soy and fish sauces to the rice vinegar and miso. Together they combine to give the fresh fish a delicious umami quality.*

MAKES 4 SERVINGS

1 tablespoon salt

1 tablespoon freshly ground white pepper

2 pounds skinless sole filets, sliced into thin, palm-sized (2-ounce) pieces

1 ounce fresh ginger, peeled and julienned

1 bunch scallions, white bulbs only, chopped

3 cups fish broth or chicken broth, prepackaged or Homemade (page 273)

6 tablespoon ponzu (citrus-seasoned soy sauce)

6 tablespoons canola oil

2 tablespoons rice vinegar

2 tablespoons lightly packed brown sugar

1 teaspoon sesame oil

1 tablespoon toasted sesame seeds

1 teaspoon sriracha sauce

1 teaspoon fish sauce

4 cups roasted corn (see note, below)

½ cup diced Roma tomatoes

½ cup julienned fresh shiitake mushrooms

4 tablespoons white miso paste

1) Preheat the oven to 350°F.

2) Sprinkle the salt and pepper on both sides of the fish. Put three pieces of ginger and 1 teaspoon of the chopped scallions on top of each fish fillet, and roll the fish to keep the ginger and onion inside. Place the fish rolls in a baking dish, seam-sides down.

3) Pour the broth over the fish rolls and cover the pan with foil. Bake for 15 minutes, until the fish is cooked through.

4) Meanwhile, prepare the miso sauce: In a large pot over medium heat, combine the miso, ponzu, canola oil, rice vinegar, brown sugar, sesame oil, sesame seeds, sriracha, and fish sauce. Whisk well and cook the mixture for 5 minutes to heat through and meld the flavors. Add the roasted corn, tomatoes, and mushrooms and bring the mixture to a boil. Pour the sauce over the fish. Serve hot.

NOTE: *To roast the corn, start by preheating the oven to 350°F and shucking five ears of corn. Brush the cleaned ears of corn with olive oil, arrange them on a baking sheet, and roast them for 3 minutes per side. Remove the roasted ears of corn from the oven and set them aside to cool. Once they are cool enough to handle, slice the kernels off the cobs.*

Shrimp Angel Hair Pasta

MY MOTHER WANTED TO CREATE A LIGHT AND HEALTHY DISH FOR HER LUNCH CROWD, *so she gave shrimp with pasta a modern Vietnamese twist. The secret to her tomato-basil sauce: a little fish sauce and Maggi seasoning sauce. They add a depth of umami flavor that's still very clean on the palate. This is a perfect dish to introduce someone to the magic of fish sauce. This recipe will give you extra tomato sauce for other dishes.*

MAKES 2 TO 4 SERVINGS

FOR THE TOMATO SAUCE:

4 tablespoons extra-virgin olive oil

6½ pounds fresh ripe Roma tomatoes, peeled, seeded, and chopped

½ cup tomato paste

½ cup diced white onion

⅓ cup chopped fresh parsley leaves

⅔ cup sugar

2 tablespoons salt

FOR THE PASTA:

1 (16-ounce) package dried angel hair pasta

4 tablespoons extra-virgin olive oil, divided

½ teaspoon salt

½ cup chopped fresh basil

1 tablespoon diced shallots

⅔ pound jumbo shrimp (size $21/25$; about 14 pieces), peeled and deveined

1½ teaspoons Maggi seasoning sauce, divided

1 teaspoon fish sauce, divided

1 tablespoon white wine

2 Roma tomatoes, peeled, seeded, and diced

Freshly grated Parmesan cheese, for serving

1] TO MAKE THE TOMATO SAUCE: Heat the oil in a large saucepan over low heat. Add the tomatoes, tomato paste, onion, parsley, sugar, and salt. Cook, stirring occasionally, until the moisture has evaporated, about 1 hour. Pour the tomato mixture into a blender or food processor and purée into a smooth sauce.

2] TO MAKE THE PASTA: Bring a large pot of salted water to a boil. Add the pasta and cook for 7 minutes or until al dente. Drain the pasta, rinse it under cold water, and then return it to the pot. Add 1 tablespoon of the oil and the salt to the pasta and mix well. Set aside.

3] Heat 2 tablespoons of the oil in a new large saucepan over medium heat. Add the shallots, sauté for 1 minute, and then add the basil. Add the shrimp and sauté until they turn opaque, about 5 minutes. Stir in 1 teaspoon of the Maggi sauce and ½ teaspoon of the fish sauce. Add the wine and deglaze the pan, stirring to scrape up the browned bits from the bottom. Stir in the remainder of the Maggi sauce and fish sauce.

(Continued to opposite page)

4] Pour the tomato sauce over the pasta to evenly coat the noodles. (Store any excess tomato sauce in an airtight container in the refrigerator up to 1 week, or in the freezer for up to 1 month.) Add the seasoned shrimp and the remaining tablespoon of olive oil to the pasta and stir well. Serve hot with the fresh diced tomato and Parmesan cheese grated over the top.

Mango Lobster Salad

THIS IS CRUSTACEAN'S BEST-SELLING ENTRÉE SALAD. *People come in every day asking for it and making sure we still have it on the menu. The secret to its fabulous taste is that rather than discarding the lobster shells, we sauté them in the pan. When lobster is boiled, much of the fabulous flavor is released into the surrounding water and then lost. Heating the shells in a pan with oil keeps these juices on hand for extra flavor.*

MAKES 4 SERVINGS

FOR THE LOBSTER MIXTURE:

2 (1½-pound) Maine or spiny lobsters, boiled in water for 3 to 4 minutes and chilled

2 tablespoons canola oil, divided

4 tablespoons chopped shallots, divided

4 tablespoons chopped fresh basil, divided

2 tablespoons white wine, divided

½ cup + 1 tablespoon Homemade Chicken Broth (page 273) or store-bought low-sodium chicken broth, divided

1 teaspoon unsalted butter

FOR THE DRESSING:

1 teaspoon miso paste

1 teaspoon rice vinegar

1 tablespoon mayonnaise

1 teaspoon extra-virgin olive oil

1 teaspoon sesame oil

1 teaspoon fish sauce

1 teaspoon freshly squeezed lemon juice

1 teaspoon honey

1 teaspoon sugar

1 teaspoon peeled, minced fresh ginger

½ teaspoon white pepper

¾ cup (2 ounces) mixed baby greens salad mix

1 mango, peeled, pitted, and sliced

8 cherry tomatoes, sliced

1] Crack the lobster open and remove the meat, discarding the feathers and tomalley. Save the body, claw, and leg shells and head as well. Cut the meat into 1-inch pieces and set aside.

2] **TO MAKE THE LOBSTER MIXTURE:** Heat 1 tablespoon of oil in a large oven-proof skillet over medium heat. Add 2 tablespoons of the shallots, 2 table-spoons of the basil, and the lobster shells (body, claw, and legs) and sauté for 5 minutes. Add 1 tablespoon of the wine, being conscious of a possible flame-up, then stir in in ½ cup of the chicken stock and cook until the liquid is reduced by half, about 10 minutes. Remove the skillet from the heat and carefully strain the sauce through a fine-mesh sieve, discarding the herbs and shells. Set aside.

3] Preheat the oven to 400°F.

(Continued)

4] Heat the remaining tablespoon of oil in the same skillet over medium heat. Add the rest of the shallots and basil and the lobster head and cook for 1 minute until the shell becomes red. Remove lobster head for plating, or discard if desired. Add the lobster meat and sauté for 3 minutes, then add the remaining tablespoon of wine, being conscious of a possible flame-up. Stir in 1 tablespoon of chicken stock and 1 tablespoon of the reserved lobster sauce and place the skillet in the oven for 3 to 5 minutes or until the sauce is bubbly and the lobster is golden brown. Add 1 teaspoon of butter to the skillet and stir until it has completely melted. Transfer the lobster mixture to a medium bowl and set aside.

5] To make the dressing: In a small bowl, whisk the miso paste into the rice vinegar until smooth. In another bowl, whisk together the mayonnaise and olive oil until smooth. Add the mayonnaise mixture to the miso mixture and whisk again until smooth. Stir in the sesame oil, fish sauce, lemon juice, honey, sugar, ginger, and white pepper. Pour 1 tablespoon of the dressing over the lobster mixture and toss gently to coat.

6] Put the salad greens in a large serving bowl, add 1 tablespoon of the dressing, and toss. Spoon the lobster mixture on top of the salad. Garnish with the mango slices and cherry tomatoes and serve.

Note: For added flavor, drizzle any extra lobster sauce over the lobster mixture on top of the salad right before serving.

OPPOSITE: Tiato garden patio.

5

bistronomy

a new generation of food

Even though it was never my mother's intention for us to follow her into the food industry—"A terribly hard job," she'd say, "Go be a doctor or a lawyer or anything else!" —we all gravitated back to it in the end. Though we tried different careers, such as design, business, banking, advertising, and engineering, the pull of working with our first love, family, and our second, food, proved too irresistible. We had all grown up in the kitchen, both in our restaurants and at home with our grandmother Diana. We all had great palates, an intuition for ingredients, and a passion for serving others.

We all joined the House of An restaurant group as managing partners and brought a new generation of ideas and innovation to our family business, including adventures in molecular dining and bistronomy.

"Growing up, my grandmother always said, 'We already have the restaurant business, you don't have be in it. Go follow your heart.' And I did. In the process of soul-searching, I studied in Botswana and China. I went to work for the designer Richard Tyler. But I missed my family. Working in this industry is so creative and gives me such a sense of satisfaction. It makes me happy."

— CATHERINE AN

enter AnQi

*M*y sister Elizabeth has always loved fashion, and for our next restaurant she came up with a concept that combined couture and cuisine. *AnQi*, a gourmet bistro in the Bloomingdale's wing of South Coast Plaza, one of the largest luxury plazas in the country, has a catwalk that runs right through the middle of the sleek dining room. In a nod to Crustacean, the 60-foot glass runway has a crystal stream that runs beneath it, and it regularly serves as a stage for fashion shows and celebrity appearances.

"I wanted the restaurant to be sexy and sophisticated, a magnetic place with a chic, loungey vibe that you couldn't stop visiting because something new and unique was always happening," Elizabeth says.

She accomplished her "dining as art" vision by designing a space that was open and flexible. The catwalk converts to additional seating when not in use, and crystallographic partitions allow for endless configurations. Named for our family and qi, Chinese for "life force," AnQi incorporates both ancient feng shui and modern sustainability based on the four elements: Earth, Water, Fire, and Wind. Antique Asian furnishings blend with eco-friendly polished concrete and pebbled floors. Undulating reclaimed wood structures backlit from behind line the walls and invoke an organic sense of the outdoors.

Throughout the restaurant the color red is used to express energy, passion, prosperity, and spice.

The menu honors our mother's culinary philosophy but with a contemporary twist. The food-forward offerings are constantly evolving from small plates and Crustacean-inspired classics to molecular gastronomy and one-of-a-kind experiential dinners dubbed "GourMondays." Aside from the main dining room, AnQi also has a state-of-the-art lounge and a noodle bar.

Another unique aspect of AnQi is The Chef Table, which offers a special sneak peek of the restaurant's Secret Kitchen. When guests at this table press a secret button, the chef can make the adjacent glass window go from frosted to clear and give them a glimpse into the Secret Kitchen.

catering and a
market garden café

Based on the success of our Oscar celebrations at Crustacean and word-of-mouth from our celebrity clientele, my mother got more and more requests to provide her delicious food for offsite special events. In answer, my sister Catherine spearheaded the launch of An Catering. However, it quickly became so popular that it threatened to overrun Crustacean's kitchen.

"Go find your own kitchen!" my mother told her, and she did. Catherine has always been very creative, and she converted a dimly lit diner in the heart of Santa Monica's media district into **Tiato**, a light-filled, eco-chic breakfast, lunch, and special events venue that now also serves as the home base for An Catering. Out went the shiny, red vinyl booths and in their place came movable banquet chairs made of sustainable wood, repurposed structures—an old rusty mattress spring form Catherine found at a flea market hangs from the center of the courtyard, covered in cascading succulents and brightly colored flowers—and lots of live plants. Catherine hired a local artist whose specialty was turning abandoned farm equipment like rusted wheelbarrows and ploughs into magnificent water features for the patio.

Accomplishing her vision of warm, natural, rustic charm wasn't easy, though. Thankfully, like my mother, Catherine is very determined and very hands-on. She doesn't just tell people what she wants; she goes out and does it. When the architect she hired to design the bar turned in a plan that was cold and too modern, she scrapped it and went to work herself, sketching her ideas on a large piece of paper well into the middle of the night. When she couldn't find the flexible divider system she had envisioned, she designed one herself, mounting wine crates on wheels that could be easily moved around for any occasion. She turned old lobster cages into light fixtures and filled large glass containers with rice and dried tea that both added color to the décor and represented the restaurant's style of cooking.

For the menu, Catherine wanted light and flavorful fare with an emphasis on organic. With full service as well as a salad bar and take-out counter, Tiato offers a range of healthy Vietnamese-American dishes that all bear the classic An family flavor profile. The chicken bánh mì burger, for instance, is seasoned with lemongrass, pickled vegetables, and chile aioli.

Named for my mother's favorite Vietnamese green-and-purple herb, Tiato has an on-site herb garden and a large garden patio that serves as an outdoor oasis for lunch customers during the week and a wonderful location for wedding receptions and special events at night and on the weekends.

STEWARDS OF THE EARTH

Being eco- and socially conscious is important to our family and something we strive to incorporate into each of our endeavors. Nowhere is this more apparent than at Tiato, where we hire locally, grow our own ingredients, and source local, healthy, and sustainable goods whenever we can. We compost everything and were the first restaurant in Santa Monica to have zero waste. We work with Carbon Fund and are proud of our dedication to the highest standards of environmental consciousness. A love for the land is part of all of our heritages.

the secret to successful events

A lifetime of hosting events—from elegant soirees for foreign dignitaries to humble family dinners, from casual Super Bowl viewing parties with friends to paparazzi-filled black-tie galas—has taught us that the venue, the décor, and the budget aren't as important as one simple thing: hospitality. When you share a celebration with someone, you're sharing your life with them. And when you make them feel like part of the party or show or event, they will remember you. We've found that the best way to do this is to simply pay attention to seating, incorporate tradition, and add just one wow.

Seating

No matter the size or scope of the event, really look at your guest list. Make sure you've invited a mix of people, not just all actors or attorneys, all married or all people without kids. People want to learn from and be inspired by others.

And don't leave seating to chance. An older gentleman doesn't want to get stuck next to a sulking toddler; a single career woman probably doesn't want to sit by a teenaged boy. Create a seating chart based on who might be interested in talking to whom. The goal is to put different people next to each other in a way that will spark great conversation. They don't need to have the same vocation or background; just one common interest, hobby, or shared vacation destination can be enough. People want to be interested and feel interesting.

Then go one step further and identify that common interest or interesting fact for your guests. Introduce them and break the ice so they don't have to. Making people comfortable through careful seating and thoughtful introductions goes a long way.

Incorporate Tradition

Another key to hosting a successful event is to incorporate traditions, both old and new. Include interesting antiques or family heirlooms in your presentation that have a story you can tell. Use photo frames as placeholders that guests can take home as a happy remembrance.

I have a friend in New York who has a black chalkboard wall in her entryway, and everyone who visits writes a note on it. The wall itself becomes an instant conversation piece. I have another friend who has a tradition of handing out puzzle pieces for guests to sign, commemorating the evening. The puzzle is later put together and framed, then hung in the house. I personally like to save all the corks from wine opened at my dinner parties. I keep them all in a large glass box set out for other people to see, comment on, and reminiscence about with me. A good event will make memories for both you and your guests.

Add One Unexpected Thing

When we throw parties, especially at our restaurants, we always want them to be the most amazing events anyone's ever attended. Rather than beat ourselves up trying to make every single aspect over-the-top, though, we focus on one wow factor, one unique thing that's never been done. It could be a food item, or how the food is displayed, or even a show.

For the Weinstein Company's VIP Golden Globes party, we created special "dragon's smoke" cookies to honor the Year of the Dragon (co-Chairman Harvey Weinstein's Chinese zodiac sign), which were dipped in liquid nitrogen and allowed guests to "breathe fire" after the first bite. At AnQi, we did a fashion show where the models wore dresses made of beautiful herbs and vegetables. For the Beverly Hills Centennial party at Crustacean, we crafted an edible "prosperity tree" food wall and had sushi geishas wearing structural "table" skirts walking around serving hors d'oeuvres.

At the end of the day, however, a great party comes down to great food. If you have great drinks and great food, your great party will fall into place.

ENTERTAINING TIPS FROM THE ANS

Throwing an affair doesn't have to be expensive. Here are some of our favorite low-cost ideas:

- *Handwrite homemade name cards*
- *Fill the table with candles instead of full floral arrangements, tucking single blooms in between*
- *Use natural found objects as chopstick rests, such as seashells or pebbles*
- *Decorate plates or passing trays with snipped herbs bundled with a ribbon*
- *Embrace the eclectic; beautiful table arrangements don't have to be perfectly matched to bring joy and start conversation*
- *Ultimately, though, food is about bringing people together. The accessories don't matter as long as you bring the love.*

Here are a few of our favorite entertaining recipes:
appetizers, small dishes, tapas, and lighter fare, some
traditional and some just beyond. All of these dishes are
guaranteed to get your gathering off to a great start.

Warm Goji Berry–Brown Rice Salad

MY MOTHER CREATED THIS SALAD TO SHOWCASE INGREDIENTS *that Eastern medicine has long believed had unique health benefits and that the Western world now recognizes as "superfoods." Goji berries and baby bok choy are rich sources of antioxidants, ginkgo nuts have been shown to reduce cholesterol, and kale is a nutrient-dense vegetable high in vitamins A and K. Brown rice is a whole grain, which makes it rich in fiber and selenium, and it is also an excellent source of manganese, an essential nutrient that can help with both weight loss and lowering cholesterol.*

MAKES 4 TO 5 SERVINGS

1 cup brown rice

1 tablespoon canola oil

¼ cup diced shallots

¼ cup thinly sliced fresh shiitake mushroom

2 tablespoons Michiu rice cooking wine or white wine, divided

3 garlic cloves, sliced

8 shelled ginkgo nuts, precooked (see note) (optional)

2 tablespoons dried goji berries

2 tablespoons shelled edamame

8 ounce Swiss chard, stems discarded, cut into thin strips and blanched

8 ounce baby bok choy, cut into thin strips and blanched

8 ounce kale, stems discarded, cut into thin strips and blanched

1 teaspoon salt

½ teaspoon freshly ground black pepper

½ teaspoon sugar

1 tablespoon grapeseed oil

1] Soak the rice in warm water for 3 hours, then drain it, rinse it under cold water, and spread it on a baking sheet to dry.

2] Heat the canola oil in a large pot over high heat. Add the shallots and mushrooms and sauté for 1 minute. Add the rice and sauté for 3 minutes. Add 1 tablespoon of the wine, being conscious of a possible flame-up. Add 2 cups of water to the pot and bring the liquid to a boil, then reduce the heat to medium low. Cover the pot and keep cooking until the rice is cooked, about 20 minutes. Drain the rice and spread it out on a baking sheet to cool.

3] Place a large skillet over high heat. Add the garlic and dry sauté for just 15 seconds until fragrant. Add the rice to the skillet, tossing and sautéing until it is light brown and dry, about 3 to 5 minutes. Add the ginkgo nuts, goji berries, and edamame and continue to cook for about 3 minute. Put the seasoned rice on a serving plate; set aside.

4] Add the Swiss chard, baby bok choy, and kale to the same skillet over high heat. Stir in the salt, pepper, and sugar and stir constantly for 2 minutes. Add the remaining tablespoon of wine, being conscious of a possible flame-up. Sauté the vegetables for 1 minute, then stir in the grapeseed oil. Spoon the vegetables on top of the rice mixture and serve warm.

NOTE: *To pre-cook shelled ginkgo nuts, bring a small pot of water to a boil. Add the ginkgo nuts and cook for 5 minutes, then drain. Let the nuts cool before handling.*

NOTE: *Goji berries can interact with certain medications for blood thinning, blood pressure, and diabetes, so check with your doctor if you are on any of these medications.*

Tiato Rolls

I'M ALWAYS AMAZED AT HOW MY MOTHER MAKES VEGETARIAN DISHES SO FLAVORFUL. *This name-sake of our Santa Monica restaurant became so popular that we carried it over to our other restaurants. The Tiato roll is my mother's reinvention of the traditional rice paper–based summer roll. This light and refreshing vegetarian roll includes the eponymous green-and-purple herb as well as tofu, sweet potatoes, eggplant, and zucchini, marinated in a cilantro chili sauce. The turmeric soy paper used inside of the rice paper completes the perfect balance of texture and flavor.*

MAKES 4 ROLLS

FOR THE CILANTRO CHILI SAUCE:

1 cup seasoned rice wine vinegar

1 cup sugar

2 tablespoons minced garlic

2 tablespoons chopped fresh cilantro

1 tablespoon chopped red chiles

1 teaspoon freshly squeezed lime juice

1 teaspoon fish sauce

FOR THE FILLING:

3 tablespoons canola oil

Firm tofu, cut into 8 (3 x ½-inch) sticks

½ zucchini, cut into 3 x ½-inch sticks

½ Chinese eggplant, cut into 3 x ½-inch sticks

½ sweet potato, cut into 3 x ½-inch sticks

½ teaspoon salt

½ teaspoon freshly ground black pepper

½ teaspoon sugar

16 fresh Vietnamese perilla (tía tô) leaves

16 fresh Thai basil leaves

4 sheets rice paper

4 sheets turmeric soy wrappers or soy paper

1] TO MAKE THE SAUCE: Combine the vinegar, sugar, and garlic in a medium pot over medium heat. Cook, stirring frequently, until the sauce is golden in color and reduces by half, about 10 minutes. Stir in the cilantro, chiles, lime juice, and fish sauce. Pour the sauce into a large bowl and set it aside.

2] TO MAKE THE FILLING: Heat the oil in a large skillet over medium heat. Add the tofu, zucchini, eggplant, and sweet potato and fry the vegetables, stirring constantly, until they are light brown and tender, about 5 minutes. Remove the skillet from the heat and transfer the vegetables to a paper towel–lined plate to drain.

3] Add the zucchini and eggplant to the sauce and set it aside to marinate for 10 minutes.

4] Place the tofu and sweet potatoes in a large bowl. Add the salt, pepper, and sugar to the vegetables and toss well. Set aside.

5] Get a clean, lint-free kitchen towel, wet it, and wring it dry. Place it on a hard surface or cutting board. Soak one square of rice paper in warm water. Remove it from the water and place it on the damp cloth; press lightly and wipe away the excess water.

6) Place the softened rice paper wrapper in front of you on a hard surface or cutting board. Place one soy paper wrapper on the center of the rice paper. Place four tía tô and four basil leaves in a line down the middle of the soy paper. Layer one of each filling ingredient—marinated zucchini, marinated eggplant, sweet potato, and tofu—on top of the herbs.

7) Fold the bottom of the wrapper over the vegetables and start rolling upward, making sure to tuck in the sides as you go. Don't roll too tightly, as that might cause the wrapper to tear. Set the roll aside and repeat this process with the remaining wrappers and filling ingredients. Eat the rolls fresh within an hour of making them.

Lobster Corn Dogs on Sugarcane

MY MOTHER LOVES WHEN HER CATERING CLIENTS HAVE SPECIAL REQUESTS; *it's a challenge for her and an excuse to experiment. Sometimes these special requests turn into regular menu items. Such is the case with Lobster Corn Dogs. Using the Vietnamese dish of grilled shrimp on sugar cane sticks (chạo tôm) as a base, she modified it to include lobster and deep-fried it in a corn dog batter. The results speak for themselves: Lobster Corn Dogs are now a popular appetizer at our restaurants. They are easy to pass around on serving trays at a home party, and they are wonderful by themselves or served with Garlic Lemon Sauce (page 274) or the aioli sauce from our Bánh Mì recipe (page 144).*

MAKES 8 CORN DOGS

FOR THE LOBSTER MIXTURE:

4 ounces lobster meat, cooked

4 ounces peeled and deveined shrimp

2 ice cubes

1 teaspoon beaten egg white

2 tablespoons finely chopped scallions, inner white part only

2 teaspoons minced garlic

1 teaspoon sugar

1 teaspoon fish sauce

2 tablespoons salted butter

1 (20-ounce) can sugarcane sticks

4 sugar cane skewers, cut in half (see note, page 178)

FOR THE CORN DOG BATTER:

1¼ cups all-purpose flour

¾ cup semolina flour

4 teaspoons sugar

1 teaspoon sea salt

1 teaspoon baking powder

¾ cup buttermilk

2 large eggs

Canola oil, for deep-frying

1] To make the lobster mixture: In a food processor, combine the lobster, shrimp, and ice cubes and pulse until the seafood is coarsely chopped. Add the egg white and process until the smooth. Transfer the mixture to a bowl. Wash out the food processor and dry it thoroughly.

2] In the clean food processor bowl, combine the scallions, garlic, sugar, and fish sauce and process until the mixture forms a smooth paste. Return the seafood mixture to the food processor and pulse until well combined.

3] Line a baking sheet with waxed paper. Lightly oil your fingers and palms. Shape about 1 tablespoon of the seafood mixture in a ball. Then shape the ball firmly around one end of a sugar cane skewer so it resembles a lollipop. Transfer the lollipop to the prepared baking sheet. Repeat this step until all the skewers are used.

4] Set up a multi-tier steamer and bring the water to a boil. Arrange the lollipops in the steamer, canes sticking up, and cover. Cook until the seafood balls look opaque, about 10 minutes.

5] To make the corn dog batter: In a large bowl, whisk together the flours, sugar, baking soda, and salt. Add the buttermilk and egg and stir until well combined.

6] Position a rack in the center of the oven and preheat to 200°F. Line a large baking sheet with paper towels.

7] Pour enough oil to come halfway up the sides of a large, deep saucepan or wok and heat the oil over high heat until reaches 350°F on a candy or deep-frying thermometer. (You can also test if the oil is hot enough by dropping in one small piece of onion. If it turns golden and floats to the top in 5 seconds, then the oil is ready.)

8] Fry the corn dogs in batches, being sure not to crowd them in the oil. Using kitchen tongs, grab a corn dog by its cane. Dip the ball end into the batter to coat, then dip the ball end into the hot oil. Fry until the ball is set, about 30 seconds. Release the stick into the oil and continue frying until the ball is golden brown, about 2 to 3 minutes. Using the tongs, transfer the corn dogs to the prepared baking sheet as they are cooked, and keep them warm in the oven. Repeat until all of the corn dogs are fried. Serve warm.

BUTTERFLIES

I remember our first Oscar party like it was yesterday. We were all so nervous and excited at the same time. It was humbling and hard to fathom that our little family from San Francisco was suddenly going to be rubbing shoulders with the Hollywood elite. To have celebrities we were used to seeing on TV right in front of us, in our restaurant, was a bit overwhelming. We were terrified that something would go wrong, but thankfully it was a fantastic event.

Even though we host exclusive industry parties and cater big events all the time now, we still get those little butterflies in our stomachs. The tension and excitement will perhaps never entirely leave us, because inside we still feel like the owners of a tiny twenty-seat restaurant in Outer Sunset.

Balsamic Chicken Pot Stickers

MY MOTHER CREATED THIS DISH FOR ANQI'S NOODLE BAR, *giving a traditional Asian dish a little European flair. Juicy chicken dumplings are pan seared like traditional pot stickers and balanced with a balsamic reduction for sweetness. A touch of butter at the end of the cooking process adds an extra flavor boost.*

MAKES 48 POT STICKERS

FOR THE POT STICKERS:

½ cup (about 1½ ounces) dried wood ear mushrooms

½ cup (about 1½ ounces) dried shiitake mushrooms

2 cups chopped white onion

2 teaspoons oyster sauce

1 tablespoon fish sauce

1 teaspoon sugar

1 teaspoon freshly ground black pepper

½ teaspoon salt

1 pound ground dark meat chicken

¾ cup finely chopped carrot (about 5 ounces or 1½ carrots)

1 (12-ounce) package dumpling skins or wrappers

Canola oil, for frying

Unsalted butter

FOR THE BALSAMIC REDUCTION:

1 cup balsamic vinegar

½ cup lightly packed brown sugar

1] Soak the mushrooms in warm water, until they soften and expand, about 1 hour. Drain the mushrooms and set aside.

2] Put a medium pan over medium heat. Add the onion and sauté for 2 to 3 minutes or until softened and fragrant.

3] To make the pot sticker filling: In a large bowl, mix together the oyster sauce, fish sauce, sugar, pepper, and salt. Add the sautéed onions and ground chicken and mix well. Fill a larger bowl with ice and set the bowl with the filling inside. Cover the bowls and refrigerate for 1 hour.

4] In a food processor or blender, grind the reconstituted mushrooms with the carrots. Stir this mixture into the chilled stuffing.

5] To make the dumplings: Fill a small bowl with cool water. Place a dumpling skin in front of you on a hard surface or cutting board. Place 1 full teaspoon of chicken filling in the middle of the dumpling skin. Moisten the edges of the dumpling skin with water. Fold one edge of the skin over to cover the filling, overlapping the other edge. Press the skin firmly around the filling to eliminate any air bubbles and press around the edges to seal. Repeat with the remaining dumpling skins and filling.

6] Bring a large pot of water to a boil. In batches, add the dumplings and cook until they float to the top of the pot, about 15 minutes. Transfer the cooked dumplings to a plate.

(Continued)

7] To make the balsamic reduction: Pour the vinegar into a medium saucepan over low heat. Stir in the sugar until it is dissolved. Continue cooking until the amount of liquid in the pan is reduced by half. Set aside.

8] Position a rack in the center of the oven and preheat to 200°F. Line a large baking sheet with paper towels.

9] To fry the pot stickers: Heat 1 tablespoon of the oil in a large skillet over medium heat. Working in batches, add 6 cooked dumplings (or whatever will comfortably fit in your pan without overcrowding) and sauté them until they are golden brown, about 5 minutes on each side. Add 1 tablespoon of butter and sauté for another minute. As they finish cooking, transfer the pot stickers to the prepared baking sheet and keep them warm in the oven. Repeat until all of the dumplings are fried.

10] Serve them warm, drizzled with the balsamic reduction.

NOTE: *This recipe makes a large batch, which as a busy mom I appreciate because it means I can freeze the extras to have a quick meal on hand for the future. To freeze, put uncooked dumplings on a baking sheet, making sure none stick together, and sprinkle them with flour. Freeze them until they are solid, then transfer them to freezer bags. To reheat the pot stickers, bring a large pot of water to a boil, add the frozen pot stickers, and boil for about 15 minutes or until they rise to the surface. Drain. At this point, you can either eat them as dumplings or fry them into pot stickers.*

Crispy Garlic Chicken Wings

AN EASY RECIPE WITH MY MOTHER'S SIGNATURE FLAVORS, *these wings are simple yet delicious. Created for our bar menu, the dish combines fish sauce, sugar, garlic, and lime for a sweet and tangy flavor that is truly finger-licking good. My husband and I have a tradition of hosting Super Bowl parties, and these wings are a staple dish that everyone looks forward to along with the halftime show. The secret to juicy wings is to steam cook them before frying, as it adds moisture and reduces the frying time.*

MAKES 4 SERVINGS

2 pounds chicken wings

2 tablespoons fish sauce

2 tablespoons sugar

2 teaspoons minced garlic

1 teaspoon salt

3 teaspoons sweet chili sauce or sriracha sauce (optional)

2 cups canola oil

4 teaspoons freshly squeezed lime juice (from 1 lime)

1) Cut the wings at the joint and discard the tips.

2) Combine the fish sauce, sugar, garlic, salt, and chili sauce, if using, in a large bowl. Mix well. Add the chicken wings and turn to coat. Cover the bowl and let the wings marinate in the refrigerator for 1 hour.

3) Take the chicken wings out of the refrigerator and place them on a steamer tray over boiling water. Steam them for 15 minutes. Set them aside to cool.

4) Heat the oil in a deep skillet over medium heat. Once the oil reaches 350°F on a candy or deep-frying thermometer, add the chicken wings in batches and cook them until the outsides turn golden brown, about 5 minutes. Using tongs or a slotted spoon, immediately transfer the fried chicken wings to a large bowl. Repeat this process with all of the chicken wings.

5) When all of the chicken wings have been fried, squeeze the lime juice over them in the bowl. Toss to coat. Serve hot.

Filet Mignon on Sesame Crisps

THESE BITE-SIZED CRISPS ARE GREAT FOR SNACKING OR FOR SERVING AS APPETIZERS. *They were created specifically for our restaurant bars as they go well with just about any kind of alcohol and are easy to share. As you probably know by now, Vietnamese food centers around balancing flavors and textures, and that idea carries through in this simple appetizer, as the crunch of the sesame crisps complements the balance of the sweet and spicy filet mignon.*

If you have trouble finding sesame crisps, you can use fried wonton skins as the base.

MAKES 4 SERVINGS

2 tablespoons canola oil

8 ounces filet mignon, cut into ⅛-inch dice

1 tablespoon white wine

2 tablespoons House Sauce (page 276)

2¼ cups (about 6 ounces) fresh enoki mushrooms, cut into 1-inch strips

1 tablespoon wasabi powder

1 tablespoon mayonnaise

¼ teaspoon salt

¼ teaspoon sugar

16 Sesame Crisps (page 59)

1 teaspoon sweet chili sauce

2 Italian Roma tomatoes, seeded and cut into ⅛-inch dice, for garnish

1 bell pepper, seeded and cut into ⅛-inch dice, for garnish

1 cucumber, seeded and cut into ⅛-inch dice, for garnish

1) Heat the oil in a large saucepan over medium heat. Add the filet mignon and sauté for about 2 minutes to brown. Add the wine, being conscious of a possible flame-up, then add the House Sauce and cook for another minute. Turn off the heat. Stir in the mushrooms and set the pan aside.

2) In a small bowl, combine the wasabi powder and 2 tablespoons of warm water. Mix well. Stir in the mayonnaise, salt, and sugar. Set aside.

3) Put a dot of chili sauce on the bottom of each crisp, then add 1 tablespoon of the seasoned filet mignon and top with a dot of wasabi paste. Garnish with the tomatoes, peppers, and cucumbers.

Saigon Steamed Pork Buns

CHỢ LỚN, THE CHINESE DISTRICT IN HO CHI MINH CITY *(formerly Saigon), is known for its Chinese-influenced street food. At our restaurants, we decided to create our own take on char siu bao, Chinese steamed buns filled with roasted pork. While traditionally pork belly is used for these street food favorites, we prefer to use pork cheek—a vastly under-hyped cut of meat—because pork cheek is moist without being fatty. These pork buns are great as an appetizer or as an afternoon snack between meals.*

MAKES 12 BUNS

FOR THE PORK:

1 tablespoon corn syrup

1 tablespoon honey

1 tablespoon caramel syrup

1 tablespoon soy sauce

1 tablespoon sugar

1 tablespoon minced Fried Garlic [page 282]

1 teaspoon freshly ground white pepper

1 teaspoon salt

1 teaspoon Chinese BBQ Char Siu Seasoning Mix

1 teaspoon oyster sauce

½ teaspoon ground ginger

1 pound whole pork cheek

FOR THE BUN DOUGH:

¾ cup hot water

¾ cup cold milk

6 cups [724 grams] cake flour

¾ cup [80 grams] powdered sugar

2½ teaspoons baking powder

½ teaspoon instant yeast

Canola oil, for sealing the buns

Pickled Carrots and Daikon [page 238]

Maggi seasoning sauce

Fresh cilantro

1) To marinate the pork: In a large bowl, whisk together the corn syrup, honey, caramel syrup, soy sauce, sugar, garlic, pepper, salt, seasoning mix, oyster sauce, and ginger.

2) Pat the pork dry with a paper towel and place it in a large resealable plastic bag. Pour in the marinade and seal the bag. Turn the pork to coat it in the marinade and refrigerate overnight.

3) To make the bun dough: In a medium bowl, whisk together the hot water and milk. Set aside.

4) In the bowl of an electric mixer fitted with the dough hook attachment, mix together the flour, sugar, baking powder, and yeast. Add the whisked milk mixture and mix until a smooth dough forms, about 3-4 minutes. Divide the dough in half and place each half in a large resealable plastic bag. Squeeze all of the air out, seal the bags, and set them on the counter to rest until the dough has doubled in size, 1½ to 2 hours.

5) Preheat the oven to 350°F.

[Continued]

6] Remove the pork from the marinade and place it on a metal rack with a baking sheet underneath to catch any drips. Roast the pork for 15 minutes, then turn it over and roast for 15 more minutes. Remove the pork from the oven and set it aside to cool.

7] Remove the dough from the plastic bags and punch it down to release any air bubbles. Cut the dough into six equal pieces, then cut those pieces in half for a total of twelve portions. Shape each portion into a ball. With a rolling pin, flatten each ball into an oval shape, about 1½-inch by 3-inches. Place plastic wrap over the ovals to keep them from drying out as you shape them in the next step.

8] Take out one oval and brush half of it with canola oil. Gently fold the oval in half lengthwise. Place it back under the plastic wrap and repeat with the remaining ovals of dough. When all of the ovals have been folded, set them aside and let them rise at room temperature until almost double in size, 1 to 2 hours.

9] Fill a wok or a large pot with an inch of water and set a steamer tray or basket in the wok or pot. Place the buns in the steamer, and bring the water to a boil over high heat. Cover the wok or pot and steam until the buns have expanded, about 8 minutes. (If you don't have a multi-tiered steaming basket, you will have to steam the buns in batches so they won't be overcrowded.) To check if the buns are finished steaming, carefully press one with your finger. If the bun springs back quickly, it is done. If not, rotate the steamers and steam for 5 more minutes. Transfer the steamed buns to a sheet pan and allow them to cool.

10] Slice the pork cheek into ⅛- to ¼-inch-thin slabs to fit in the buns. Take a bun, open it up, and fill it with four pieces of pork. Top the pork with pickled daikon and carrots, and season it with salt and pepper and a couple drops of Maggi seasoning sauce. Garnish with cilantro. Repeat with the remaining buns and fillings.

Crab Puffs

A FINGER FOOD FAVORITE FROM OUR RESTAURANT AND CATERING MENUS, *crab puffs are another example of my mother fusing European and Asian techniques and flavors. To make this recipe, she took a traditional wonton wrapper and, instead of just filling it with crabmeat, she created a special crab cake–like stuffing, complete with cream cheese. For a final, fun flourish, she twists the wonton skins to look like a tiny crab with claws.*

MAKES 16 CRAB PUFFS

FOR THE DIPPING SAUCE:

1 cup Homemade Chicken Broth [page 273] or store-bought low-sodium chicken broth

1 cup white wine

2 tablespoons peanut sauce

2 tablespoons mayonnaise

1 tablespoon Dijon mustard

1 tablespoon honey

FOR THE FILLING:

¼ cup (2 ounces) cream cheese

3 tablespoons creamy peanut butter

1 tablespoon sugar

4 teaspoons honey

2 teaspoons Fried Shallots [page 281]

1 teaspoon Fried Garlic [page 282]

1½ teaspoons salt

1½ teaspoons freshly ground black pepper

½ teaspoon fish sauce

8 ounces snow crab meat

1 (12-ounce) package wonton skins or wrappers

2 cups canola oil

1] To make the sauce: In a medium bowl, combine the chicken broth, wine, peanut sauce, mayonnaise, mustard, and honey. Mix well, cover the bowl, and refrigerate until ready to use.

2] To make the filling: In a food processor, combine the cream cheese, peanut butter, sugar, honey, shallots, garlic, salt, pepper, and fish sauce. Pulse to combine, then add the crabmeat and process until smooth.

3] To assemble the puffs: Fill a small bowl with cool water. Place a wonton skin in front of you on a hard surface or cutting board. Place 1 full teaspoon of the filling in the center of the wonton skin. Moisten the edges of the wonton skin with water. Fold one edge of the skin over to cover the filling, overlapping the other edge. Press the skin firmly around the filling to eliminate any air bubbles and press around the edges to seal. Grab the two open ends of the puff and twist them slightly until you have a candy wrapper–like shape. Repeat with the remaining wonton skins and filling.

4] Position a rack in the center of the oven and preheat to 200°F. Line a large baking sheet with paper towels.

5] Heat the oil in a deep skillet over medium heat. Once the oil is hot, 350°F on a candy or deep-frying thermometer, add the crab puffs in batches and cook until the outsides turn golden brown, about 5 minutes. As they are finished cooking, transfer the crab puffs to the prepared baking sheet and keep them warm in the oven. Repeat until all of the crab puffs are fried.

6] Serve the crab puffs warm with dipping sauce on the side.

Steamed Black Mussels

IN VIETNAM, ĂN NHẬU IS LIKE AMERICAN "HAPPY HOUR," *when friends get together to share small tapas and enjoy a drink or two. The name comes from the Vietnamese words ăn, "to eat," and nhậu, "to drink." The food eaten during ăn nhậu is lighter with strong flavors and meant to go well with beer or wine. Steamed mussels are a popular ăn nhậu treat, which my mother reinvented for our restaurants. The secret to this delicious dish is to get the freshest mussels you can find and to not overcook or over-season them. A simple pairing of nước chấm (garlic lemon sauce) and mỡ hành (scallion oil) is all that's needed to bring out the sweet and savory flavors of the mussels.*

MAKES 4 SERVINGS

2 cups white wine

2 pounds mussels, scrubbed

4 tablespoons Garlic Lemon Sauce (nước chấm) (page 274)

¾ cup canola oil

½ cup chopped scallions, green stalks only

4 tablespoons Roasted Peanuts (page 281)

1] Preheat the oven to 200°F.

2] Pour the wine into a large pot over medium heat and add 2 cups of water. Add the mussels to the pot, cover, and steam until they open. Remove the mussels and discard any that didn't open or have broken shells. Clean the grassy beards from the mussel shells.

3] Place the mussels on a baking pan and warm them in the oven for 5 minutes. Take them out and drizzle them with the nước chấm.

4] Meanwhile, heat the oil in a medium saucepan. Add the scallions and immediately turn off the heat. Pour the scallion oil over the mussels in the baking pan. Sprinkle with the roasted peanuts and serve hot.

Tofu and Fried Eggplant in Tía tô Leaves

THIS DISH WAS INSPIRED BY A SNACK MY MOTHER ENJOYED IN HER YOUTH. *Her eldest sister, Chu, was an amazing chef who loved to cut eggplant into long, thin strips, sort of like French fries, and fry them in a very hot wok. For our restaurant dish, my mother added baked tofu for protein and lots of fragrant herbs to lighten the dish.*

MAKES 4 TO 6 SERVINGS

5 tablespoons white rice flour

1 tablespoon sea salt

2 medium eggplants, cut into long, ⅔-inch-thick strips

Canola oil, for frying

3 garlic cloves, minced

2 ounces baked tofu, cut into long, ½-inch-thick strips

3 tablespoons House Sauce (page 276)

⅓ cup coarsely chopped fresh Thai basil

¼ cup coarsely chopped fresh Vietnamese perilla (tía tô) leaves

1) Put the rice flour on a small tray or in a shallow bowl and set it aside. Fill a large bowl with cold tap water, and stir in the salt. Soak the eggplant strips in the salt water for 5 minutes. Remove the strips, pat them dry, and then dredge them in the rice flour, coating them well and shaking off any excess.

2) Heat 2 inches of oil in a large skillet or wok over medium-high to high heat until a deep-frying or candy thermometer reads 350°F. Line a baking sheet with paper towels. In batches, add the coated eggplant strips and cook until golden, about 3 to 4 minutes, turning frequently with a long-handled spoon so they brown evenly. As they are finished cooking, remove the fried eggplant strips from the oil and transfer them to the prepared baking sheet to drain.

3) Place a new skillet over high heat and sauté the garlic for 1 minute. Add the baked tofu and sauté for 1 minute, then add the fried eggplant strips to the pan. Instead of stirring, which will break the tender eggplant strips, toss the pan three times, like you are flipping an egg or a pancake. Add the House Sauce and cook for 2 minutes, tossing the contents of the pan a few more times. Add the basil, toss one more time, and then transfer the eggplant, tofu, and basil to a plate. Garnish with tía tô leaves and serve hot.

NOTE: *To test if the oil is hot enough for frying, drop in one small piece of onion. If it turns golden and floats to the top in 5 seconds, then the oil is ready.*

THE SECRET TO DEEP FRYING

While it can seem daunting to submerge healthy vegetables into cooking oil, if you do it correctly, the oil will only crisp the food and not seep into it. The secret is to make sure your oil is hot enough for frying, and to presoak vegetables in salt water, which decreases the amount of oil that they can absorb. Hot oil will form a crust on the outside of food, while oil at lower temperatures will soak in and make food soggy.

Vietnamese Steak Tartare with Honey Truffle Dijon Sauce

THIS CRUSTACEAN DISH IS A FRENCH-STYLE STEAK TARTARE *with Vietnamese flavors. In Vietnam, we don't typically eat tartare; instead, Vietnamese carpaccio is king. My mother infused that traditional dish with European techniques by turning it into a tartare served with aioli. The aioli is lemongrass-flavored, and roasted rice powder adds a hint of the nutty smokiness found in Vietnamese carpaccio. If you'd like, serve sprinkled with roasted peanuts or hazelnuts.*

MAKES 4 SERVINGS

FOR THE SAUCE:

1¼ teaspoons honey

1¼ teaspoons Dijon mustard

½ teaspoon white truffle oil

FOR THE TARTARE:

2 tablespoons finely diced red onion

2 tablespoons capers, crushed

1 teaspoon finely sliced fresh Vietnamese coriander (rau răm) leaves

1 teaspoon chopped fresh chives

1 teaspoon roasted rice powder

1 tablespoon Lemongrass Dressing (page 280)

4 ounces filet mignon, cut into ¼-inch dice

1] Keep all the ingredients chilled until ready to use.

2] To make the sauce: In a small bowl, mix together the honey, mustard, and truffle oil until well blended. Taste the sauce and add more honey if needed.

3] To make the tartare: In a large bowl, add the onions, capers, rau răm, and chives. Sprinkle the rice powder over the top and mix well. Add the sauce and the Lemongrass Dressing to the bowl and mix well. Add the filet mignon and mix until thoroughly combined.

4] Serve the tartare with toasted crostini or shrimp crisps.

NOTE: *Eating raw meat is not recommended if you are elderly, pregnant, or have a compromised immune system.*

THE SECRET TO TARTARE: NEAT CUTS

For a successful tartare, aside from having high-quality meat, the shape of the solid ingredients is extremely important. Vegetables and meat alike should be diced into neat, uniform squares. This is accomplished by first slicing the ingredient into long, thin strips that resemble matchsticks—a julienne cut—and then cutting those sticks into even cubes. A small dice cut results in ¼-inch cubes (about the smallest you can get for meat); ⅛-inch cubes are called brunoise cuts, while ¹⁄₁₆-inch cubes are fine brunoise. The cutting takes time and patience, but more than anything it requires a good, sharp knife.

Salmon Tartare

ANOTHER POPULAR APPETIZER FROM OUR CRUSTACEAN MENU, *this dish showcases how French and Vietnamese cooking work so beautifully together. While lime, chili sauce, and fish sauce are hallmark flavors of Vietnam, mustard is not a traditional ingredient, however, my mother often uses it because she loves French cooking. The bites from the Vietnamese sauces are rounded out by the earthiness of the French mustard.*

Considered a delicacy in Asia, quail eggs have a stronger, slightly gamier flavor than chicken eggs. If you can't find any in your go-to Asian or specialty grocery store, check your local farmers' markets. In a pinch (or if you prefer), you can substitute the yolk from a small chicken egg.

MAKES 4 SERVINGS

FOR THE SUNDRIED
TOMATO PASTE:

¾ cup sundried tomatoes

1 tablespoon chopped fresh parsley

1 tablespoon chopped fresh basil

FOR THE TARTARE:

8 ounces fresh sushi-grade salmon, skinned and cut into ¼-inch dice (see note, page 224)

1 ounce anchovies (3 to 5 fillets), cut into ¼-inch dice

1 teaspoon freshly squeezed lime juice

1 tablespoon sweet chili sauce

1 tablespoon Dijon mustard

1 teaspoon Tabasco pepper sauce

1 teaspoon fish sauce

¼ teaspoon salt

¼ teaspoon freshly ground white pepper

¼ cup chopped red onion

2 tablespoons chopped scallions, inner white bulb only

4 quail egg yolks

1 Persian cucumber, sliced into half-moons

1 tablespoon capers

1 tablespoon minced fresh parsley

1 tablespoon chili oil

½ French baguette loaf, sliced

SPECIAL EQUIPMENT:

3-inch ring mold

1) To make the sundried tomato paste: In a food processor, purée the sundried tomatoes with the parsley and basil. Set aside.

2) To make the tartare: Add the salmon and anchovies to a large bowl. Pour in the lime juice and mix well to coat. Stir in the sweet chili sauce, Dijon, Tabasco, fish sauce, salt, and pepper. Add the red onions and scallions and toss well.

(Continued)

3] Place the ring mold on a plate and fill it with the salmon mixture, leaving a hole in the center. Remove the mold. Carefully place the egg yolk in the hole. Arrange the cucumber half-moons around the tartare. Sprinkle with the capers and parsley and drizzle with the chili oil.

4] Toast the baguette slices and top them with the sundried tomato paste. Serve with the tartare.

NOTE: *Eating raw meat or raw eggs is not recommended if you are elderly, pregnant, or have a compromised immune system.*

HOW TO BUY FRESH SALMON

If you've never had raw salmon before, this dish is a good introduction, as the lime juice cures the fish, giving it a refreshing, crisp finish. However, since the fish isn't cooked, it's imperative that you buy the best, freshest salmon you can find.

Good, fresh salmon will not smell "fishy" or like ammonia; if it even has a smell, it should be fresh and mild or slightly buttery. The flesh of fresh salmon should be firm and shiny, not dull. It should spring back when pressed; if it doesn't, keep looking. Finally, fresh salmon shouldn't have any discoloration or darkening around the edges.

The safest choice is to go to a reputable fish market and ask the fishmonger to help you pick a suitable fillet for tartare. Ideally, you want sushi-grade salmon as fresh as possible, since it's iced thoroughly as soon as it's caught.

6
sides

the perfect accompaniments

For me, cooking is about bringing people together. While we grew up eating together as a family, as we've now started families of our own, that precious time of gathering around the table to feast together is mostly reserved for special events and holidays. When we do get together, my grandmother Diana and my mother will still plan an elaborate menu, as they did in the past. However, now my sisters (who are all wonderful cooks in their own right) and I try and do all of the cooking to give my mother a break. "Try" is the operative word, though, as my mother doesn't like to sit still and will do her best to pop into the kitchen to see how we're faring.

Like our traditional appetizers and entrées, Vietnamese side dishes are also easy and flavorful, and appeal to all of the senses. Bright colors, wonderful aromas, crisp sounds, delicious tastes, and pleasing textures delight the eyes, ears, and nose while simultaneously appealing to our sense of taste and touch.

Vietnamese meals almost always include a vegetable side dish—whether raw or steamed, stir-fried or pickled. Here are nine of our favorite vegetable dishes, including one magical meat accompaniment, a fairy floss of crunchy protein that just might change your culinary life!

Candied Heirloom Carrots

THESE ROASTED CARROTS WITH ASIAN SPICES *make a wonderful vegetarian dish and are great with any kind of meat, especially roasted chicken or fish. We serve these at Thanksgiving with our Turkey Stuffed with Sticky Rice (page 137).*

MAKES 6 SERVINGS

⅓ cup extra-virgin olive oil

3 teaspoons freshly squeezed lime juice

3 teaspoons ground cumin

¼ teaspoon cayenne pepper

10 garlic cloves, crushed

¼ cup honey

¼ cup Garlic Lemon Sauce (page 274)

1 tablespoon unsalted butter

1 knob ginger, peeled and cut into long, thin strips

15 to 20 baby heirloom or young carrots, or 6 to 8 large carrots, unpeeled

1) Preheat the oven to 400°F.

2) In a medium bowl, mix the olive oil and lime juice with the ground cumin, cayenne pepper, and crushed garlic. Set aside.

3) In a medium saucepan over medium-low heat, combine the honey, garlic-lemon sauce, butter, and ginger. Bring the mixture to a simmer and cook, stirring frequently, until the ginger loses its sharpness, about 2 to 3 minutes. Remove the pan from the heat and set it aside.

4) Line a baking sheet with aluminum foil and place the carrots on the prepared baking sheet. Drizzle the olive oil–lime juice mixture over the carrots and transfer the baking sheet to the oven. Roast until the carrots are lightly browned and caramelized around the edges, about 15 minutes. Remove the baking sheet from the oven.

5) Drizzle the honey-ginger sauce over the carrots. Serve hot.

Wok-Tossed Water Spinach

POPULAR AND ABUNDANT IN VIETNAM, *water spinach is traditionally stir-fried in a wok to make rau muống xào chao. The high heat binds the flavorful sauce to the spinach and the quick cooking time makes this a great side dish. Water spinach can be chewy, however, so it's important to tear the pieces by hand and then roll them in your palms to help break down the plant's fibers before cooking. This recipe also works wonderfully with any other leafy green.*

We use shrimp paste, which does have a strong aroma, but don't shy away from this condiment. Just like anchovies or anchovy paste often used in Italian cooking, shrimp paste gives a sweetness and depth of flavor that fish sauce alone cannot do.

MAKES 2 TO 4 SERVINGS

1 tablespoon Homemade Chicken Broth (page 273) or store-bought low-sodium chicken broth

½ teaspoon shrimp paste

½ teaspoon salt

½ teaspoon sugar

2 tablespoons canola oil

10 garlic cloves, smashed

1 pound water spinach *(rau muống)*

1) Mix the chicken broth, shrimp paste, salt, and sugar together in a medium bowl. Set aside.

2) To prepare the water spinach: Twist off and discard the hard parts of the spinach, keeping only the tender partleaves. Tear the tender bits into 4-inch pieces and then lightly crush them between your palms.

3) Heat the oil in a wok or large skillet over high heat. Add the garlic and sauté until fragrant, about 2 minutes. Add the water spinach and toss vigorously for 2 minutes, then add the chicken broth mixture and toss for 1 more minute. The water spinach is done when it is al dente, or wilted but with a slight crunch.

Baby Bok Choy in Garlic Sauce

LIKE AMERICAN KIDS WITH PEAS OR GREEN BEANS, *children in Asian households grow up getting their regular vegetable fix from bok choy. The cabbage-like vegetable tastes like sweet, nutty spinach. Baby bok choy is more tender than full-grown bok choy, and with my mother's garlic sauce recipe, it makes a quick, simple, and delicious side to any meal. This recipe is also great with other leafy green vegetables like spinach.*

MAKES 2 TO 4 SERVINGS

8 ounces (about 5 heads)
baby bok choy

1 teaspoon oyster sauce

½ teaspoon fish sauce

½ teaspoon Maggi seasoning sauce

1 tablespoon minced garlic

½ teaspoon sugar

1 tablespoon unsalted butter

½ teaspoon sesame oil (optional)

1) Rinse the bok choy well to remove any dirt or sand stuck in the leaves. Trim off any brown root ends, and then cut the bok choy in half lengthwise.

2) Bring a large pot of water to a boil. Fill a large bowl with ice water and set it nearby. Add the bok choy and blanch, cooking until they turn bright green, about 40 seconds. Drain the bok choy and immediately transfer it to the ice water bath to stop the cooking. Drain the bok choy once more and set it aside on a plate.

3) In a medium bowl, mix together the oyster sauce, fish sauce, Maggi seasoning sauce, garlic, sesame oil (if using), and sugar.

4) Place a wok or large skillet over medium heat. Add the sauce mixture and stir in the butter. Add the bok choy and cook, tossing repeatedly, until the bok choy is heated through, about 2 to 3 minutes. Serve hot.

Pickled Vegetables

PICKLING VEGETABLES, A TIME-HONORED TRADITION, *served two important purposes in Vietnam: it prolonged the edible life of fresh produce and it allowed cooks to work with vegetables even when they weren't in season. Of course, it also made the vegetables taste amazing. Pickling gives food a refreshing taste and balances out other strong flavor profiles: for instance, pickled vegetables pair well with a salty dish like caramelized black cod.*
    We always have something pickling in our kitchen. Here's how to make our favorite preserves.

PICKLING BRINE

MAKES ABOUT 3 QUARTS

1 quart white vinegar

4¼ cups sugar

1 teaspoon sea salt

1) In a glass mixing bowl that can hold at least 4 quarts of liquid, mix the vinegar with 2 quarts of warm water. Add the sugar and salt and stir until they dissolve.

NOTE: *Tap water is fine to use unless you have hard water. If so, use purified water instead.*

NOTE: *Be sure to use sea salt without any additives, as certain chemicals can make the brine cloudy.*

PICKLED CAULIFLOWER

MAKES 2 PINTS

1 head cauliflower

Pickling Brine (above)

SPECIAL EQUIPMENT:

Canning jars or tempered-glass containers with lids, sanitized

1) Break the cauliflower into bite-size pieces.

2) Bring a large pot of water to a boil. Fill a large bowl with ice water and set it nearby. Add the cauliflower and boil for 20 seconds. Drain the cauliflower and immediately transfer it to the ice water bath to stop the cooking. Drain again.

3) Divide the cauliflower among glass jars or containers. Pour the pickling brine into the jars, covering the cauliflower completely but stopping within ½ inch of the top of the jars. Place the lids on the jars or containers and refrigerate for at least 24 hours before serving. Pickled cauliflower can be kept in the refrigerator for up to a month.

PICKLED CARROTS

MAKES 5 PINTS

5 pounds carrots, peeled

5 tablespoons sugar

Pickling Brine [page 237]

SPECIAL EQUIPMENT:

Canning jars or tempered-glass containers with lids, sanitized

1] Cut the carrots into ⅛-inch-thick rounds. Place the carrot slices in a large bowl.

2] Sprinkle the sugar on top of the carrots, tossing well to coat. Set the bowl aside on the counter and let the carrots marinate for 2 hours.

3] Drain the carrots and discard any accumulated juices.

4] Divide the marinated carrots among glass jars or containers. Pour the pickling brine into the jars, covering the carrots completely but stopping within ½ inch of the top of the jars. Place the lids on the jars or containers and refrigerate for at least 24 hours before serving. Pickled carrots can be kept in the refrigerator for up to 1 month.

VARIATION: *For Pickled Daikon Radish: Replace carrots with daikon radish in steps above, however, make sure that the daikon is thoroughly dried and all water is squeezed out before placing in the brine. Pickled daikon keeps crisp for just 5 days.*

A TIME-SAVING TIP FOR PEELING CARROTS

While you may be inclined to peel carrots over a compost bin or trash can, which is fine for one or two carrots, restaurant cooks know this process has its pitfalls. For one, you risk dropping the carrot and wasting the food (which we never like!). And two, it wastes time, which can add up when you have pounds of carrots to peel.

Even though most standard handheld vegetable peelers have a double-sided blade, most people peeling over an open container only use one side as they swipe downwards, lift the blade back to the top, and swipe again. You can cut peeling time in half by using both blades. Here's how:

Take one carrot and hold it at a 45-degree angle over a cutting board with the bottom tip resting on the board. Starting halfway down the carrot, slide the blade down toward the tip then back up again without lifting your blade. Continue this up-and-down motion, rotating the carrot until the bottom half is peeled. Now turn the carrot over and repeat with the top half.

PICKLED CHAYOTE

MAKES 3 PINTS

4 chayote, peeled

3 garlic cloves, sliced

1 teaspoon salt

Pickling Brine (page 237)

SPECIAL EQUIPMENT:

Canning jars or tempered-glass containers with lids, sanitized

1) Cut the chayote into 3 x ½-inch strips (the size of your index finger) and put them in a large bowl. Fill the bowl with water, mix in the salt, and let the chayote marinate at room temperature for 10 minutes.

2) Drain the chayote and rinse it well under cold water.

3) Divide the chayote among glass jars or containers. Pour the pickling brine into the jars, covering the chayote completely but stopping within ½ inch of the top of the jars. Place the lids on the jars or containers and refrigerate for at least 2 days before serving. Pickled chayote can be kept in the refrigerator for up to a week.

PICKLED MUSTARD GREENS

MAKES 3 PINTS

FOR THE PICKLING BRINE:

1 cup rice vinegar

1 cup sugar

½ teaspoon sea salt

5 pounds (about 2 bunches) mustard greens

5 tablespoons sugar

1 tablespoon salt

SPECIAL EQUIPMENT:

Canning jars or tempered-glass containers with lids, sanitized

1) To make the brine: In a glass mixing bowl that can hold at least 4 quarts of liquid, mix the rice vinegar with 2 quarts of warm water. Add the sugar and salt and stir until they dissolve. Set aside.

2) Chop the mustard greens into 2-inch pieces and put them in a large bowl.

3) Sprinkle the sugar and salt on top of the mustard greens; toss well to coat. Set the bowl aside and let the mustard greens marinate at room temperature for 1 hour.

4) Drain any excess liquid from the mustard greens and discard any accumulated juices.

5) Divide the mustard greens among glass jars or containers. Pour the pickling brine into the jars, covering the mustard greens completely but stopping within ½ inch of the top of the jars. Place the lids on the jars or containers and refrigerate for at least 3 hours before serving. Pickled mustard greens can be kept in the refrigerator for up to 1 month.

PICKLED CUCUMBERS

MAKES 2 PINTS

20 Persian cucumbers

3 tablespoons sugar

Pickling Brine (page 237)

SPECIAL EQUIPMENT:

Canning jars or tempered-glass containers with lids, sanitized

1] Cut the cucumbers in half lengthwise and scoop out and discard the soft seed-filled centers. Cut the seeded cucumbers into 1½-inch-thick half-moons and put them in a large bowl.

2] Sprinkle the sugar on top of the cucumbers, tossing well to coat. Set the bowl aside and let the cucumbers marinate at room temperature for 30 minutes.

3] Drain the cucumbers and then squeeze out any excess liquid. Discard any accumulated juices.

4] Divide the cucumbers among glass jars or containers. Pour the pickling brine into the jars, covering the cucumbers completely but stopping within ½ inch of the top of the jars. Place the lids on the jars or containers and refrigerate for at least 24 hours before serving. Pickled cucumbers can be kept in the refrigerator for up to 4 days.

Oven-Roasted Curried Cauliflower

ROASTING VEGETABLES IS MORE OF A FRENCH TECHNIQUE *than a common Vietnamese method of cooking, but my mother fused the two using Asian flavors. This side dish is easy to make and great to throw in the oven and not worry about—perfect for when you're entertaining and don't want to be in the kitchen missing your guests. You can of course use just white cauliflower, but the multi-colored veggies are so much more aesthetically appealing, and they can even be a great conversation starter!*

MAKES 6 SERVINGS

1 head yellow cauliflower

1 head purple cauliflower

1 head green cauliflower

1 tablespoon Madras curry powder

2 teaspoons ground cumin

2 teaspoons ground turmeric

1 teaspoon five-spice powder (see note, page 175)

½ teaspoon ground cinnamon

3 tablespoons plus 2 teaspoons extra-virgin olive oil, divided

1 shallot, julienned

1 garlic clove, finely grated

Kosher salt

Zest of 2 lemons

⅛ teaspoon crushed red pepper

1) Preheat the oven to 400°F.

2) Clean the heads of cauliflower, cut them into bite-sized florets, and put them in a large bowl.

3) In a new medium bowl, mix together the curry powder, cumin, turmeric, five spice powder, and cinnamon.

4) Drizzle 3 tablespoons of the olive oil over the cauliflower, add the spice mix, and toss to coat. Transfer the seasoned cauliflower to a baking pan and roast until the cauliflower reaches your desired tenderness, 7 to 10 minutes.

5) Meanwhile, heat the remaining 2 teaspoons of oil in a small saucepan over medium heat. Add the shallots and garlic and sauté until fragrant, about 2 minutes. Remove the pan from the heat and set aside.

6) Remove the cauliflower from the oven, add the sautéed garlic and shallots, lemon zest, and crushed red pepper to the baking pan, and toss well. Taste the cauliflower and adjust the seasonings with more olive oil and salt to taste. Serve hot.

Shredded Chicken [Ruốc]

SINCE MY MOTHER'S FAMILY HAD TO MOVE A LOT DURING THE WARS, *ruốc was one food they made in large batches and always had on hand because it is full of protein and does not spoil easily. The closest thing I can think of in American cuisine to the classic staple of Vietnamese shredded meat [ruốc] is jerky, but only because they are both dried meats that last a long time. Like jerky, ruốc is great as a fast snack on the go, but unlike jerky, it's sprinkled over other dishes such as rice, porridge, or even sandwiches. The stovetop drying process turns the meat into a salty-sweet sensation with a fluffy, cottony texture that you can add to any other dish or as I discovered can be eaten with white rice and two sunny-side-up eggs for an ideal meal any time of day.*

MAKES 8 SERVINGS

2 (8-ounce) boneless, skinless chicken breasts

1 cup Homemade Chicken Broth [page 273] or store-bought low-sodium chicken broth

3 tablespoons fish sauce

3 tablespoons sugar

1 teaspoon freshly ground white pepper

1 tablespoon canola oil

1 teaspoon salted butter

1] Put the chicken breasts and chicken broth in a medium pot over medium heat and bring the broth to a boil. Add the fish sauce, sugar, and white pepper, reduce the heat to low, and poach the chicken for 10 minutes, then cover the pot, and remove it from the heat, letting it cool down. Remove the chicken breasts from the pot, reserving the broth mixture.

2] Once the chicken breasts are cool enough to handle, cut each breast along the grain into ten small pieces. Place one chicken piece into a large mortar or bowl, and smash it along the grain with a pestle. Repeat with all of the pieces, shredding any bigger chunks by hand. [You can also use a food processor to shred the chicken.]

3] Heat the oil in a large skillet over medium heat. Add the shredded chicken and, using a wooden spoon, stir in a circular motion for 5 minutes, pressing the chicken down into the skillet. Reduce the heat to low and add 1 teaspoon of the reserved poaching liquid, continuing to press the chicken down with the wooden spoon. Once the chicken is relatively dry, add another teaspoon of the poaching liquid and repeat the process. When the broth is gone and the shredded chicken is completely dry, add the butter and press it into the chicken for 1 minute. The chicken will be slightly toasted.

4] Serve the dried chicken over rice or porridge, or on a buttered baguette.

NOTE: Ruốc can be stored unrefrigerated for two weeks. It will last for one month if stored in an airtight container in the refrigerator.

7

desserts

creating sweet memories

I n the early years of our restaurants, we couldn't afford a pastry chef, so my mother and grandmother and even my father experimented to create new desserts. Our home kitchen bubbled with the smell of banana breads, chè, and French pastries. My sisters and I were the lucky ones who tested each dish and gave the thumbs up or down. Even today, there is a friendly debate about who in the family gets the credit for our popular home desserts.

In my family, desserts are more than just the sweet ending to a fabulous meal. They are a composition of memories from our past. Each dessert carries a story about the inspiration behind it or the memory of how the final recipe came to be. Here are some of our favorite desserts, a mix of family classics and restaurant favorites.

Coconut Cake with Strawberry Sauce

STRAIGHT FROM OUR RESTAURANT DESSERT MENU, *these beautiful individual cakes hold layer after layer of surprises: a double coating of sugared rum syrup and luscious coconut cream filling on the inside and homemade frosting with two kinds of coconut flakes on the outside. You can make the strawberry sauce just before serving, or you can make it the day before and store it in the refrigerator.*

The secret to perfectly whipped frosting is to use a metal bowl and metal whisk that have been pre-chilled in the freezer, and to keep the heavy cream cold in the refrigerator until the moment you are ready to use it.

MAKES 24 MINI CAKES

FOR THE RUM SYRUP:

2 cups (300 grams) sugar

1 teaspoon Bacardi rum (optional)

FOR THE FILLING:

6 (12-ounce) cans coconut milk

3 (14-ounce) cans sweetened condensed milk

¾ cup (100 grams) cornstarch

Juice of ½ lemon

FOR THE FROSTING:

1 quart heavy cream

1 tablespoon powdered sugar

FOR THE STRAWBERRY SAUCE:

1 cup fresh strawberries

1 cup corn syrup or ½ cup sugar

FOR THE CAKE:

9 large eggs

1½ cups sugar

2½ cups (250 grams) cake flour

1 cup unsweetened coconut flakes

1 cup sweetened coconut flakes

Special equipment: 2½-inch plain round biscuit cutter

1] Preheat the oven to 350°F. Line a 18x26 sheet pan or two half sheet pans (18x13) with parchment paper.

2] To make the rum syrup: Bring 4 cups of water to a boil. Add the sugar and cook, stirring regularly, until it dissolves. Remove the pan from the heat and stir in the rum. Set aside.

3] To make the coconut cream filling: In a large pot, combine the coconut milk, condensed milk, cornstarch, and lemon juice over high heat. Bring the liquid to a boil and cook, stirring constantly, until the mixture thickens to a custard-like consistency. Remove the pot from the heat and set aside.

4] To make the frosting: In the bowl of an electric mixer fitted with the whip attachment, beat the heavy cream until firm peaks appear. Carefully fold in the powdered sugar with a rubber spatula or wooden spoon. Cover and refrigerate until ready to use.

(Continued)

5 ⌋ To make the strawberry sauce: Combine the strawberries and corn syrup in a medium pot over low heat. Cook until the strawberries are very soft, 15 to 20 minutes. Remove the pot from the heat and allow the strawberry mixture to cool. Once cooled, blend the mixture in a food processor or blender and then strain the sauce through a fine-mesh sieve into a clean bowl. Cover and refrigerate until ready to use.

6 ⌋ To make the sponge cake: In the bowl of an electric mixer fitted with the paddle attachment, combine the eggs and sugar. Beat well. Fold in the cake flour and mix until just combined. Pour the cake batter into the prepared baking sheet. Increase the oven temperature to 450°F. Put the baking sheet in the oven, and bake the cake for 5-6 minutes until lightly golden; do not overbake. Remove the baking sheet from the oven and set it aside to cool. Once the cake as cooled, use a 2¾-inch diameter biscuit cutter to cut it into 48 circles.

7 ⌋ To assemble the cakes: Brush the top of one cake circle with rum syrup, and then spoon on a 1½-inch layer of coconut cream filling. Place a second cake circle on top of the coconut cream and brush the top with more rum syrup. Repeat with the rest of the cake circles, syrup, and filling, making twenty-three more cakes. Set the cakes aside overnight in the refrigerator so the cream can harden.

8 ⌋ Cover the entire cake—the top and sides—with frosting. Repeat with the other twenty-three cakes. Mix the coconut flakes together in a large, shallow bowl and roll the cakes in the coconut flakes. Serve the cakes drizzled with the strawberry sauce.

NOTE: *For this recipe, we preheat the oven at 350°F, then raise it to 450°F for baking so the sponge cake doesn't burn before the inside is cooked.*

Vietnamese Yogurt

ADDICTIVE IS THE ONLY WORD TO DESCRIBE MY MOTHER'S YOGURT. *Unlike Greek or American yogurt, Vietnamese yogurt is lighter in texture and slightly sweet and tart. While people today use special low-heat incubating machines, my mother's method is very basic: she just puts the yogurt jars in a hot tray of water in the oven, where they stay nice and warm while they set. Another one of her tips: she saved our baby food jars for storing the yogurt, since they were the perfect serving size.*

MAKES ABOUT 16 SMALL SERVINGS

5¼ cups (42 ounces) whole milk

1 (14-ounce) can sweetened condensed milk

1 cup all-natural plain yogurt

Special equipment: 4- or 8-ounce canning jars or tempered-glass containers with lids, sanitized

1) Pour 1¾ cups of water into a large bowl. Add the whole milk, condensed milk, and yogurt and mix well. Strain the yogurt mixture through a fine-mesh sieve into a clean bowl. Pour the strained mixture into the jars, stopping ½ to 1 inch from the top. Place the jars on a deep-sided tray.

2) Bring 12 cups of water to a boil. Once it boils, remove it from the heat and set it aside to cool until it's no longer bubbling, about 2 minutes.

3) Pour the hot water into the tray of jars. Do not submerge the jars in water; the water should be at the yogurt line or a little above, but no more. Screw lids on the jars or use foil to cover the pan if your jars do not have lids.

4) Place the tray of yogurt jars in the oven for 8 hours to allow the yogurt to set.

5) Refrigerate the yogurt and serve cold.

Vietnamese Affogato

ON THE SURFACE, AFFOGATO IS A VERY SIMPLE DESSERT—*just two primary ingredients—yet everyone has their own way of personalizing it. Some people use a specialty ice cream or finish it off with chocolate or nutty toppings, while others add a shot of amaretto or hazelnut liqueur. My father is the inspiration behind our version of affogato, as he prefers using Vietnamese coffee rather than espresso and adding a touch of sweetened condensed milk, as in café sua, a Vietnamese coffee recipe.*

Vietnamese coffee is known for its intense, dark roast—a perfect balance to the cool ice cream and sweet condensed milk.

MAKES 1 SERVING

2 scoops vanilla bean ice cream

2½ tablespoons ground Vietnamese coffee

1 tablespoon sweetened condensed milk

Special equipment: Vietnamese coffee filter or metal drip filter

1) Two hours before serving: Scoop the ice cream into a heat-tolerant glassware cup or small bowl and place it in the freezer.

2) When ready to serve: Boil 2 cups of water in a kettle and then remove the kettle from the heat. Add the ground coffee to a stainless steel Vietnamese coffee filter and gently tap the sides of the filter with a spoon to settle the coffee evenly. Attach a filter insert on top of the coffee grounds.

3) Place the coffee filter on top of a coffee cup and slowly pour two tablespoons of the hot water from the kettle into the filter to wet the coffee grounds. Wait about 30 seconds for the initial pour to drain, and then fill the coffee filter with the hot water to near the top of the filter; discard the excess water.

4) Place a lid on the coffee filter and allow the coffee to brew until it stops dripping from the filter, about 4 minutes. Remove the filter.

5) Retrieve the glass or bowl of ice cream from the freezer and drizzle the condensed milk over top. Pour the coffee over the ice cream, or pour it into a mug to serve alongside. Serve immediately.

Banana Pudding with Tapioca Pearls and Coconut Milk

MY AUNT BAC TRANG, MY MOTHER'S SISTER, *was unable to escape when Southern Vietnam fell to the Communists. With her home lost and her possessions confiscated, she turned to cooking to support her family of eight children. She hoped that she might be able to make a living if she went door-to-door selling her wonderful homemade desserts. Happily, she did more than just get by. She did so well, in fact, that even today her desserts are still served in Saigon.*

Bac Trang was famous for her version of this dish, called chè chuối chưng in Vietnamese. Chuối is Vietnamese for "banana;" chưng roughly means "infused with flavor;" and chè is the word given to our delicious sweet soups and dessert stews. Chè is slightly thinner than pudding and can be served in a bowl and eaten with a spoon or in a glass as a beverage. Chè is infinitely customizable, and there is a street food market in Saigon that has a whole section of just chè vendors.

This is one of our favorite versions of chè to make at home. You'll know the tapioca balls are cooked when they turn translucent. Just be careful not to pop them when stirring or they'll flavor the chè too early.

MAKES 4 TO 6 SERVINGS

5 bananas

3 cups coconut milk

4 tablespoons small tapioca pearls

2 tablespoons sugar

3 tablespoons sweetened condensed milk

1 teaspoon freshly squeezed lime juice

4 cups water

4 teaspoons crushed Roasted Peanuts (page 281), for garnish

4 teaspoons finely ground toasted sesame seeds, for garnish

1) Peel and cut each banana in half lengthwise, then cut them into 2-inch pieces and place them in a large bowl. Sprinkle with 2 tablespoons of the sugar and let the bananas sit at room temperature for 15 minutes.

2) Bring 4 cups of water to a boil in a large pot over high heat. Add the tapioca pearls and reduce the heat to medium. Stir gently for a couple of minutes. Reduce the heat to low and continue to simmer uncovered for 20 minutes, stirring every couple of minutes so that the tapioca pearls do not stick to the bottom of the pot and burn. The pearls are finished when they are translucent.

3) Add the sweetened bananas, condensed milk, coconut milk, and lime juice to the pot, and continue to simmer uncovered for 10 minutes, stirring constantly. Remove the pot from the heat.

4) Serve the pudding hot or at room temperature with roasted peanuts and sesame seeds.

Crème Caramel

MY GRANDMOTHER, HAVING LIVED IN FRANCE *while my father studied abroad in Paris as a teen, was a connoisseur and student of French cooking. It's no surprise that my father and grandfather loved French desserts—my grandmother loved making them. One of their favorites was crème caramel, also known as flan or caramel pudding. My sister Cathy and I used to help my grandmother make the custard dessert when we were little, one of us stirring the caramel pot while the other stirred the custard bowl.*

MAKES 12 SERVINGS

2½ cups sugar, divided

6 eggs plus 1 egg white

2 cups whole milk

2 cups heavy cream

¼ teaspoon vanilla extract

Special equipment: 12 (4-ounce) ramekins or mini metal cake tins

1] Preheat the oven to 325°F.

2] To make the caramel: Put 1 cup of sugar and ¼ cup of water in a small pot over medium heat. Cook, stirring constantly until the sugar turns golden brown. Remove the pot from the heat and divide the caramel evenly among the ramekins, tilting the cups to create a nice thin layer of caramel at the bottom.

3] To make the custard: In a large bowl, combine the eggs and the remaining 1½ cups of sugar. Gently stir until the egg yolks are blended and the sugar has dissolved. Add the milk, heavy cream, and vanilla to the bowl and gently stir until all of the ingredients are incorporated. Strain the custard through a fine-mesh sieve into a clean bowl, then divide it evenly among the ramekins.

4] Bring a large pot of water to a boil. Place the ramekins in a large roasting pan. Fill the pan with boiling water up to about ¼ the height of ramekins, and cover the whole pan with foil. Put the roasting pan in the oven and bake for 25 to 30 minutes (see note).

NOTE: *Every oven is different, but flan is delicate and can't take too much heat. To prevent overcooking, check the flan with a toothpick after 25 minutes of baking (or less if your oven runs really hot). If a toothpick inserted into the flan comes out clean, the flan is ready. If the toothpick comes out wet, then cook the flan for 5 more minutes.*

Rum-Soaked Vietnamese Banana Cake

NOTHING MAKES A KITCHEN SMELL MORE INVITING THAN A FRESHLY BAKED BANANA CAKE, *and my sisters and I always loved when my mother made this for us. It was the ultimate comfort food and a delicious snack, and now it's great for weekend afternoon tea with friends. There's no better use for day-old baguettes or slightly-past-their-peak bananas, in my opinion.*

MAKES 12 SERVINGS

12 ripe bananas

2 cups sugar

¼ cup Bacardi rum

1½ cups whole milk

1 (12-ounce) can coconut milk

1 French baguette

½ cup unsalted butter, melted

1] Peel the bananas and cut them at an angle into ⅛-inch diagonal slices. Place them in a large bowl. Cover with the sugar and rum and set aside to marinate for 30 minutes.

2] Meanwhile, in another large bowl, mix together the milk and coconut milk. Cut the baguette into ¼-inch slices and press them into the milk; let the bread soak at room temperature for 10 minutes.

3] Preheat the oven to 300°F.

4] Line the bottom of a 12 x 8-inch baking pan with a single layer of the soaked bread slices. Top with a layer of marinated banana slices. Repeat the process with all of the bread and banana slices, ending with banana on top. Bake for 1 hour. To test for doneness, insert a toothpick into the center of the cake; it's ready when the toothpick comes out clean.

5] Remove the cake from the oven and spread the butter on top. Bake for 5 more minutes until golden brown. Serve warm.

8

drinks

libations for any meal

Whether you own a restaurant or are hosting a party at home, having good drinks is just as important as having good food for your guests. To ensure success, your drinks should pair well with your food, they shouldn't be too strong, and like in all other cuisine, they should be made with as many fresh ingredients as possible.

Since almost every cook has a kitchen garden in Vietnam, plucking a fresh sprig of mint to muddle into a sparkling limeade or a picking an orange right off the tree for a freshly squeezed flavored iced tea is common practice. My Grandmother Diana continued this tradition when she moved to San Francisco. Since my family lived with my grandparents until I was nine, I was lucky enough to be able to help my grandmother with her garden. She had an amazing rose garden with roses that would bloom to the size of large rice bowl, kumquat trees, and a variety of Vietnamese herbs and vegetables that were otherwise hard to find in San Francisco at that time.

While San Francisco is not known for its warm weather, at the end of September and early October there is an "Indian Summer" of beautiful warm weather which, if we were lucky, would last for two weeks. During those warm lazy days, the fog that hangs over the Sunset district dis-sipates, and my grandmother's house which faces the ocean would get incredibly hot. My grandmother was always one to experiment and loved to make things from scratch. She mixed sparkling soda with freshly squeezed kumquat and orange juice, brown sugar and minced tía tô leaves and poured the concoction over a tall glass of ice. Without realizing it, she created her own version of a virgin mojito. While not much of a drinker, she enjoyed making her own wine, fermenting grapes, peaches, pears, persimmons, lychees, and other fruits especially for holidays. These are fond memories and traditions that I plan to pass on to my children.

Here are some of our favorite drinks—both alcoholic and non—from our home and our restaurants. As with our food, we hope that you, like Grandmother Diana, use them as a base and then experiment, creating your own perfect libations.

DECONSTRUCTED
WHITE RUSSIAN
with
VIETNAMESE
COFFEE MARTINI

LAVENDER
MOJITO

PEAR FUSION

THE FRANKIE

DARK AND
STORMY

THE BEVERLY

alcoholic

Lavender Mojito

LAVENDER HAS A PLEASANT, FLORAL FRAGRANCE, *so most people are surprised to know that it gives a slight peppery kick when added to food and drinks. Infusing lavender into simple syrup and muddling it with black-berries and mint leaves creates a mojito-style concoction that is sweet with a mild bite. It is a refreshing drink to be enjoyed year round, especially in hot summer months.*

A sprig of mint usually refers to a stem of mint with 3 or 4 leaves, but you can substitute a sprig with 6 to 8 loose mint leaves. This recipe uses leaves for the drink and a sprig for the garnish.

MAKES 1 DRINK

5 organic blackberries

2 ounces white rum

1 ounce freshly squeezed lime juice

1 ounce lavender syrup

6 to 8 fresh mint leaves

2 ounces sparkling soda

1 sprig fresh mint, for garnish

1〕 In a cocktail shaker, muddle three of the blackberries with the white rum, lime juice, lavender syrup, and mint leaves. Add the sparkling soda and ice. Shake hard for a few seconds.

2〕 Strain the cocktail into a highball glass filled with ice. Garnish with the remaining blackberries on a toothpick and the fresh sprig of mint.

Mint is one of those herbs that's easy to grow at home and best when picked fresh from the plant. In my New York apartment, I used a window planter of mint, basil, rosemary, and thyme to produce the freshest herbs for all of my dishes and drinks.

Pear Fusion

PEAR AND ELDERFLOWER FLAVORS COMBINE IN THIS CRISP AND CLEAN COCKTAIL *that is a mainstay at our Crustacean Beverly Hills restaurant. There are more than ten varieties of pears, each with its own unique flavor profile. Many (Comice, Seckel, Forelle) go well raw with wine and cheese, while others (Green Bartlett) should only be baked, canned, or processed for the best flavor. In our Pear Fusion, we prefer to use the Asian pear for its sweet flavor and ability to hold up as a garnish in the drink. If you can't find Asian pears at your grocery store, try a Comice, Green Anjou, or Seckel pear instead.*

MAKES 1 DRINK

½ Asian pear, cut into ⅛-inch-thick slices

1 ounce simple syrup

2 ounces Grey Goose La Poire Vodka

1 ounce Saint Germain liqueur

¾ ounce freshly squeezed lemon juice

1) Muddle 3 slices of pear and the simple syrup in a cocktail shaker. Add ice, then pour in the vodka, Saint Germain, and lemon juice. Shake hard for 10 seconds.

2) Fine strain the cocktail into a coupe glass. Garnish by floating a pear slice over the drink.

Dark and Stormy

IN THE EARLY DAYS OF THANH LONG, *my father was heavily involved in all areas of the restaurant, including the bar menu. He loved to experiment with cocktails by adding a twist of his own so that they paired well with my mother's dishes. While the official "Dark 'N Stormy" is a highball cocktail that originated in Bermuda and is traditionally made with Gosling's Black Seal Rum and Gosling's Stormy Ginger Beer, my father added a splash of lime and ginger juice to give it a tangy, warm finish. This popular drink is still on our menus today.*

MAKES 1 DRINK

4 ounces ginger beer

1 ounce simple syrup

½ ounce freshly squeezed lime juice

½ ounce ginger juice

2 ounces Gosling's black rum

1 lime wedge, for garnish

1) Fill a highball glass three-fourths full with ice cubes. Pour the ginger beer, simple syrup, lime juice, and ginger juice over the ice. Stir gently to mix.

2) Slowly float the dark rum into the glass, creating a perfect dark and stormy look. Garnish with the lime wedge.

Deconstructed White Russian with Vietnamese Coffee Martini

ADDING VIETNAMESE COFFEE AND CONDENSED MILK TO THE CLASSIC WHITE RUSSIAN *adds another level of bittersweet yin-yang balance, and the coffee gives the drink a little kick that makes this one of my favorites. You can mix the cream and condensed milk into the drink if you wish, but I prefer to layer the liquids. Deconstructed, this drink looks great and has a sweet finishing taste.*

MAKES 1 DRINK

¼ ounce sweetened condensed milk

2 ounces vodka

1 ounce black Vietnamese Coffee [*café den*], chilled (see variation, page 269)

1 ounce coffee liqueur

1½ ounces heavy whipping cream

1] Pour the condensed milk into a martini glass and set aside.

2] Pour the vodka, chilled coffee, and coffee liqueur into a cocktail shaker filled halfway with ice cubes. Shake well for 10 seconds and then strain the mixture into the martini glass over the back of a spoon to create a second layer above the condensed milk.

3] Add the cream to a clean cocktail shaker and shake for 10 seconds until fluffy. Float a thin layer of the cream into the martini glass to top the drink. Enjoy the drink in its deconstructed state or mix before consuming.

The Beverly

MOST MAJOR CITIES HAVE A COCKTAIL TO CALL THEIR OWN. *There's the Parisian, the London Buck, the Singapore Sling, and of course the Manhattan. Los Angeles was without a cocktail of its own until Crustacean created The Beverly in 2008 to celebrate being in Beverly Hills for more than ten years. This fashionably pink cocktail delivers warm citrus notes from the fresh juices, and the peach vodka imparts a smooth finish. Since the unveiling of this cocktail, other Beverly Hills restaurants have added The Beverly to their menu—and now you can, too!*

MAKES 1 DRINK

2 ounces peach vodka

¼ ounce freshly squeezed lemon juice

¼ ounce freshly squeezed lime juice

¾ ounce freshly squeezed orange juice

¾ ounce pomegranate juice

¾ ounce simple syrup

Twist of lime peel, to garnish

1] Add all the ingredients to a cocktail shaker filled with ice cubes. Shake hard for 10 seconds.

2] Strain into a coupe glass. Garnish with the twist of lime peel.

SIMPLE SYRUP

Instead of adding granulated sugar to a drink for sweetness, simple syrup is a liquid in which sugar has already been dissolved. You can buy simple syrup at most liquor stores, or make your own. Here's how:
Add 1 cup of granulated sugar to 1 cup of water in a medium pot over medium heat. Stir until the sugar dissolves. Bring the sugared water to a boil, then reduce the heat to medium and simmer for 3 minutes. Pour the simple syrup into a bowl and set in a second bowl of ice to chill. Simple syrup can be stored in the refrigerator in an airtight container for up to 2 weeks.

The Frankie

SPICY AND FRUITY, WITH ITS RICH, GOLDEN COLOR, FRESH CITRUS SCENT, *and oversized ice cube, The Frankie is a simple drink that adds sophistication to any home bar. Its roots are in the Vieux Carré French Quarter cocktail that Crustacean Beverly Hills reinvented as The Frankie. Unlike other rye whiskey cocktails that call for simple syrup, The Frankie uses sweet vermouth and Bénédictine liqueur for sweetness.*

MAKES 1 DRINK

1 ounce rye whiskey

1 ounce Armagnac

½ ounce sweet vermouth

½ ounce Bénédictine liqueur

3 dashes Angustora bitters

Orange peel, for garnish

Large ice cube or ice sphere

1) Pour all the ingredients into a crystal beaker filled with ice. Stir gently for 10 seconds. Put a large ice cube or ice sphere into a rocks glass strain the cocktail over the ice.

2) Twist an orange peel over the drink to release oils, rub it around the rim of the glass, and then drop it into the drink as a garnish.

non-alcoholic

Sparkling Kumquat Limeade

CALLED CHANH SO DA IN VIETNAMESE, OR "LIME SODA," *this naturally refreshing caffeine-free drink can be found in almost every restaurant in Vietnam. It consists of lime juice, soda water, and crushed sugar. Since my grandmother has a huge kumquat tree in her backyard, she adds kumquat to this classic. She always made sparkling kumquat limeade for her grandchildren on warm summer days, and I loved the tangy, crushed-sugar taste. You can add more or less sugar depending on your personal sweetness preference.*

MAKES 1 DRINK

3 ounces freshly squeezed lime juice

1 ounce freshly squeezed kumquat juice

2 tablespoons sugar, plus more to taste

Sparkling soda water

Lime twist, for garnish

1 sprig fresh mint, for garnish

1) Add the lime juice, kumquat juice, and sugar to a cocktail shaker. Muddle together to crush the sugar crystals into the juice. Add crushed ice and fill with sparkling soda water. Shake well for 10 seconds.

2) Strain into a tumbler glass filled with ice. Garnish with a lime twist and mint sprig.

Corn Silk Tea

VIETNAMESE PEOPLE DON'T LIKE TO WASTE ANY PART OF AN ANIMAL OR PLANT, *in their food or in their drinks. As such, even the silk on corn, usually discarded in America, is used to steep a special tea that the women in my family have been making for generations. Corn silk tea has many health benefits, including diuretic and anti-in-flammatory properties, and it can help eliminate toxins from the body. Adding sugar or agave syrup and ice makes this a surprisingly refreshing drink to complement your next barbeque.*

Use organic, pesticide-free corn so that the tea is free from toxins that might otherwise have accumulated on the corn silk.

MAKES 4 SERVINGS

Silk from 4 ears of fresh organic sweet corn

Sugar or agave syrup to taste (optional)

1) Place the silk in a medium pot. Add 6 cups of water and bring it to a boil over high heat, then reduce the heat to low and simmer for 10 minutes.

2) Remove the pot from heat and allow the tea to cool. Strain the silk from the tea, and enjoy warm or cold. Corn silk tea can be stored in an airtight container in the refrigerator for up to 2 days.

Sweetened Vietnamese Coffee

VIETNAM IS SECOND ONLY TO BRAZIL IN COFFEE EXPORTS, *but, surprisingly, the rich flavors of Vietnamese coffee are relatively unknown outside of the realm of coffee connoisseurs. Ground from robusta, a type of coffee bean introduced by the French colonists in the late nineteenth century, Vietnamese coffee is strong and full-bodied with an earthy undertone. It's considered by some to be more bitter than coffee made from Arabica-type beans, but many local Vietnamese roasters add butter and fish sauce to bring out chocolate notes. When served with sweetened condensed milk, as we do here, it's called café sua.*

Vietnamese coffee is brewed by the cup using a small, metal drip filter (phin), which my husband jokes is the original single-serve coffee pod machine. You can find a stainless steel Vietnamese coffee filter kit online for less than $10. To use it, you simply pack the filter with coffee grounds and set it on top of any coffee cup.

Experiment with different coffee brands and the measures of coffee and condensed milk to find your preference for the perfect cup.

MAKES 1 SERVING

2 tablespoons ground Vietnamese coffee

1½ tablespoons sweetened condensed milk, or to taste

Special equipment: Vietnamese coffee filter or metal drip filter

1] Pour the milk into a coffee cup.

2] Boil 2 cups of water in a kettle and then remove the kettle from the heat.

3] Add the ground coffee to a stainless steel Vietnamese coffee filter and gently tap the sides of filter with a spoon to settle the coffee evenly. Attach a filter insert on top of the coffee grounds.

4] Place the coffee filter on top of the coffee cup and slowly pour two tablespoons of the hot water from the kettle into the filter to wet the coffee grounds. Wait about 30 seconds for the initial pour to drain, and then fill the coffee filter with the hot water to near the top of the filter; discard the excess water.

5] Place a lid on the coffee filter and allow the coffee to brew until it stops dripping from the filter, about 4 minutes. Remove the filter, stir the coffee to mix with the milk, and enjoy. (If your brew takes significantly less than 4 minutes, then next time pack the coffee a little tighter before adding water; similarly, if the brew takes more than 4 minutes, do not pack coffee as tightly next time.)

VARIATION: For cold coffee, follow the instructions above, but increase the amount of coffee in the filter to 2½ tablespoons to brew stronger coffee, and instead of using a coffee cup, use a tall glass filled with ice cubes.

VARIATION: For black Vietnamese Coffee (*café den*), follow the instructions above but omit the sweetened condensed milk.

9

broths, sauces, dressings, and special ingredients

broths

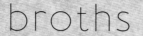

A good broth or stock is the foundation for a great meal. While you can buy it prepackaged, by making it at home you are able to ensure the quality of all the ingredients, regulate the addition of salt, and eliminate the use of chemicals. It also allows you to experience the Vietnamese tip-to-tail philosophy of using every part of an animal, including the bones and rich marrow. My mother makes her own broth every day and this is a key component to her delicious recipes.

Since you can't hurry a good broth, Vietnamese people typically make very large pots of it at one time. You can easily scale the recipes down, or refrigerate or freeze the extras.

Homemade Beef Phở Broth

MY MOTHER'S BEEF BROTH IS GREAT FOR ANY NUMBER OF RECIPES, *including Mama's Beef Phở (page 53). If you're not going to use the broth within 2 hours of cooking it, you can refrigerate it or freeze it. It will keep in an airtight container in the refrigerator for 3 to 4 days and in the freezer for 4 to 6 months. If you need more or less broth, you can scale the recipe accordingly.*

MAKES ABOUT 6 QUARTS

4 pounds beef knuckle bones

2 pounds beef oxtail

¼ cup plus 1 tablespoon sea salt, divided

5 whole star anise

1 (3-inch) cinnamon stick

2 black cardamom pods

20 black peppercorns

2 large white onions, charred and then peeled (see note, page 55)

1 (4-inch) piece fresh ginger, charred and then peeled (see note, page 55)

6 tablespoons (70 grams) rock sugar

1) Put the beef knuckle and oxtail in a very large stockpot and add water until the bones and meat are covered. Add 1 tablespoon of the salt. Bring the water to a boil and cook for 5 minutes. Drain the oxtail and bones and rinse them well under cold water. Discard the liquid and rinse the pot.

2) Return the bones and oxtail to the pot and add 6 quarts of water. Bring the water to a boil over medium heat, skimming the surface often to remove any fat, froth, and impurities. Continue to cook until most of the impurities are gone and the broth is almost clear, about 15 to 20 minutes.

3) Meanwhile, in a small, dry skillet over medium heat, lightly toast the anise, cinnamon, cardamom, and peppercorns. Cook until slightly browned and fragrant, about 3 to 5 minutes. Remove from heat and carefully wrap the spices in cheesecloth to make a pouch.

4) Add the spice bag, charred onions, and ginger to the pot of beef broth. Boil for 15 minutes, then reduce the heat to low and simmer uncovered for 2 hours.

5) Add the rock sugar and salt and continue to simmer uncovered for 1 hour, checking the pot periodically and skimming off any remaining fat or froth that floats to the top.

6) Remove and discard the bones. (If you wish, you may save any meat remaining on the bones to use in another dish. We save the oxtail meat to eat with beef phở.) Remove and discard the spice pouch, onion, and ginger. Strain the broth through a fine mesh colander to remove any impurities. The broth should be clear. (If it is not, strain it again.)

VARIATION: For a basic beef broth, omit the star anise, cinnamon, and cardamom.

Homemade Chicken Broth

THE SECRET STAR OF MANY OF MY MOTHER'S DISHES, *this recipe can easily be halved or doubled depending on how much you need. If you're not going to use the broth within 2 hours of cooking it, refrigerate it in an airtight container for 3 to 4 days. Homemade chicken broth will last for 4 to 6 months in the freezer. A great trick: pour the broth into 8-ounce freezer-safe containers, then, once frozen, pop the individual servings of frozen broth into a large plastic bag for convenient 1-cup cooking.*

MAKES ABOUT 6 QUARTS

5 pounds chicken bones

3 large white onions, charred and then peeled (see note, page 55)

2 (3-inch) pieces fresh ginger, charred and then peeled (see note, page 55)

¼ cup sea salt

5 tablespoons (60 grams) rock sugar

1] Put the chicken bones in a very large stockpot and add 6 quarts of water. Bring to a boil over medium heat, skimming the surface often to remove any fat, froth, and impurities. Continue to cook uncovered until most of the impurities are gone and the water is almost clear about 15 minutes.

2] Add the charred onion and charred ginger to the broth and continue cooking uncovered over medium heat for 1 hour. Add the salt and sugar, reduce the heat to low and simmer for 45 minutes.

Homemade Fish Broth

UNLIKE BEEF OR CHICKEN BROTH, *in which the bones take a long time to release their flavor, fish bones broth comes together rather quickly. Homemade fish broth can be made in well under an hour. In fact, you should resist the urge to boil the bones any longer, as the broth can start to turn bitter.*

MAKES ABOUT 1½ QUARTS

2 teaspoons sea salt, divided

2 pounds heads and bones of non-oily white fish such as halibut

1 onion, peeled and halved

2 garlic cloves

2 ounces fresh ginger, smashed

3 celery stalks

2 leeks, trimmed, each stalk cut into thirds

1] Add 1 teaspoon of salt to a large bowl of water and stir. Add the fish bones and soak for 5 minutes. Drain the bones, rinse, and drain again.

2] Add 2 quarts of water and 1 teaspoon of salt to a large pot. Add the washed bones; the water should cover the bones. Add the onion, garlic, ginger, celery, and leeks, and bring to a boil. Cook uncovered over medium heat for 20 to 30 minutes. Turn the heat off and let the pot sit for 10 minutes.

3] Remove and discard the bones and vegetables. Strain through broth through a cheesecloth into a clean container, leaving any residue behind. The broth should be clear. (If it's not, strain it again.)

sauces

Sauces aren't just for dipping, they can actually help speed up meal preparation. My mother uses sauces as both condiments and ingredients in her cooking. Sauces can be added as the final flourish to a dish, or they can be used from the very beginning as a masterful marinade. You can pour the sauces directly over vegetables, poultry, seafood, or meat for a quick stir-fry, or into little bowls for your guests to sample as they please.

Garlic Lemon Sauce (Nước Chấm)

NAMED FOR THE VIETNAMESE WORDS FOR "WATER" *(nước)* and *"dip" (chấm), this is an essential dipping sauce for all Vietnamese households. We use it as a dip for spring rolls, to brighten seafood, to add a tang to protein, as a dressing for noodles and rice, and as a marinade for meat. It's a unique combination of sweet, sour, salty, savory, and spicy that will enhance almost any dish.*

MAKES ABOUT 5⅔ CUPS

1 cup sugar

1 cup fish sauce

⅓ cup freshly squeezed lemon juice

⅓ cup rice vinegar

1 tablespoon minced garlic

1 teaspoon bird's eye chile, seeded and cut into thin strips, or 1 table-spoon chili paste

Add 3 cups of warm water to a large bowl. Mix in the sugar and stir until completely dissolved. Add the fish sauce, lemon juice, rice vinegar, garlic, and chile. Stir well.

NOTE: *The sauce can be kept in a covered container in the refrigerator for up to 2 weeks.*

Ginger-Balsamic Sauce

1 (3-inch) piece fresh ginger, peeled and finely chopped

2 garlic cloves, chopped

2 cups sugar

⅓ cup balsamic vinegar

⅓ cup soy sauce

1 teaspoon fish sauce

1] Heat the oil in a large saucepan over medium heat. Add the ginger and garlic and sauté until the ginger is tender, about 3 to 5 minutes. Reduce the heat to low.

2] Carefully add 2 cups of water, the sugar, balsamic vinegar, fish sauce, and soy sauce and simmer for 20 minutes. Strain the sauce through a fine-mesh sieve into a bowl and set it aside to cool. The sauce can be kept in a covered container in the refrigerator for up to 2 weeks.

Caramel Sauce

1 cup sugar

1] In a medium bowl, combine the sugar with ½ cup warm water and stir until the sugar is completely dissolved.

2] Preheat a medium pot over medium heat for 1 minute. Add the sugar water and cook, stirring frequently, until it turns dark golden brown, about 10 to 12 minutes.

3] Remove the pot from the heat and immediately, but carefully, add ½ cup of cool water to stop the cooking process. Add 1 more cup of water and mix well, then return the pot to medium heat and simmer for 10 minutes. The sauce should be dark brown and have a thick, caramel consistency. The sauce can be kept in a covered container at room temperature for up to 1 month.

House Sauce

MAKES ABOUT 3 ½ CUPS

2 tablespoons canola oil

2 tablespoons finely chopped
fresh ginger

2 tablespoons finely chopped garlic

2 tablespoons finely chopped
scallions, tender inner white
bulb only

2 cups soy sauce

½ cup rice vinegar

¼ cup Homemade Chicken Broth
(page 272) or store-bought low-
sodium chicken broth

¼ cup lightly packed brown sugar

2 tablespoons white wine

2 tablespoons chili oil

2 tablespoons hoisin sauce

2 tablespoons sriracha sauce

1) Heat the canola oil in a small skillet over medium heat. Add the ginger, gar-lic, and scallions and sauté until the ginger is tender, about 2 to 3 minutes. Remove the skillet from the heat and set it aside.

2) Add the soy sauce, vinegar, and chicken broth to a medium pot over medium heat. Stir in the brown sugar. Add the wine, chili oil, hoisin sauce, and sriracha sauce and cook for 5 minutes. Add the sautéed ginger, garlic, and scallion, and cook for 5 minutes. Remove the pot from the heat and let the sauce cool slightly before serving. The sauce can be kept in a covered container in the refrigerator for up to 2 weeks.

Spicy Satay Sauce for Grilled Meat

MAKES ABOUT 5 CUPS

2 to 3 fresh lemongrass stalks

5 tablespoons canola oil

2 pounds white onions, chopped

14 ounces shallots, chopped

¼ cup chopped fresh ginger

¼ cup chili paste

2 (12-ounce) cans coconut-flavored soda

½ cup fish sauce

½ cup light soy sauce

½ cup pineapple juice

1½ cups lightly packed brown sugar

½ cup sesame oil

1 pear, sliced

3 (½-inch thick) fresh pineapple rings, chopped

1 teaspoon freshly ground black pepper

1] Separate the tender inner white lemongrass bulbs from the tough outer stalks, but save both pieces. Cut the white bulbs into thin slices, and set aside. Crush the outer lemongrass stalks to release the flavor, and then tie the stalks into a bunch, and set aside.

2] Heat the canola oil in a medium pot over medium heat. Add the lemongrass bulbs, the bundle of lemongrass stalks, the onions, shallots, ginger, and chili paste. Sauté until the mixture is very fragrant. Add the coconut soda. Stir in the fish sauce, soy sauce, pineapple juice, and brown sugar.

3] Reduce the heat to low. Add the pear slices, sesame oil, and pineapple pieces. Add the black pepper and cook for 15 minutes. The sauce can be kept in a covered container in the refrigerator for up to 2 weeks.

White Sauce

MY MOTHER'S FRENCH-INSPIRED WHITE SAUCE IS LIKE A ROUX. *We use it as a thickener and a base for many of our recipes. Since some of our dishes are vegetarian, we use water in this recipe; for additional flavor, you can replace the water with chicken broth.*

MAKES ABOUT 8 CUPS

3 tablespoons canola oil

3 garlic cloves, crushed

1 medium white onion, chopped

2 teaspoons all-purpose flour

1 teaspoon sea salt

1 teaspoon sugar

1 〕 Heat the oil in a large pot over medium heat. Add the garlic and sauté until it turns golden, about 1 minute. Add the onions and sauté until the onions sweat and begin to soften, about 5 minutes.

2 〕 Sprinkle the flour into the pan and, using a wooden spoon, stir it into the other ingredients for 5 minutes. Add the salt and sugar. Pour in 8 cups of water and continue to cook for 10 minutes, stirring continuously with the wooden spoon so the flour won't clump. Reduce the heat to low and cook for 15 more minutes. Strain the sauce through a fine-mesh sieve into a large bowl and set it aside to cool. The sauce can be stored for 4 to 5 days, covered with plastic wrap, in the refrigerator.

Bean Sauce

TO MAKE THIS SAUCE *vegetarian, you can substitute water for the chicken broth. You can also garnish the sauce with roasted peanuts when serving.*

MAKES 2 CUPS

2 tablespoons dried white beans

½ teaspoon sea salt

4 garlic cloves, 1 left whole and 3 minced

1 sprig fresh thyme

1 tablespoon canola oil

½ teaspoon chili paste

2 cups Homemade Chicken Broth (page 272) or store-bought low-sodium chicken broth

1 tablespoon sugar

1 tablespoon hoisin sauce

1 teaspoon vegetarian oyster sauce

2 tablespoons creamy peanut butter (optional)

Roasted Peanuts (page 281) (optional)

1] Bring a small pot of water to a boil over medium heat. Add the beans, salt, 1 clove of garlic, and the thyme. Cook until the beans are soft, about 15 minutes. Strain out the garlic and thyme. Drain the beans, rinse with cold water, and set aside.

2] Heat the oil in a medium saucepan over medium heat. Add the minced garlic and chili paste and sauté for 30 seconds. Carefully pour in the chicken broth. Stir in the sugar, Hoisin sauce, vegetarian oyster sauce, and peanut butter, if using, whisking well to dissolve the peanut butter. Reduce the heat to low and simmer for 5 minutes. Remove from heat and set aside to cool. The sauce can be stored in an airtight container in the refrigerator for 2 weeks.

dressings

Helene's Lemon-Sugar Dressing

THIS DRESSING GOES ESPECIALLY WELL WITH SHAKEN BEEF *(page 64). At Tiato, we pour it over butter lettuce and sliced tomatoes, and at Crustacean we use it to dress an arugula and cabbage salad. The dressing can be stored in an airtight container in the refrigerator for 3-4 days.*

MAKES ABOUT 4 TABLESPOONS

3 tablespoons freshly squeezed lemon juice

3 tablespoons sugar

½ teaspoon sea salt

½ teaspoon freshly ground black pepper

1 tablespoon grapeseed oil

Combine all the ingredients in a medium bowl. Whisk until smooth.

Lemongrass Dressing

MAKES 2 CUPS

1 jalapeño

1 tablespoon finely chopped fresh lemongrass

1 tablespoon minced shallots

1 teaspoon minced ginger

½ cup olive oil

½ cup sugar

¼ cup rice wine vinegar

¼ cup fish sauce

Combine all the ingredients in a food processor or blender and purée until smooth. The dressing can be stored in an airtight container in the refrigerator for 3-4 days.

special ingredients

Fried Shallots

3 whole shallots
(about 4 ounces total)

2 cups canola oil

1] Soak the shallots in a bowl of water for 15 minutes, and then peel and wash them.

2] Slice the shallots thinly and set them in a colander to drain until they are completely dry, about 15 minutes.

3] Heat the oil in a wok or large skillet until it registers 350°F on a deep-frying or candy thermometer. Add half of the shallots to the oil and fry them until they are golden brown and crisp, about 45 seconds. Using a skimmer or slotted spoon, scoop out the shallots and put them on a tray lined with paper towels to dry up the oil and let them cool. Repeat with the second batch of shallots. Fried shallots can last for 10 days at room temperature in an airtight container.

NOTE: *To test if the oil is hot enough, drop in one small piece of onion. If it turns golden and floats to the top in 5 seconds, then the oil is ready.*

Roasted Peanuts

Unsalted peanuts, shelled

1] Preheat the oven to 350°F.

2] Spread the peanuts out in a baking pan. Roast until golden brown, about 10 to 15 minutes.

NOTE: *The roasted peanuts can be kept in a airtight container at room temperature for up to a month.*

Fried Garlic

MAKES ABOUT ½ CUP

½ cup canola oil

4 garlic cloves, finely chopped

1) Heat the oil in a small pan or skillet until it registers 350°F on a deep-frying or candy thermometer. Add the garlic and fry until it is a medium golden color, about 45 seconds. Scoop out the garlic and put it on a tray lined with a paper towels to dry up the oil. Reserve the oil in the pan.

2) Once the garlic oil has cooled to room temperature, transfer it to an air-tight container. Add the garlic to the oil, seal the container, and store it in the refrigerator for up to two weeks. You can use both the garlic and the oil.

NOTE: *To test if the oil is hot enough for frying, drop in one small piece of onion. If it turns golden and floats to the top in 5 seconds, then the oil is ready.*

Scallions in Hot Oil

Known as mở hành in Vietnam, this is a simple garnish that goes well with many dishes, especially grilled meats.

MAKES ABOUT 1½ CUPS

1 cup canola oil

½ cup thinly sliced scallions, green stalks only

Heat the oil in a medium saucepan over medium heat. When the oil just starts to simmer, after about 2 minutes, add the scallions and stir for 1 to 2 seconds. Remove the pan from the heat. The scallions can be kept in a covered container in the refrigerator for up to 4 days.

VARIATION: To make a smaller amount, just 2 tablespoons, use 2 tablespoons thinly sliced scallions in 2 tablespoons of oil.

Tamarind Juice

TAMARIND JUICE, ALSO KNOWN AS TAMARIND WATER, *is not actually as thin as the name implies. Rather than a pure liquid, it has a thicker consistency more like ketchup.*

Bottled tamarind juice can be purchased in gourmet markets and online, but you can easily make your own from dried tamarind pulp, which is sold in small blocks in specialty ethnic markets (and is sometimes labeled "paste").

MAKES 1½ CUPS

1 (5-ounce) block seedless tamarind pulp

1] Bring 1 cup of water to a boil in a small pot.

2] Place the tamarind pulp in a heatproof bowl and pour the boiling water over it. Set the tamarind pulp aside to soak for 15 minutes.

3] Place a fine-mesh strainer over a large bowl. Pour the tamarind pulp (now more of a paste) into the strainer, then use a spoon to press the juice out of the paste and into the bowl. The tamarind juice can be stored in an airtight container in refrigerator for up to two weeks.

ACKNOWLEDGMENTS

I would like to thank my husband, Eli, for his tireless work assisting me with this book. Thank you for burning the midnight oil as my personal editor, layout designer, recipe taster, and Mr. Mom to our 2-year-old and newborn sons. This book would not be if it weren't for your support in all matters and belief in me.

I would like to thank my mother, father, and grandmother for inspiring all of us daughters to do better and eat better. I grew up listening to our family story as told in our kitchen and at the dinner table. Thank you Mom and Bà Nội for cooking wonderful meals and for letting me be your sous-chef. You instilled in me a love for food and discovery that is shaped by the importance of our heritage. Mom, thank you for spending countless hours with me testing recipes in the kitchen, telling stories while I took notes, and just being a wonderful mom throughout it all. Dad, you taught all your daughters the importance of eating well and eating deliciously, and not cutting corners to achieve that. My love for food and cooking are a reflection of your love and care. Thank you.

Thank you to my amazing sisters for keeping the restaurants going as Mom and I dove into creating this book. Writing Mom's first cookbook was no small undertaking, and I see why no one attempted it in the past! Our love and support for each other is the real secret to our success.

Helene and I are sincerely grateful for the hard work of our restaurant staff and wonderful chefs. You are the support behind the scenes, and we are grateful for your contributions. Thank you to Chef Tony Nguyen and Chef Van for preparing all the dishes for the camera, and a special thanks to Chef Tony Nguyen for plating.

Thank you Evan Sung and Nidia Cueva for your time and effort in capturing my mother's cuisine so beautifully and artfully. You turned our humble dishes into magical photographs.

Heather Maclean, where do I begin? You were our partner in this book from the start, and I thank you for the advice, contributions, and countless hours you gave to bring this book to the finish line. Your energy, creativity, and dedication never ceased to amaze us.

Thank you to our publisher Running Press and Editor Jennifer Kasius for being a true partner with us on this journey.

Finally, thank you to our clients and fans that visit our restaurants every day. Without your support and love for our food, we wouldn't have the opportunity to create this book to share our family stories and recipes. I hope you enjoy recreating our dishes at home! — JACQUELINE AN

Our Favorite Brands

Sauces

Fish Sauce – Phu Quoc Fish Sauce by Viet Huong Fish Sauce Company or Red Boat Fish Sauce

Chili Sauce – Sambal Oelek Ground Fresh Chili Paste by Huy Fong Foods, Inc.

Sweet Chili Sauce – Sweet Chilli Sauce by Yeo's

Hoisin Sauce – Hoisin Sauce by Lee Kum Kee and Hoisin Sauce by Koon Chun

Oyster sauce – Panda Brand Oyster Flavored Sauce by Lee Kum Kee

Ponzu citrus seasoned soy sauce – Ponzu Citrus Seasoned Soy Sauce by Mitsukan

Soy Sauce – All-Purpose Naturally Brewed Soy Sauce by Kikkoman

Sriracha sauce – Sriracha Hot Chili Sauce by Huy Fong Foods, Inc.

Seasoning Powders

Curry powder – Indian Curry Càri Ấn Độ by Zesty Foods Distributor

Wasabi powder – Powdered Wasabi by Hime Brand

Pastes

Miso paste – Organic Miso Paste by Hikari

Shrimp Paste – Shrimp Sauce (Finely Ground) by Lee Kum Kee

Oils

Sesame Oil – Pure Sesame Oil by Kadoya Brand

Noodles & Wraps

Phở Noodles – We buy fresh pho noodles. For dried noodles: Rice Stick Noodles, BÁNH PHỞ TƯƠI by Lucky K.T. Co., Inc.

Rice Vermicelli – Guilin Rice Vermicelli (Ông Già Quê Hương) by Oldman Que Huong Brand

Rice Paper Wrappers – Rice Paper Feuilles De Riz Bánh Tráng by Coconut Tree Brand

Sesame Rice Paper – Bánh Tráng Mè Đen Black Sesame Cracker by First World Brand

Dumpling wrapper – Dumpling Wrapper by Twin Marquis

Wine and Beer Pairings for Main Entrées

1] SIMPLE DIVINITY

Mama's Beef Pho

Wine: Chateauneuf-du-Pape, Delas, Southern Rhone, France

Beer: Amber Ale, Anderson Valley Brewing, 'Boont Amber,' Boonville, California

Oven-Roasted Lemongrass Chicken

Wine: Gamay, Domaine Dupueble Pere et Fils, Beaujolais, France

Beer: Lager, Saigon Export, Vietnam

Vietnamese Chicken Coriander Cabbage Salad

Wine: Chardonnay, Landmark Vineyards, 'Overlook,' Sonoma County

Beer: Lager, Saigon Export, Vietnam

Caramelized Black Cod

Wine: Pinot Noir, Flowers, Sonoma Coast

Beer: Pilsner, Spaten, Munich, Germany

Fried Rice with Shrimp, Chicken, and Chinese Sausage

Wine: Riesling, Domaine Schlumberger, 'Les Princes Abbey,' Alsace, France

Beer: Golden Ale, Duvel, Belgium

Filet Mignon Shaken Beef

Wine: Malbec, Terrazas de Los Andes, 'Las Compuertas,' Mendoza, Argentina

Beer: India Pale Ale, Bear Republic, 'Racer 5,' Sonoma County, California

Spicy Chicken & Shrimp Ramen in Cognac XO Sauce

Wine: Chardonnay, Cakebread Cellars, Napa Valley

Beer: Lager, Saigon Export, Vietnam

2] INDOCHINE REVERIE

Cognac Crab and Asparagus Soup

Wine: Pinot Noir, Tantara, Santa Maria Valley, California

Beer: Brown Ale, Lost Coast Brewing, 'Downtown Brown, Eureka, California

Red Snapper Tamarind Soup

Wine: Marsanne, Bello Family Vineyards, Napa Valley

Beer: White Ale, Lost Coast Brewing, 'Great White,' Eureka, California

Crispy Chicken Spring Rolls

Wine: Chardonnay, Kistler, 'Les Noisetiers,' Sonoma Mountain, California

Beer: Hefeweizen, Paulaner, Munich, Germany

Lotus, Chicken & Shrimp Salad

Wine: Sauvignon Blanc, Duckhorn Vineyards, Napa Valley, California

Beer: Belgian White Ale, Hoegarden, Belgium

Shrimp Summer Rolls

Wine: Sauvignon Blanc, Cakebread Cellars, Napa Valley, California

Beer: Lager, Saigon Export, Vietnam

Sizzling Shrimp Crepes

Wine: Sauvignon Blanc, Craggy Range, 'Te Muna Road Vineyard,' New Zealand

Beer: Blonde Ale, Mission Brewing, San Diego, California

Hot Pastry Pies, Pate Chaud

Wine: Pinot Noir, Gary Farrell, Russian River Valley, California

Beer: India Pale Ale, Strand Brewing, 'Atticus,' Manhattan Beach, California

Slow-Roasted Pork with Ginger Glaze

Wine: Pinot Noir, Craggy Range, 'Te Muna Road Vineyard,' New Zealand

Beer: Pale Ale, North Coast Brewing, 'Red Seal,' Ft. Bragg, California

Snapper Baked in Banana Leaf

Wine: Chardonnay, Jayson by Pahlmeyer, Sonoma County, California

Beer: Blonde Ale, Wychwood Brewery, 'Wychcraft,' Bedford, England

Crispy Turmeric Fish with Fresh Dill

Wine: Viognier, Darioush, 'Signature,' Napa Valley, California

Beer: Pilsner, North Coast Brewing, 'Scrimshaw,' Ft. Bragg, California

3] NEW HOME COMFORT

Chicken Phở with Kaffir Lime

Wine: Chardonnay, Chalk Hill, Russian River Valley, California

Beer: Pale Ale, Sierra Nevada, Chico, California

Green Papaya, Long Bean, and Tomato Steak Salad with Tamarind Dressing

Wine: Rose of Pinot Noir, Skywalker Vineyards, Marin County, California

Beer: Pilsner, Uinta, '801,' Salt Lake City, Utah

Spicy Beef & Lemongrass Soup

Wine: Syrah, Tantara, 'Gary's Vineyard,' Santa Lucia Highlands, California

Beer: India Pale Ale, Shipyard Brewing, 'Monkey Fist,' Portland, Maine

Beef Stew with Vietnamese Spices

Wine: Cabernet Sauvignon, Faust, Napa Valley, California

Beer: Russian Imperial Stout, Mission Brewing, 'Dark Seas,' San Diego, California

Lotus Soup with Pork

Wine: Pinot Noir, Davis Bynum, 'Jane's Vineyard,' Russian River Valley, California

Beer: Amber Ale, Lost Coast Brewing, 'Alleycat Amber,' Eureka, California

Ragout Eggplant with Tofu & Vietnamese Herbs

Wine: Grenache/Syrah Blend, Tablas Creek, 'Esprit de Tablas,' Paso Robles, California

Beer: Amber Ale, Anderson Valley Brewing, 'Boont Amber,' Boonville, California

Lemongrass Beef Vermicelli

Wine: Merlot, Provenance, Rutherford, California

Beer: White IPA, Lost Coast Brewery, 'Sharkinator,' Eureka, California

Seared Steak Salad with Garlic Lemon Dressing

Wine: Shiraz, Molly Dooker, 'Blue-Eyed Boy,' McLaren Vale, Australia

Beer: Saison, North Coast Brewing, 'Le Merle,' Ft. Bragg, California

Turkey Stuffed with Sticky Rice

Wine: Chardonnay, Rochioli, Russian River Valley, California

Beer: Pale Ale, Strand Brewing, '24th Street Pale,' Manhattan Beach, California

Leftover Turkey Porridge

Wine: Vermentino, Guado Al Tasso, Bolgheri, Tuscany, Italy

Beer: Saison, Allagash Brewing, Portland, Maine

Pork Chops with Caramel Marinade

Wine: Garnacha/Syrah Blend, Sims de Porrera, 'Solanes,' Priorat, Spain

Beer: Amber Ale, Strand Brewing, 'Beach House Amber,' Manhattan Beach, California

Helen ok Noodles with Stir-Fried Vegetables

Wine: Sancerre, Comte Lafond, 'Grand Cuvee,' Loire Valley, France

Beer: Pilsner, Oskar Blues, 'Mama's Little Yella' Pils,' Lyons, Colorado

Báhn Mì with Tropical Marinated Flank Steak

Wine: Grenache Blend, John Duval, 'Plexus,' Barossa Valley, Australia

Beer: Bourbon-Barrel Aged Ale, Allagash, 'Curieux,' Portland, Maine

Vietnamese Chicken-Stuffed Cabbage

Wine: Viognier, Melville Winery, 'Verna's Vineyard,' Santa Rita Hills, California

Beer: Belgian White Ale, Chimay, 'Cinq Cents Tripel,' Belgium

Cashew Chicken

Wine: Pinot Blanc, Domaine Schlumberger, 'Les Princes Abbey,' Alsace, France

Beer: Golden Ale, North Coast Brewing, 'Pranqster,' Ft. Bragg, California

Chicken and Potatoes in Curry Lemongrass Sauce

Wine: Chardonnay, Summerland, 'Teresa's Vineyard,' Santa Maria Valley, California

Beer: Pale Ale, Anderson Valley Brewing, 'Poleeko Gold,' Boonville, California

Caramelized Lemongrass Shrimp

Wine: Pinot Grigio, Jermann, Friuli-Venezia-Giulia, Italy

Beer: Lager, Saigon Export, Vietnam

Coconut Spareribs

Wine: Shiraz, Darioush, 'Signature,' Napa Valley, California

Beer: Double IPA, Mission Brewing, 'Shipwrecked,' San Diego, California

4] EVERYDAY GOURMET

French Onion Phở With Beef Ravioli

Wine: Falanghina, Feudi di San Gregorio, Campania, Italy

Beer: White Ale, Cismontane Brewing, 'Whiting's Wit,' Rancho Santa Margarita, California

Baked Tofu with Julienned Snap Peas

Wine: Albarino, Mar de Frades, Rias Baixas, Spain

Beer: Lager, Saigon Export, Vietnam

Drunken Crab

Wine: Meursault, Louis Jadot, Burgundy, France

Beer: Lager, Hue, Vietnam

Grilled Turmeric Calamari

Wine: Gavi, La Scolca, 'Black Label,' Piedmont, Italy

Beer: Lager, Saigon Export, Vietnam

Five-Spice Duck Salad

Wine: Pinot Noir, Paul Hobbs, Russian River Valley, California

Beer: Red Rice Ale, Hitachino, 'Nest,' Japan

Mongolian Fried Chicken

Wine: Chardonnay, Chateau Montelena, Napa Valley, California

Beer: Pale Ale, Stone Brewing, Escondido, California

Kobe Beef Meatballs on Sugar Cane

Wine: Syrah Blend, Justin, 'Savant,' Paso Robles, California

Beer: Abbey Ale, North Coast Brewing, 'Brother Thelonious,' Ft. Bragg, California

Sweet Shoyu Short Ribs

Wine: Cote Rotie, E. Guigal, Northern Rhone, France

Beer: India Pale Ale, Ballast Point Brewing, 'Sculpin,' San Diego, California

Grilled Mongolian Lamb Lollipops

Wine: Chateauneuf-du-Pape, Chateau de Beaucastel, Southern Rhone, France

Beer: Brown Ale, Samuel Smith's Nut Brown Ale, England

Steamed Filet of Sole with Miso Sauce

Wine: Chardonnay, Frank Family, 'Reserve,' Napa Valley, California

Beer: Pilsner, Oskar Blues Brewing, 'Mama's Little Yella' Pils,' Lyons, Colorado

Shrimp Angel Hair Pasta

Wine: Riesling, Marcel Deiss, 'Schoenenbourg Vielles Vignes,' Alsace, France

Beer: Lager, Hue, Vietnam

Mango Lobster Salad

Wine: Sauvignon Blanc, Cliff Lede, Napa Valley, California

Beer: Pilsner, North Coast Brewing, 'Scrimshaw,' Ft. Bragg, California

5] BISTRONOMY

Warm Goji Berry Brown Rice Salad

Wine: Pinot Blanc, WillaKenzie, Willamette Valley, Oregon

Beer: Pilsner, North Coast Brewing, 'Scrimshaw,' Ft. Bragg, California

Tiato Roll

Wine: Sauvignon Blanc, Kim Crawford, 'Spitfire,' Marlborough, New Zealand

Beer: Pale Ale, Abita Brewing, 'Restoration,' Abita Springs, Louisiana

Lobster Corn Dogs on Sugar Cane

Wine: Sauvignon Blanc, Cloudy Bay, 'Te Koko,' Marlborough, New Zealand

Beer: Pale Ale, Oskar Blues Brewing, 'Dale's Pale Ale,' Lyons, Colorado

Balsamic Chicken Pot Stickers

Wine: Chardonnay, DuMol, Russian River Valley, California

Beer: Saison, North Coast Brewing, 'Puck Petite Saison,' Ft. Bragg, California

Crispy Garlic Chicken Wings

Wine: Dry Riesling, Trefethen Vineyards, Napa Valley, California

Beer: India Pale Ale, Shipyard Brewing, 'Monkey Fist,' Portland, Maine

Filet Mignon on Sesame Crisps

Wine: Pinot Noir, Duckhorn Vineyards, 'Goldeneye,' Alexander Valley, California

Beer: India Pale Ale, Victory Brewing, 'Hop Devil,' Downingtown, Pennsylvania

Saigon Steamed Pork Buns

Wine: Gamay Beaujolais, Louis Jadot, Beaujolais, France

Beer: White Ale, Unibroue Brewery, 'Blanche de Chambly,' Quebec, Canada

Crab Puffs

Wine: Rose, Kenzo Estate, 'Yui,' Napa Valley, California

Beer: Lager, Saigon Export, Vietnam

Steamed Black Mussels with Garlic Lemon Sauce

Wine: Chardonnay, Ponzi Vineyards, 'Reserve,' Willamette Valley, Oregon

Beer: India Pale Ale, Strand Brewing, 'Atticus,' Manhattan Beach, California

Tofu and Fried Eggplant in Tía Tô Leaves

Wine: Chardonnay, Cakebread Cellars, Napa Valley, California

Beer: Saison, Adelberts Brewery, 'Philosophizer,' Austin, Texas

Vietnamese Beef Tartare with Honey-Truffle Dijon Sauce

Wine: Merlot, Shafer, Napa Valley, California

Beer: Abbey Ale, Chimay, 'Blue Label,' Belgium

Salmon Tartare

Wine: Chardonnay, Merry Edwards, 'Olivet Lane,' Russian River Valley, California

Beer: Blonde Ale, Uinta Brewing, 'Monkshine,' Salt Lake City, Utah

INDEX